JoyknPress.com
29.07.'16
DanaPoint,
Calif.
#92629

A TIME FOR
ACTION

A TIME FOR
ACTION

EMPOWERING THE FAITHFUL TO RECLAIM AMERICA

RAFAEL CRUZ

FOREWORD BY **GLENN BECK**
EPILOGUE BY **SENATOR TED CRUZ**

 WND Books

A TIME FOR ACTION

Published by WND Books, Washington, D.C. WND Books is a registered trademark of WorldNetDaily.com, Inc. ("WND")

Book designed by Mark Karis

Hardcover ISBN: 978-1-944229-00-9
eBook ISBN: 978-1-944229-01-6

Library of Congress Cataloging-in-Publication Data Available Upon Request

Printed in the United States of America
15 16 17 18 19 20 MPV 9 8 7 6 5 4 3 2 1

I DEDICATE THIS BOOK TO AMERICA

America, offering me a safe haven when I escaped tyranny
America, the land of the free and the home of the brave
America, where all your dreams can become reality
America, where I found true freedom in Jesus Christ.

America, where in one generation,
an immigrant without money and not knowing the language
could see his son as a leader in the US Senate,
and potentially the next president of the United States.

and

to the American people,
who have the privilege and the responsibility,
as courageous conservatives,
to preserve and protect America,
our shining city on a hill,
to the glory of God.

CONTENTS

FOREWORD

Dads are arguably the most influential people on the planet. The power they wield over their children is immeasurable. Something as simple as an approving glance can fill a child with confidence, security, and love. On the other hand, as all dads have surely experienced, a moment of indifference or outburst of anger can crush a tiny, fragile soul. You've probably heard the phrase "Behind every good man is an even better woman," and that's true. But an even greater truth is that behind every great man is an even greater father.

When Ted Cruz first landed on my radar screen, I didn't know what to make of him. I liked what he was saying about the Constitution, liberty, and God. I admired his ability to effortlessly articulate conservative principles and values, a quality shockingly absent among most if not all GOP candidates in the past several decades. One of the great failures of the Republican Party has been the failure to vigorously defend these principles and values. It's a spectacular failure because not only are they the bedrock of this nation, but they have the added bonus of a proven track record. They work! Conservatives have the incredible advantage and luxury of the winning argument being on their side, yet few if any candidates have demonstrated the ability and the confidence to speak this truth boldly.

Ted Cruz has this ability. But here's the rub. I've seen this song and dance before. Candidate comes along and tickles ears with soaring rhetoric and quotes from Ronald Reagan. We make signs, donate time and perhaps even money, defend them in public and on the air. We propel them into office and wait for them to start working on everything they promised out on the campaign trail. Then we notice something is wrong. I don't know whether it's a calculated choice or not, but something happens when they arrive within the city limits of Washington, DC. The constitutional conservative we all fell in love with disappears, swallowed up by the progressive establishment GOP. Next thing we know, they're supporting all kinds of giant government legislation, and we're back to square one. So, I was cautiously optimistic but certainly not convinced about the authenticity of Ted Cruz.

Then I met Ted's father, Rafael Cruz, and any shred of doubt quickly vanished. I was fascinated as he told me his incredible story of growing up in Cuba and becoming a revolutionary fighter in the 1950s with Fidel Castro's army. While most seventeen-year-olds were finishing up high school, Rafael Cruz was leading a group of insurgents in a plot against Cuban dictator Fulgencio Batista. Cruz was caught, thrown in jail, and brutally tortured. This horrific experience only emboldened him to continue the fight, but eventually he decided it was better to get out. He fled to America and ended up at the University of Texas. He had barely any money to his name and could hardly speak English, but he was determined. While he was at UT, he learned that Castro, with whom he'd been fighting, was a communist. He realized it was wrong to have fought for him and actively did what he could to now fight against him. This time his weapons were letters and the power of persuasion as he tried to convince his former band of brothers that this was not the cause they should be fighting for.

Rafael Cruz understood the horrors of socialism and communism better than most. He suffered both physically and mentally and barely survived his youth. Most of the candidates you will see onstage in this election cycle do truly appreciate and value freedom, but they'll never be able to relate in the same way Ted Cruz can. You see, dads wield incredible amounts of power. And when Rafael Cruz told his teenage son about the torture, the fighting, the oppression, the murder, and the communist hellhole he grew up in—there's no doubt that imagery shook his young son to the core and burned an unforgettable image and feeling that would never, ever go away.

Many candidates throw around constitutional clichés in hopes of moving the approval rating a few points. The fight for freedom is very real for the Cruz family. The Constitution holds extremely emotional and personal value for them because they know firsthand what it's like *not to have it.* Most Americans take freedom for granted and assume it will always be here no matter whom we elect into office. In the history of humankind, freedom is the rarest of societal experiments. More than 95 percent of all human civilization has lived under what could be considered oppressive regimes. Truly free countries, such as America, have existed only 5 percent of the time since humans have walked the earth. What an incredible gift and privilege we have been given to live in such a time and in such a place. Trapped in our comforts, we cannot comprehend this. I would go so far as to wager that some candidates cower to political correctness because they don't really believe deep down to their core that freedom is under attack. They don't really believe that your rights under the Constitution will ever be stripped away. They just see it as a way to gain supporters and eventually power.

Ted Cruz will do anything to protect and preserve freedom. He has shown this time and time again in the belly of the beast in Washington, DC. He has fearlessly stood up not just to Democrats but to the kingmakers in the GOP as well. Think of the attacks this man has withstood. The brunt of his own party has been thrust down on him many times—he singlehandedly has been blamed for shutting down the government. It's one of the most ludicrous arguments ever made, but Ted had to grin and bear it because he stood for what he believed while few had the courage to stand alongside him. Some have accused him of creating political stunts and grandstanding, but this is simply not accurate. Those are the actions of a weak, greedy, selfish person. Ted's motivation stems from a very real, authentic, and personal place. He is doing this because he believes it. And he believes it because his father taught him and told him everything he experienced.

You'd be hard-pressed to find a better American story than this one: former Cuban revolutionary flees to America with no money and can't speak the language—and now his son is a sitting United States senator who is running for president.

How awesome is that?

Behind every great man is an even greater father. And let it be stated for the record unequivocally: Rafael Cruz is one of the greatest freedom fighters of his generation.

—GLENN BECK

hee! hee!

a Oerode of Fools,
misfits,
+
Imposters!!!

INTRODUCTION

I do solemnly swear . . .

Sitting in the Senate chambers, my eyes filled with tears and meandered down my cheeks. Watching my son take the oath of office nearly caused my heart to burst. Was I dreaming?

. . . that I will support and defend the Constitution of the United States . . .

The Constitution. Not many families spend their evening dinners discussing the finer points of this foundational document. But ours did—and my son Ted's love for it drove him into the legal profession *noT $*
and ultimately to a life of public service. Few people understand and *$ 9 $!!!*
defend the Constitution like Ted Cruz. Regrettably, too many politi- *B.S. !*
cians bend it, twist it, and try to change it. If they succeed, our nation *Dolfmm S.*
will crumble.

. . . against all enemies, foreign and domestic . . .

The United States of America is in danger. ISIS, Boko Haram, and other Muslim extremists threaten our security and way of life. Vladimir *lie !!*
Putin is leading Russia back into the Cold War. But our greatest enemy doesn't reside outside our borders. Perhaps our greatest enemy is apathy among the American people.

. . . that I will bear true faith and allegiance to the same . . .

I blinked my eyes and refocused. The vice president of the United States was administering the oath to my son!

. . . that I take this obligation freely . . .

Only in America could the son of a Cuban immigrant who came to this great country with nothing and unable to speak the language be elected to the US Senate and potentially become the president of the United States. Only in America! Fewer than six decades before, I had fought against oppression in my homeland to win the freedoms that Americans enjoy.

> "Our Constitution was made only for a moral and religious people. It is wholly inadequate to the government of any other."
>
> —JOHN ADAMS

. . . without any mental reservation or purpose of evasion . . .

But our freedoms are eroding. Americans are trading liberty for the oppression and control I once knew in Cuba.

. . . and that I will well and faithfully discharge the duties of the office . . .

We desperately need true patriots who love America— uncommon men and women committed to rescuing this nation from economic, moral, and spiritual collapse. Men and women with the resolve to abide by the Constitution without hesitation.

. . . on which I am about to enter . . .

Our country yearns for leaders who will awaken the sleeping giant and call us to the greatness of our Founding Fathers.

. . . so help me God.

But we cannot do this without God's help. Without it, our nation and our way of life will no longer exist. Former president John Adams once said, "Our Constitution was made only for a moral and religious people. It is wholly inadequate to the government of any other."[1]

We need elected officials who rely on God for wisdom and strength and who will protect America from the attacks of those who seek to undermine it.

This is America's time for action.

* * *

In the summer of 1957, I arrived in America. After being imprisoned and tortured in my native Cuba for my involvement in the revolution against the Fulgencio Batista government, I knew that if I didn't escape, I would be killed. With very little money and unable to speak English, I paid my way through school at the University of Texas by working first as a dishwasher and later as a cook.

In 1959, after Castro came to power, I returned to Cuba, believing that he would rid the country of corruption and align with America to make it a bulwark of freedom and democracy. But the Communist/Marxist policies he had instituted shocked me.

Disillusioned, I left Cuba three weeks later, never to return again. And when I landed on American soil, I knew I had found my permanent home, the land of the free and the home of the brave.

Within seven years of leaving college, my wife and I had founded and owned a small business in oil and gas exploration. Then in the late 1970s, I was shocked once again when the Jimmy Carter administration began implementing policies reminiscent of the bearded dictator I had left behind in Cuba. In addition to befriending communist strongmen like Fidel Castro, Yugoslavia's Josef Tito, and Romania's Nicolae Ceaucescu, Carter advocated the redistribution of wealth by taxing the rich and giving to the poor, which promoted greater dependency upon the government. He also returned the Panama Canal to Panama and their communist-leaning dictator Omar Torrijos.

After Castro came to power, hundreds of thousands of Cubans immigrated *legally* to the United States—not to mention the countless others who have risked their lives floating on dilapidated boats across the Gulf of Mexico. According to the US Census Bureau, as of 2013, 1,144,000 Cuban immigrants were living on American soil.[2]

And how many Americans have immigrated to Cuba since 1959? A handful. And most of them were criminals trying to evade the US government.

People who have tasted Communism firsthand can readily identify it—more than people who have spent their lives enjoying the fruits of freedom and democracy. After seeing how it ravaged my homeland, I decided to do everything within my power to prevent history from repeating itself in America.

In late 1979, I joined the State Board of the Religious Roundtable, a coalition of Christians and Jews charged with mobilizing millions of people of faith to elect Ronald Reagan, whom I consider the greatest president since Abraham Lincoln. My son, Ted, had just turned nine.

Throughout 1980, our dinner conversations centered on why we needed to get rid of a liberal, progressive president like Jimmy Carter and replace him with a constitutional conservative like Ronald Reagan. So Ted got a dose of conservative politics from a Christian worldview every day for a year before he was even a teenager! I must have told my son a dozen times, "You know, Ted, when I faced oppression in Cuba, I had a place to flee. If we lose our freedom here, where do we go?" Those words profoundly impacted Ted's life.

Psalm 37:23 tells us that "the steps of a good man are ordered by the Lord, and He delights in his way." Indeed, through Craig and Paige Moore, our clients and friends, Ted met Rolland Storey, the founder of the Free Enterprise Institute. They introduced him to the writings of Adam Smith, John Locke, Milton Friedman, Ludwig von Mises,

Friedrich Hayek, and Frédéric Bastiat, as well as to the Federalist Papers, the Anti-Federalist Papers, and other important works.

The Institute formed a group of five high school students, including Ted, and called them the Constitutional Corroborators. With the help of a memory expert, those five teenagers memorized the US Constitution, and for the next four years they toured Texas giving approximately eighty speeches on free-market economics and the Constitution. Before Ted graduated from high school, he was passionate about the Constitution, the Declaration of Independence, free enterprise,

> "When I faced oppression in Cuba, I had a place to flee. If we lose our freedom here, where do we go?"

limited government, and the rule of law. This passion became like "fire in his bones." (See Jeremiah 20:9 NLT.) I know my son, Ted, will not compromise his principles in Washington because that fire is as alive today as it was thirty years ago!

Those early years shaped my son's life as well as mine. We grew keenly aware of how fragile freedom is, even in this great country of ours. As Ted immersed himself in America's founding documents and the lives of their framers, so did his mother and I. My wife, Eleanor, invested a great deal of time working with Ted and driving him to various events. I coached him on his speech organization and delivery, and soon he excelled in his presentations. Watching him speak was nothing short of exhilarating!

This only confirmed what I had long sensed about Ted. Even when he was a young boy, I knew Ted had a special calling on his life. Every day, I immersed him in prayer, asking God to protect him and grant him wisdom. And I told Ted over and over, "God has given you remarkable talents, and you must use those gifts to His glory." Ted knew in his heart that he would dedicate his life to fighting for the preservation

> The only way we can dig out of our political hole is by involving ourselves in civic society and restoring the Judeo-Christian principles that have undergirded America, the driving force behind American exceptionalism.

of our precious liberty and serving "We the people."

While we share similar passions, my role differs from Ted's. He is a political leader; I am a minister. A message for the American people burns deep inside me, and I cannot keep it silent: *stop complaining about our political woes and do something about them.* The only way we can dig out of our political hole is by involving ourselves in civic society and restoring the Judeo-Christian principles that have undergirded America, the driving force behind American exceptionalism.

The Obama administration has intensified our progression into an age of lawlessness. This includes:

- attacking our civil and religious liberties

- deteriorating our quality of life and destroying businesses through excessive taxation and regulation

- jeopardizing the future of our children and grandchildren by accumulating ever-increasing national debt

- fostering massive unemployment and underemployment

- creating a dependent society in bondage to the government

- trampling the Constitution, the rule of law, separation of powers, and limited government

- leading our nation away from Judeo-Christian values and into secular humanism

I feel compelled to "shout [it] from the housetops," as Jesus exhorted us to do (see Matthew 10:27 NLT), which is why I constantly crisscross the country, speaking at churches, pastors' conferences, Tea Party meetings, 9/12 meetings (a volunteer-based movement focusing on building and uniting our communities), homeschool gatherings, and political rallies. I'll speak where anyone will listen, to conservatives, Libertarians, independents . . . anyone. In person or through radio and television interviews, I will do all I can to tirelessly share the message of restoration for America.

This book not only explains how we got to the condition in which we find ourselves today, but more important, how to restore this great nation to the "shining city on a hill" that Ronald Reagan so eloquently described.[3] You'll read about my life in Cuba and the harrowing story of my escape to America. Then I'll show you how America is tragically following the same path that Cuba did a half century ago. We'll explore seemingly innocuous philosophies that undermine our country. Next, I will chart a path to true freedom. You won't want to miss the appendices at the end, disclosing fascinating research about humanism, communism, and the spiritual foundations of our country that the liberal media try to suppress. Finally, my son, Ted, will offer some words on his optimistic vision for the future.

There are more of us than there are of them. The problem is that far too many of "us" are asleep at the wheel. Well, the time has come for the American people to wake up and get active! It is time for us to put our hearts and souls into restoring this great nation of ours to that "shining city on a hill." It is a time for action!

But we can accomplish this only as we all work together, with no one lagging behind. The future of America is at stake, the future of our children and our children's children. It is for them that we must fight with all our might. Remember President Ronald Reagan's words:

> Freedom is never more than one generation away from extinction.
> We didn't pass it on to our children in the bloodstream. It must be
> fought for, protected, and handed on for them to do the same, or

one day we will spend our sunset years telling our children and our children's children what it was once like in the United States where men were free.[4]

I hope that you will stand with me. I am not willing to have that conversation with my children and grandchildren. I will fight now, while we still have time. America is worth saving! May we be willing to covenant with one another before God, as did the signers of the Declaration of Independence:

And for the support of this Declaration, with a firm reliance on the protection of divine Providence, we mutually pledge to each other *our lives, our fortunes and our sacred Honor.*[5]

1

FREEDOM: A UNIVERSAL QUEST

Stand fast therefore in the liberty by which Christ has made us free, and do not be entangled again with a yoke of bondage.

—GALATIANS 5:1

The American dream is not that every man must be level with every other man. The American dream is that every man must be free to become whatever God intends he should become.

—RONALD REAGAN

A dot of perspiration trickled down my temple and past my cheek, deliberately finding its way to my chin. I could feel it hanging there, but I no longer cared. Tears threatened, and my nose began to run, a telltale sign that I was no longer in control. All my life, I had lived according to my rules. The desire for freedom oozed from every pore in my body. As a teenager I resisted the totalitarian Batista regime in Cuba. Then, the about-face of Fidel Castro, who shared a similar hunger for control as his predecessor, made it obvious that I needed to live in the land of the free. Once in America, I took the bull by the horns and graduated from the University of Texas on time, despite not knowing even a smattering of English when I enrolled my freshman year. Within a few short years I was running my own geophysical company in the oil industry. But I still didn't feel free.

Which brought me to Darrell and Betty Lassonde's living room in 1975. The guilt of abandoning my wife and four-year-old son two thousand miles away weighed on me as if I were swimming in the ocean with a cinder block tied around my neck. The weight finally brought me to my knees. Literally.

> Every man and woman since the beginning of time has yearned for freedom.

Dear God, I prayed. I can't go on like this. I need You to come into my life. I need You to heal my family and heal my heart. Please forgive me of my sins, which I know are many. Jesus, I give my life to You right now. I promise to live for You. In Jesus' name, amen.

As I concluded my prayer, I felt as if somebody snipped the cord that had enslaved me to that massive weight.

I was free. Finally, totally free!

Every man and woman since the beginning of time has yearned for freedom. From our terrible twos through the teenage years, we struggled with our parents over this very issue. Addiction clinics and support groups encourage us to fight the personal demons that control us. People and countries are willing to lay down their lives to live free from their oppressors.

All of us find ourselves on a universal quest for freedom. Two thousand years ago, the apostle Paul wrote in Galatians 5:1: "Stand fast therefore in the liberty by which Christ has made us free, and do not be entangled again with a yoke of bondage."

Following in his footsteps, our American forefathers wrote in the preamble of the Declaration of Independence: "We hold these truths to be self-evident, that all men are created equal, that they are endowed by their Creator with certain unalienable Rights, that among these are Life, Liberty and the pursuit of Happiness."

Freedom. Liberty. The right to live and act in accordance with our consciences and before our God without fear of oppression and undue control. We cannot obtain it, nor is it learned. While still in the womb, our Creator endowed us—every person—with the longing to live free.

This book is about the freedom to live and to act. I share parts of my story because I believe you share similar desires.

So how did it all begin?

* * *

Rafael, I think we caught something!"

My best friend, Mayito, and I were shark fishing on a small rowboat a mile off the shore (you read that right) in the dark blue waters of Matanzas Bay on the north side of Cuba. Matanzas is called the "City of Bridges" for the many bridges that cross the three rivers in the city. Tourists often refer to it as the "Venice of Cuba." At that moment, we wished we were standing on one of those bridges. Anything solid.

After attaching a two-pound chunk of tuna on a number 25 hook, we threw the four-hundred-yard line into an area in the bay known for its sharks. Not long after that, the boat jerked. Thirty yards away, a six-foot shark surfaced for a moment at the end of our line and then disappeared.

"Mayito, if we can pull that shark in, we'll be the heroes of Matanzas!"

Together we engaged in a mighty tug-of-war with the powerful animal. Our boat began picking up speed as the shark pulled us out to sea. Then suddenly, the line went slack.

"Mayito, did you see how big that shark was?"

Wham!

Water began flooding into the boat. In the moment, we thought the shark had taken a big bite out of it but later realized it had rammed the side, breaking off a big sliver of wood between the side and bottom. Terrified, we cut the line and headed back to shore as fast as we could. While Mayito rowed, I bailed water with a bucket. Our fear of being eaten by the shark or drowning in the bay fueled us with enough adrenaline to work as fast and hard as we could. And we needed it because we were a mile out at sea, and the water was rushing in faster than I could bail.

Finally, three hundred yards from shore, the rowboat submerged. Mayito and I jumped out and paddled as hard as we could, pushing the boat to shore.

Just another day growing up in Cuba. Seventeen years *young* and carefree.

* * *

In 1901, Agustin Cruz and his wife, Maria, with their one year-old son, Rafael, boarded a ship in the Canary Islands, Spain, bound for the New World. Their hearts brimmed with anticipation and a sense of adventure for their lives in the Spanish-controlled Caribbean island of Cuba.

Romantic stories and ideals brought them and others to the West from faraway lands. Conquistadors like Hernando de Soto led an expedition of seven hundred followers in 1539 from Havana into the southeastern United States in search of gold.

Two decades earlier, another conquistador, Hernán Cortés, may have been the first European to taste chocolate (in a frothy drink) following a meal with the famous Aztec emperor Montezuma. The native peoples called it the elixir of the gods. Only royalty could drink it, and warriors just before a battle. Now chocolate bistros were scattered throughout Europe.

Hernández de Boncalo introduced tobacco to Europe; not surprisingly, Columbus's first scouts reported their discovery of the leafy plant in Cuba. Within short order, Europeans across the continent were using tobacco in its various forms. Many Spaniards like Agustin and Maria were told that the land in Cuba was so fertile that anything would grow in its tropical climate. It sounded exciting!

The West represented freedom and opportunity.

So they boarded their crowded ship and sailed into the unknown. In spite of their lingering seasickness, their spirits remained high . . . because they had a dream!

Upon arrival, Agustin worked from sunrise to sunset, energized by the goal of owning a farm. His relentless hard work and determination finally paid off, and after a few years he purchased a few acres of land and started a successful business. His dream had become a reality!

Work at the farm was a family affair and the kids went to school only long enough to learn the three Rs—reading, [w]riting, and [a]rithmetic. Then they helped with many chores throughout the day.

But fate took an ugly turn, and in 1917 Agustin became one of the millions of fatalities of the worldwide influenza epidemic. Agustin left behind his wife, Maria, and six children, the oldest of whom was my father, Rafael, who was only seventeen at the time. Overwhelmed by her depression and despair, Maria fell prey to a con artist who swindled her out of their farm. They lost everything.

Unsure about what to do next, Maria and her children moved to a sugarcane plantation. The owner offered work for her older boys cutting sugarcane in exchange for a hut with a dirt floor where they could live.

Life at the plantation was extremely difficult. About a hundred huts formed a circle in the small village. The lone general store, owned by the sugar mill, sold everything the people needed, from food to tools to clothing and shoes. The store gave the families credit (up to a certain limit), and the sugar mill paid the people's salaries through the store, which used the money to pay their debt and give them any remaining money (there never was any). Basically, they were de facto slaves of the system established by the sugar mill!

One day a bus driver stopped in the village, offering five dollars and a sandwich to anyone willing to attend a political rally in Matanzas, the capital of the province by the same name. The offer sounded pretty good to my father, who viewed it as an opportunity to escape the indentured servitude of the sugar mill. He boarded the bus and never returned.

After the rally ended, my father walked down to the beach and met the owner of a fruit stand. He asked the owner for a job and the man hired him on the spot. Since my father was broke, the owner let him sleep on the floor of the fruit stand. When he got paid, he sent some of his salary to his mother and tried to save as much as possible.

A couple of years later the owner opened a restaurant across the street, and my father bought the fruit stand. Just like his father, he now owned his own small business . . . a magnificent beachfront fruit stand.

Despite his third-grade education, my father knew how to manage his money (and he could add numbers faster than anyone I have ever known). Soon his younger brother joined him in Matanzas. After a few years he had saved enough to open a grocery store a few blocks from the fruit stand. With hard work he became a successful businessman, just like his father.

About a quarter mile from the grocery store, Juan Diaz and his wife, Lola, owned a small ranch where they lived with their eight children, five boys and three girls. Laudelina was the youngest of the three girls. My father, Rafael, courted Laudelina for five years before they married.

With the many responsibilities of running a successful business, he hired his youngest brother to help him. Unfortunately, the young lad was more interested in women and booze than in being a responsible business partner, and before long he ran the business into the ground.

Although my father knew how to grow a business, he was also very generous . . . to a fault. After a strike at a nearby textile factory left many workers without income, my father offered them credit at his grocery store. "Your families will not go hungry while I have a grocery store," he promised them. Unfortunately, when the strike was settled, many of those workers stopped coming to the store and never paid him back. Between the irresponsible brother and the delinquent accounts, my father had no choice but to close the business.

Proverbs 24:16 says, "A righteous man may fall seven times and rise again." This certainly characterized my father. To him, failure was an opportunity to learn, not an excuse to give up.

After closing the grocery store, my father worked as a commissioned salesman for RCA, selling radios and other appliances—which he continued doing until he left Cuba. He excelled at his job and eventually became RCA's number one salesman in all of Cuba after television entered the island in 1950. My father valued relationships with his customers, which in turn built trust and repeat business—and enabled him to quickly become aware of their need for other appliances. But his focus on satisfying the needs of his customers before making the sale guaranteed plenty of business. He knew the men enjoyed watching boxing matches, the women preferred variety shows, and the teenagers *loved* Elvis Presley.

He also mastered a sales technique called the "Puppy-Dog Close." What's the easiest way to sell a puppy? Let it live with a family for a few days. Then they won't want to return it.

Dad always had fifteen or twenty TVs on loan to different people at any one time. "Did you know that Pedro Vargas and Libertad Lamarque are going to be on TV this Friday?" he'd ask someone. (Vargas was a famous tenor from Mexico, and Lamarque was a renowned tango singer from Argentina.) Or, "Your kids will love watching the cartoons on TV, and you certainly would enjoy watching the news when you come home from work. And I am sure your teenage kids would love to see the rock-and-roll craze that is going on in the United States—do you want to see it?" Then he'd tell them, "I'll lend you one of my TVs so you can watch it."

"I'm not interested in buying a TV," the unwitting prospect would invariably respond.

"Who's talking about buying? Look, I have a dozen TVs sitting in the back of the store, doing nothing. Keep it for a couple of weeks and I'll pick it up when I need it."

You can guess what happened.

My father embodied the universal quest for freedom and the desire to live without any unnecessary outside control. He was also a man of deep integrity, the kind of person Psalm 15:4 describes as one "who swears to his own hurt and does not change." On several occasions he told me, "Rafael, integrity takes a lifetime to develop, but only a second to lose." I never forgot that lesson!

One day, his integrity was put to the test. The Admiral Television Corporation offered my father a job that paid twice the commission he was earning at RCA. But he turned them down.

"Why don't you take the job?" I asked him.

"I can't do it," he answered, "no matter how much they pay me. After I have been telling people for years that RCA is the best, which I truly believe, how can I now tell them that Admiral is the best?"

What a great legacy of integrity I received from my father! Proverbs 20:7 says, "The righteous man walks in his integrity; his children are blessed after him." I benefitted from my father, and I now see his example benefitting my son.

* * *

My mother worked as an elementary school teacher most of her life. After graduation from teachers' college, she taught in a country school. To get there, she rode on a bus for an hour and then rode a horse for half an hour. But she never complained and considered it "paying the price" to fulfill her calling. After a few years she transferred to another school in a small town *only* a forty-five minute bus ride from home. She thought she was in heaven! She remained at that school for the rest of her teaching career.

Education was my mother's passion; she was deeply committed to her students and invested her life in them. Even in her old age, several of her former students found her in the United States and called her, thanking her for her positive influence and the inspiration she had been in their lives.

Into this environment, my mother gave birth to me on March 22, 1939. My parents named me Rafael Bienvenido Cruz. A few years later, my mother gave birth to my sister, Sonia. Until I left Cuba, I lived within a block of the beach. Consequently, I have always felt an affinity for the sea. As far back as I can remember I could always swim, and I imagine that my father did as well.

Incidentally, when Ted was about seven months old, my parents joined my family for a vacation at a resort in the mountains of British Columbia. Eleanor and I were swimming in a pool that was fed by hydrothermal springs while my parents sat nearby, watching the baby. All of a sudden my father picked Ted up and tossed him into the pool next to me. My wife and my mother screamed while my father and I laughed. Ted sank in the water and almost immediately came up paddling and giggling. He swam before he could walk!

When we were young children, my father would take the family swimming early in the morning before he left for work. He was a very strong swimmer and always loved the water. My sister, Sonia, and I would hold on to his feet while he swam on his back in what he called "the train."

I also loved fishing and normally spent every Friday night in the bay with a friend on a rowboat. In the morning we returned with whatever fish we had caught. We never fished with a rod and reel, but typically with a forty-four-pound monofilament line that we held in our hands. Even reeling in a two- or three-pound fish caused the monofilament to burn or cut us as we let it slide between our index fingers and our thumbs. Our fish stories normally included showing the cuts on our index fingers!

During baseball season, my father and I attended baseball games on Sunday afternoons, usually sitting between home plate and first base. My father loved baseball, and so did I. Our favorite team, the Havana Sugar Kings, played Triple-A baseball, farming players to the Cincinnati Reds. Minnie Miñoso, the Chicago White Sox Hall of Famer, started his career playing outfield for the Matanzas team in the Cuban League, so we always rooted for him in the States. My father would spend every game screaming and telling the players what to do.

Other Sunday afternoons our family drove in our 1952 Buick thirty minutes to idyllic Varadero Beach, known for its snowy-white powder sand and crystal clear water. My mother prepared a big pot of *arroz con pollo* (chicken and rice) or *empanadas* (meat pies with ground beef, olives, and raisins) which we enjoyed when we weren't swimming in the water.

Although my father could be very loving and caring in all those fun-filled activities, he was also authoritarian and demanded absolute obedience and a straight walk. My father only spanked me two times that I can remember—and I will never forget them!

The first time I was probably eight or nine. My father was showing my mother a box with a dozen beautiful pens.

"Papa, can you give me one?" I asked.

"No, *Felito*, they are gifts for my clients."

After he went to bed, I took one of the pens from his briefcase and brought it to school the next day. When I came home, my mother told me that my father knew I had stolen one of his pens. Terrified, early in the evening before my father came home, I took off my clothes (a grave mistake) and went to bed. When he arrived home, he walked straight to my bedroom, took off his belt, and pulled me out of bed. I was wearing only my underwear, with virtually no padding.

"While I am alive, my son will not be a thief!" he screamed, as he drove home his point on my backside.

The second time I was about thirteen or fourteen. I had sipped a bottle of rum one evening with three or four other boys by the beach a couple of blocks from the house. A friend of my father's saw us and told him. He walked to the beach, grabbed me by the arm, and whipped me all the way home. I don't even remember going to bed. When I woke up the next morning, my mother was standing at the foot of my bed. She didn't say a word, but she gave me a strong look of disapproval. That hurt as much as my whipping.

I felt so ashamed that I spent the next week painting the house!

Parents today seem so reticent about disciplining their children. They're so afraid of hurting their children's feelings that they wind up raising self-absorbed young men and women with no sense of right or wrong. The writer of Proverbs wisely instructs parents:

> Train up a child in the way he should go, and when he is old he will not depart from it. (Proverbs 22:6)

> Foolishness is bound up in the heart of a child; the rod of correction will drive it far from him. (Proverbs 22:15)

While I learned discipline, integrity, and a strong work ethic from my father, my mother instilled in me the importance of excellence and the value of a good education. She always insisted that we do our very best, especially in school. Because she was blessed with a photographic memory, she spent a good amount of time teaching us memory skills. She loved poetry and encouraged me to memorize long poems and read as many books as I could. Because of her influence, I always earned straight As in my classes. This served me well later on, when I attended the University of Texas and spoke little English.

Scripture affirms the values she passed on to me:

> And whatever you do, do it heartily, as to the Lord and not to men. (Colossians 3:23)

> The excellence of knowledge is that wisdom gives life to those who have it. (Ecclesiastes 7:12)

While I enjoyed a carefree Cuban childhood, little did I know that Cuba—and my childhood—would soon face dramatic changes.

While I learned discipline, integrity, and a strong work ethic from my father, my mother instilled in me the importance of excellence and the value of a good education.

2

BATISTA, CASTRO, AND MY FIGHT FOR FREEDOM

If men could learn from history, what lessons it might teach us! But passion and party blind our eyes, and the light which experience gives us is a lantern on the stern, which shines only on the waves behind us!

—SAMUEL TAYLOR COLERIDGE

But when a long train of abuses and usurpations, pursuing invariably the same Object evinces a design to reduce them under absolute Despotism, it is their right, it is their duty, to throw off such Government, and to provide new Guards for their future security.

—US DECLARATION OF INDEPENDENCE

LUCY RICARDO: This whole thing is Ricky's fault.

RICKY RICARDO: MY FAULT?

LUCY RICARDO: Yeah, if you hadn't have left Cuba to come to America, we wouldn't have gotten married and we never would've come to Switzerland in the first place.[1]

What most Americans know about 1950s pre-Castro Cuba comes from watching *I Love Lucy*. The popular black-and-white television series, which ran from 1951 to 1957, starred Lucille Ball and Cuban-born Desi Arnaz. Together they played the husband-and-wife team Lucy and Ricky Ricardo. The Emmy Award–winning show featured Ball's comedic antics and Arnaz's musical skills.

Arnaz and his orchestra introduced the broader American audience to Cuba's rich musical stylings, which remain popular to this day. Incidentally, Arnaz's family immigrated to the United States after his father was jailed and their property confiscated during the Batista regime.

Ricky Ricardo's 1950s Cuba enjoyed social and economic prosperity like few countries in the Latin American world. However, their infant mortality rate ranked first in Latin America and thirteenth in the world. Life expectancy in 1955 was 63 years, which may seem low, but compared to the rest of Latin America (52), Asia (43), and Africa (37), the Cuban people thrived. Their educational system and literacy rates compared favorably to industrialized countries. Pre-Castro Cuba boasted 58 different newspapers and ranked eighth in the number of radio stations (160), more than Austria (83), the United Kingdom (62), and France (50). And thanks in part to my father, they ranked first among Latin American countries in television sets per capita and fifth in the world.[2]

About a third of Cuba's population in the 1950s were classified middle class.[3] Akin to Americans, people in Cuba could achieve the "Cuban Dream." The bustling island featured American retailers, such as Woolworth's and Sears, and even hosted a Hilton Hotel. Three times a week, a ferry service operated between Key West and Havana with one-way fare costing $13.50 and round trip fare $26 ($213.00 in 2015 dollars). The peso was virtually interchangeable with the dollar.

Movie theaters, skating rinks, and amusement parks abounded. Hot dogs and other American convenience foods were so readily available that traditional Cuban foods could be hard to find in the larger cities.

The sun, around which the rest of Cuba revolved, was Havana, home to a sixth of the country's population. Energizing the city was its sizzling nightlife, exemplified by the Tropicana Club, frequented by American celebrities and notables such as Marlon Brando, Rita Hayworth, John F. Kennedy, and Ernest Hemingway. Nat King Cole, who performed there to sellout crowds, was one of the most popular performers in Cuba. The city's casinos, paired with the nightlife, drew the wealthy from around the world.

If New Orleans married Las Vegas and settled in Miami, you would get 1950s Havana.

* * *

The exact meaning of the name *Cuba* is unclear but most likely comes from the Taino words *cubao*, meaning "where fertile land is abundant," and *coabana*, meaning "great place."

Columbus landed on the northeast coast of Cuba on October 28, 1492, a little over two weeks after stepping foot in the New World. Cuba was one of the earliest colonies established by Spain, and served as the launching point for the conquistadors' expeditions into Central and South America. Havana quickly became an important port for shipping gold from Mexico and Peru to Spain, which meant it also attracted pirates seeking to prey on ships sailing the route on the high seas.

The Spaniards who joined Christopher Columbus on his four journeys and settled in Cuba were unscrupulous and practically decimated the entire native population. In fact, Matanzas, the city of my birth, literally means "massacre," because the Spaniards killed everyone in the original native village. Legend has it that it wasn't until Columbus's fourth trip home that he decided to bring one of the few remaining Cuban natives to Spain. Queen Isabella then decreed they were human beings and should be converted to Catholicism, which stopped the killing. Unfortunately, they had practically been wiped out!

In contrast, when the Spaniards landed in Mexico and expanded their expeditions to Central and South America, they encountered a very large indigenous population. To a substantial degree, they assimilated their two cultures, creating the rich culture common across Latin America today.

As the Spaniards began settling in Cuba, they faced a dilemma.

> If New Orleans married Las Vegas and settled in Miami, you would get 1950s Havana.

Because the native population was virtually nonexistent, they could no longer find anyone to work their sugarcane fields, which required a substantial number of laborers. Not wanting to do the work themselves, they began forcibly importing slaves from Africa.

On October 10, 1868, Carlos Manuel de Céspedes, a sugar mill owner, issued a manifesto similar to the US Declaration of Independence, stating a series of grievances against the government of Spain. He freed his slaves and asked them to join him in the war of independence from their mother country. Máximo Gómez, a former Spanish officer in the Dominican Republic, joined Céspedes, and together they led the people in a long war against Spain, lasting ten years (1868–1878), followed by a much shorter war (1879–1880), both of which failed.

> Every totalitarian regime throughout history has tried to disarm its population.

After the Ten Years' War, the Spanish government made it illegal for any Cuban to own a weapon. Only Spanish soldiers could carry weapons, which forced the Cuban rebels to pilfer or plunder anything they could from the Spanish army. They adopted a battle strategy similar to ancient armies with horses and swords, except they used machetes (two-foot-long blades used for cutting sugarcane). At the cry of "*Al machete*," they would ambush the Spanish army against their gunfire. It is worthwhile to point out that every totalitarian regime throughout history has tried to disarm its population, removing their inhabitants' ability to defend themselves. History offers us a grim lesson in the dangers of gun control:

In 1911, the Ottoman Empire (in present-day Turkey) implemented full gun control. From 1915 to 1917, the government killed 1.5 million defenseless Armenians in what is now known as the Armenian Holocaust.[4]

In 1929, the Soviet Union abolished gun ownership among its citizens. This empowered Joseph Stalin to arrest and exterminate anyone who opposed, disagreed with, or even irritated him. Between 1929 and his death in 1953, 40 million people were murdered.[5]

In 1938 Adolf Hitler reinforced the already-restrictive German gun control laws established by the Weimar government. Jews could no longer own firearms and were barred from businesses involving them. Without the means to defend themselves, 6 million Jews perished, as well as countless gypsies, homosexuals, and the mentally ill.

According to Trevor-Roper and Weinberg's book *Hitler's Table Talk, 1941–1944: Secret Conversations*, Hitler reportedly said:

> The most foolish mistake we could possibly make would be to allow the subject races to possess arms. History shows that all conquerors who have allowed their subject races to carry arms have prepared their own downfall by so doing. Indeed, I would go so far as to say that the supply of arms to the underdogs is a *sine qua non* for the overthrow of any sovereignty. So let's not have any native militia or native police.[6]

In 1935, China established gun control laws rendering political dissidents powerless to defend themselves. Between 1948 and 1952, 20 million people were exterminated.[7] Later, during Chairman Mao Zedong's 1966–1971 Cultural Revolution, as many as 3 million more lives were taken.[8]

Guatemala (1960–1981), Uganda (1971–1979), and Cambodia (1975–1979) also serve as examples of how gun control laws cost lives. Some estimates indicate that as many as 70 million people were killed in the twentieth century because they couldn't defend themselves against totalitarian governments.[9]

The Obama administration's push to integrate data from health care professionals and the Social Security Administration in order to arbitrarily decide who can own a gun evokes these tragic efforts at citizen disarmament found throughout history. Our Founding Fathers established the Second Amendment to enable their citizens to arm and defend themselves against totalitarian governments from within and without.

* * *

In 1891, Cuban poet José Martí immigrated to the United States and began soliciting America and other Latin American countries for support to free Cuba from Spain. In early 1895, Martí returned to his homeland, just as the war of independence began. He was killed fewer than three months after the first shot was fired.

Greatly outnumbering the rebels, the Spanish troops rounded up the rural population into *reconcentrados,* which later served as a model for Hitler's concentration camps. Between two hundred thousand and four hundred thousand civilians died from starvation and disease in those camps.[10]

Finally, at the beginning of 1898, the United States government sent a battleship, the USS *Maine,* to the port of Havana in an attempt to protect the lives of Americans living in that city. Two weeks later an explosion sank the *Maine,* killing all crew members on board. Under pressure from the US media to respond to the unprovoked attack, President William McKinley, with the approval of the US Congress, declared war against Spain in support of the rebels. Americans landed near Santiago, on the southeastern end of the island, and made Guantánamo Bay their base of operations.

> The Obama administration's push to integrate data from health care professionals and the Social Security Administration in order to arbitrarily decide who can own a gun evokes these tragic efforts at citizen disarmament found throughout history.

Teddy Roosevelt, who was later elected US president, joined the war effort and led his voluntary cavalry of "Rough Riders" to victory, capturing San Juan Hill. This war was short-lived, and on December 10, 1898, the United States and Spain signed the Treaty of Paris, granting Cuba its independence.

From 1899 until 1902 a US provisional military government ruled Cuba. During that period, many American entrepreneurs invested in Cuban sugar mills, tobacco plantations, and mines, and established a multitude of other businesses. Protestant denominations, such as the Baptists, the Congregationalists, and the Methodists, sent missionaries to build their flocks and provide an array of social services and educational programs.

Finally, in mid-1902, Tomás Estrada Palma was elected the first president of the Republic of Cuba. A 1903 treaty gave the United States permanent use of Guantánamo Bay.

During Gerardo Machado's presidency in the 1920s, tourism began to flourish. Hotels, nightclubs, golf clubs, restaurants, and casinos began appearing in Havana, catering to wealthy American jet-setters. Baseball, which was introduced to the country in the 1860s, became a national obsession. Dolf Luque—"the Pride of Havana"—whose career spanned twenty years, was one of seventeen Cubans to play in the American big leagues between 1911 and 1929.

Cuban music became a driving force during this time. Combining elements from Spain and Africa, the rumba and other Cuban musical styles kept Americans dancing.

The country established a constitution and selected a series of democratically elected presidents until 1933, when army sergeant Fulgencio Batista led a military coup, overthrowing President Machado. Batista then named himself the Army Chief of Staff, with the rank of colonel, essentially giving himself power over the presidency. He ruled through a series of puppet presidents until 1940, when he was elected president. In 1944 Batista's handpicked candidate lost to Ramón Grau. Concerned for his safety, Batista left the island and went into self-exile in the United States.

In 1952 Batista successfully staged another military coup and ruled Cuba with a combination of control and fear. He bolstered his defense against his opposition by raising the salaries of the military and giving them great power. The people suffered under the backhand of the military's strong arm as Batista and his henchmen imposed the kind of "protectionism" reminiscent of the Prohibition-era mobs in Chicago, extracting money from businesses, both large and small, by extortion, with dire consequences for anyone who dared to resist. A reign of terror prevailed, with dissidents being shot, beaten, or imprisoned.

Batista embraced mobsters from Chicago and Las Vegas, who exported prostitution, drugs, racetracks, and casinos into the country. Marijuana and cocaine were so plentiful that an American magazine remarked, "Narcotics are hardly more difficult to obtain in Cuba than a shot of rum. And only slightly more expensive."[11]

Of course, the dictator demanded a piece of the action. Through his partnership with American mobsters Meyer Lansky and Lucky Luciano, Batista amassed a personal fortune of several hundred million dollars.

> In seven years as Cuba's dictator, Batista was reportedly responsible for the murder of twenty thousand people.

His cut from some of the casinos was reportedly 30 percent.[12]

The corruption at the top trickled down to his ministers and even his ministers' secretaries, who enriched themselves at every opportunity. Police officers killed as they pleased. Every day, stories circulated about people being tortured and killed, with their bodies thrown in the sea so the sharks would dispose of them. People began avoiding the clubs and movie theaters for fear of being harmed, brutalized, even kidnapped. By intimidating the citizens with open displays of cruelty, Batista maintained control. In seven years as Cuba's dictator, he was reportedly responsible for the murder of twenty thousand people.[13]

Under the heavy hand of oppression, resistance surfaced. Despite the threat of police brutality, students began organizing anti-Batista demonstrations. Then on July 26, 1953, a young lawyer named Fidel Castro and his brother Raul led a contingent of 135 armed men, who stormed the Moncada army garrison in Santiago. Plagued with miscommunication, disorganization, and a lack of weapons, and outnumbered ten to one, the insurgency failed miserably. Nine rebels were killed in combat, and Castro and a handful of men were imprisoned.

Cubans consider this the beginning of the Cuban Revolution.

While in prison, Castro penned a now-famous speech, "History Will Absolve Me," which he smuggled out of his cell page by page. In memory of the attack, he renamed his group the "26th of July Movement."

Imprisonment afforded Castro the time to read the works of Marx, Lenin, and Martí and formulate his communist philosophy and strategy for moving forward. Believing that he was no longer a threat, Batista released Castro and his comrades in 1955. *53 → 55 ; 2yrs.*

But Castro was indeed a threat. He returned to Havana and began conducting radio interviews and press conferences. With Castro's fiery rhetoric fueling the ever-increasing resistance and escalating violence, Batista decided to throw Fidel and Raul back into prison. Before they could be arrested, the brothers fled to Mexico.

While in Mexico City, the brothers befriended a Marxist doctor from Argentina named Ernesto "Che" Guevara. After an extended conversation with Fidel the first time they met, Guevara decided to join the 26th of July Movement. Che and Fidel formed a synergistic friendship that planted the seeds of revolution in countries for years to come. While Guevara underwent military training with other members of the movement, Castro headed to the United States in search of wealthy sympathizers. While stateside, Batista's agents allegedly failed an assassination attempt on his life.

With Castro out of the country, it was up to high school and university students to form the major opposition to the Batista regime. Two student organizations led this effort: the FEU, or *Federación Estudiantil Universitaria* (University Student Federation), and the DR, or *Directorio Revolucionario* (Revolutionary Directorate). This took the form of an underground movement, not dissimilar to the French resistance during World War II, carrying out sabotage, propaganda, recruiting, training, acquisition and movement of weapons, and other related activities.

Into this landscape, I decided to join the rebellion . . .

* * *

I was just fourteen when Fidel Castro attacked the Moncada army garrison. Shortly thereafter, high school and university students began demonstrating all over the island. Batista's army typically broke up the demonstrations by beating the demonstrators with billy clubs. As a result, seeing students with head bandages was quite common.

Initially the student council–led demonstrations were spontaneous. But as the military began killing the protestors and destroying local businesses, they began coordinating their efforts. This led to the formation of the FEU and the DR. After Castro went into exile, the third group, the 26th of July Movement, was formed.

The FEU operated primarily in Havana and was led by José Antonio Echevarría, the president of the student council at the University of Havana. They concentrated their efforts on attacking political leaders until Echevarría was killed while leading a group trying to storm the presidential palace.

The two groups worked in close collaboration with one another, pursuing the same ultimate goal of putting an end to the Batista regime. The other group's approach was more systematic and long-term, and began by establishing an underground resistance movement.

As a leader in my high school student council, I was invited to join the underground movement. Seeing the corruption in Batista's administration and horrified by the manner in which they killed any dissidents, I was easily convinced. The underground was composed of a series of units operating in a semi-independent manner one from another.

In the evening hours we met in the high school (I can't remember how we were able to get in). We removed the guns we had hidden under a platform in a classroom and were taught how to use them. Our leaders also trained us in propaganda, logistics for recruitment, and how to identify and monitor spies. Because Batista had issued a 10:00 p.m. curfew for the city, we did our best to end our meetings on time.

After an initial period of training, I began recruiting and forming my first unit. For security reasons, the members of my unit did not know the identity of my superior. My unit concentrated on propaganda, weapons movement and acquisition, and some acts of sabotage within the city.

In September 1956, I enrolled at the University of Santiago and met Frank País, the urban coordinator of the 26th of July Movement. Five years older than me, Frank was the son of a Baptist pastor. His small band of insurgents prepared for Castro's return from Mexico on the sixty-foot cabin cruiser the *Granma*. Accompanying Castro were his brother Raul, Che Guevara, and seventy-nine other rebels. Castro chose the disembarkment location to mirror José Martí, who had sixty-one years earlier landed in the same area during the war of independence from Spain.

On November 29, the night before Castro's expected arrival, País divided us into two groups and gave us our final instructions. He led the first group, which planned to attack the police headquarters. I participated in the second group, which prepared to join Castro and his men in attacking the Moncada army barracks in the morning at the same time.

The next morning, we gathered near the barracks but didn't carry guns, to avoid suspicion. Just before our attack, a truckful of weapons was scheduled to pull in front of us so we could grab our guns and begin our assault. As we waited for the *Granma*'s arrival, one of our men arrived yelling, "Abort! Abort!" We scattered immediately. Later, we were informed that the boat had encountered some problems and our plans were thwarted.

While our unit successfully avoided the police, the other unit didn't fare so well. Apparently Frank and his men never received word about the delay. After four days of fighting, several men were killed. Frank País escaped, but seven months later, the police shot him in the back of the head, killing him. In response to his death, workers throughout Santiago declared a strike, which was the biggest demonstration in that city up to that point.

With army troops everywhere, four of us from Matanzas decided to leave Santiago by car and return home. As we departed the city, an army patrol captured us and escorted us to the Moncada army garrison. When we stepped off the army truck, soldiers began screaming, *"¡Al paredón, al paredón!"* ("To the firing squad, to the firing squad!").

Just when we thought this was the end, a fellow student from the university and son of an army major walked by.

"Erasmo, Erasmo!" we cried out. The army had picked him up by mistake and had just released him.

"What are *you* doing here?" he asked us.

"We don't know," a voice from our group answered. "We were just driving out of town and these men stopped us. Please help us and tell them that we aren't revolutionaries!" He wasn't aware that we were part of the underground.

"Señores," he told the soldiers. "I give you my word that these men are not rebels. I know them well. We attend the university together. Let them go. Please."

And with that, the soldiers released us. Although my faith was minimal at that time, I'm reminded today of God's promise: "'For I know the plans I have for you,' declares the LORD, 'plans to prosper you and not to harm you, plans to give you hope and a future'" (Jeremiah 29:11 NIV).

Castro and his men finally landed on December 2. Because the army was on high alert, the men immediately escaped to the mountains—but not without casualties. Sixty-three men were either captured or killed.

When I returned to Matanzas, I resumed control of the first unit and formed a second unit, focusing on sabotage throughout the province and disrupting communications and transportation. Again, to protect the identity of the members of the underground, the members of one unit did not know the members of the other.

Perhaps the most difficult task of all was pretending to be a different person. Considering that government informants were everywhere, to avoid suspicion I acted in public as if I did not care at all about politics, never expressing any opinions unless I absolutely knew who the other person was, and even then it was not wise to do so. I also warned my unit members to be careful whom they talked to.

Unfortunately, I did not follow my own advice and trusted a young man who expressed a desire to be involved in the revolution. I recruited him, and he turned out to be a government informant. Soon Batista's henchmen arrested me and brought me to the army garrison in Matanzas.

Four soldiers entered my interrogation room and pummeled me with an instrument similar to a billy club. When I fell to the ground under the barrage of hits, they kicked me and stomped on me. As the beating continued, a soldier kicked me on the back of my head, driving my face into the concrete floor, breaking my nose, and crushing my four front teeth. Then they picked me up and threw me into a seven-by-seven foot cell. With no bed, I stretched my shaky body on the hard concrete floor. Blood gushed from several cuts on my face, but I was so numb from the beating that I felt no pain. My body was in shock.

After about four hours, every bone in my body hurt. Then the soldiers entered my cell and escorted me to the interrogation room again, where they subjected me to good cop/bad cop questioning, followed by another brutal beating. This procedure was repeated multiple times for several days.

My father knew I was involved in the underground and grew concerned when he hadn't heard from me for days. So he began searching for me, jail by jail, until he finally found me in the Matanzas army garrison.

Before my arrest, I had heard that several other members of the underground had been captured. After the soldiers had broken their wills, the rebels confessed their involvement in the revolution and shared the names of other collaborators. A few days later the informants were found dead on the streets. The authorities claimed they were shot while trying to attack an army patrol. Not wanting to suffer a similar fate gave me the strength to endure and refuse to compromise the names of other members of the underground.

One morning a soldier entered my cell.

"The colonel wants to see you. Follow me."

Walking down the corridor, I wondered what would happen next. A firing squad? A hanging? Another beating? My hands and legs were already numb, so I doubted the pain could get much worse.

I entered the colonel's office.

"Please have a seat."

Up to that point, I had resisted every command from the opposition—but this time I complied.

"I am going to release you," he said. "But if a bomb explodes in this city, I'm coming to get you."

"How can you hold me responsible for what other people do?" I asked.

"I don't care," he answered. "If a bomb explodes in this city, I'm coming to get you."

My father picked me up at the army garrison and drove me home.

An hour after I arrived home, a lady from the underground came to my house.

"Two people from the army have been assigned to follow you twenty-four hours a day in shifts of eight hours," she informed me. "They want to use you to find your superiors; that's why they released you. The underground recommends that you get out of the country as soon as possible."

"I need to get to the mountains and try to join the rebels," I said. "Can you help me?"

"Batista's army has secured every route. I doubt you can get past them."

"Then I'll just figure out how to get out of the country."

Since I was a straight-A student, I decided the best way out of Cuba was with a student visa. So I applied to three American universities: the University of Miami, the University of Texas, and Louisiana State University. The University of Texas accepted me first—and that is how I became a Texan!

With my passport and acceptance letter, I was able to acquire a student visa from the US embassy in Havana. Only one hurdle remained between me and freedom: an exit permit from the Batista regime. With help from a lawyer friend, a Cuban government official was convinced to stamp my passport with the permit.

My father scrounged whatever cash he could find, and my mother, afraid that someone would rob me while I slept on the bus, sewed a pocket in my underwear to hold my money. In my pocket I kept a few dollars for the bus fare from Key West, Florida, to Austin, Texas, and to buy a couple of hamburgers along the way.

One early morning in August 1957, I lay on the backseat of my father's car inside the garage. My father pulled the car out of the garage and drove to Havana, to the docks in the harbor. There I caught the ferry from Havana to Key West.

> I do not know what the future holds, but I know Who holds the future.
>
> —AUTHOR UNKNOWN

When it came time to say our good-byes, my mother and sister embraced me and cried while my father tried to encourage me and give me strength. At the same time feelings of exhilaration overwhelmed me about going to "the land of the free and the home of the brave." After reading so much about the United States of America, its great heritage, the land of opportunity, a place where anyone, with hard work and perseverance, could achieve their dreams, I was determined to make the best of it.

Finally boarding the ferry, I felt apprehensive about leaving my family. Would I ever see them again? Would I ever come back? What did the future hold for me?

3

MY ESCAPE TO THE LAND OF THE FREE

My God! How little do my countrymen know what precious blessings they are in possession of, and which no other people on earth enjoy!

—THOMAS JEFFERSON

And for the support of this Declaration, with a firm reliance on the protection of Divine Providence, we mutually pledge to each other our Lives, our Fortunes, and our sacred Honor.

—LAST WORDS OF THE US DECLARATION OF INDEPENDENCE

My seven-hour ferry ride to Key West gave me plenty of time to think. For the first time in my life, I was leaving my family, friends, and home in Cuba. At eighteen, I didn't know if I would ever return. One thing I knew for sure: I couldn't return with Batista in power. My life depended on it.

The SS *Havana* was a sizable ferry for its day, transporting 500 passengers and 125 cars. After a few moments on the deck, watching the Havana skyline disappear in the distance, I stepped inside. The air-conditioning offered a welcome respite from the sticky August day. I strolled through the gift shop, imagining the many choices at my disposal when I arrived in America. Then I walked by the snack shop. While I wanted to buy a hot dog, I knew I needed to conserve my money—and fortunately my mother had packed an *empanada* (meat pie) and *mariquitas* (thinly sliced plantain chips) for my ferry ride.

I returned to my chair on the deck and savored my lunch, knowing it would probably be my last Cuban meal for a long time. Between bites, I opened my passport and examined my exit permit. Again, I could hardly believe my eyes. My next stop would be in America. The land of the free and the home of the brave. The place where dreams can become reality. Passengers all around me were speaking English, and although I didn't know the language, I resolved to make it my own.

A short five hours later, buildings began to appear on the horizon. I couldn't wait to step on land. Finally the ferry docked and passengers began to disembark. Blood surged through my veins as fast as my myriad of thoughts: *Will Cuba ever achieve this same freedom? Did I do the right thing by leaving? Should I have stayed? Am I endangering the lives of others?*

Stepping on American soil was a memory I will never forget. As I walked down the ramp, I took a deep breath of American air. *Smells just like Cuba.* Stories I had learned in school about the American patriots fighting for independence from England came to mind. They had sacrificed their lives for the cause of freedom—and now I was about to freely enjoy the liberties they had bestowed upon future generations. What a remarkable legacy!

I boarded a Greyhound bus in Key West, heading to Miami, and then boarded another bus bound for Baton Rouge. My fishing buddy, Mayito, had left Cuba and was studying at LSU, so I spent a day with him. The following day I boarded one more bus for Austin, Texas.

Finally, I arrived at the University of Texas, about a month before classes started, and immediately walked to the Foreign Students Office. Because of my limited resources, the director recommended that I live at a place called Campus Guild. This was a house that was cleaned and maintained by the students, which made room and board very afford-able. It housed eighty-four students on four wings with twenty bunk beds each. Only the four officers who ran the place had private rooms.

In order to help pay my way through school, I was able to find work in the chemistry department. With a letter from the university, I was able to register with the IRS and obtain a Social Security card. I then found a job working at a restaurant as a dishwasher. I figured that I didn't need to speak English to wash dishes. My salary was fifty cents an hour.

Back then, not every restaurant owned an automatic dishwasher—including this one. So I washed every dish by hand. One sink held soapy water for washing, and the other held scalding hot water for rinsing. My manager gave me rubber gloves to wear, but within the first hour the hot water seeped inside my gloves several times, which really burned. I decided to take off my gloves and never wore them again. Because of this, my arms always looked red, like a boiled lobster.

As you can imagine, my early inability to speak English caused communication problems. One day during my first week on the job, my manager asked me to empty and clean the ice machine because a waiter had broken a glass inside of it. Out of that whole discourse, I only understood one word: "glass." Since I had just washed about fifty glasses, I figured that she said the glasses were dirty—so I picked them all up and washed them again.

Everyone in the kitchen thought my misunderstanding was hysterical. Only after I had finished rewashing the glasses did a bilingual employee explain what my manager had said.

Before I left Cuba, a high school English teacher gave me an invaluable piece of advice for learning English quickly: go to the movies every day. So, every day after I finished washing dishes, I rushed to the movie theater. Then I watched the same movie three times in a row. Back then, the theater wasn't emptied between showings, so I stayed and watched the next showing. Each time, I concentrated on associating words with corresponding actions and objects. By the third showing I had a pretty good idea of what the movie was about. After following that daily routine for a month, I began thinking in English.

To counteract the language barrier, I also sat in the front row in every class, paying close attention and taking copious notes in my broken English. I was extremely focused, and usually studied with an open Spanish–English dictionary next to my textbooks. Between work and study, I had minimal spare time.

One day, the Office of Foreign Students at the university offered me a "Good Neighbor Scholarship" which covered my two-hundred-dollar-per-semester tuition. This must have been an act of God, because I hadn't applied for it.

By the next semester, I found a "better" job at a Toddle House restaurant (the chain no longer exists). They served breakfast twenty-four hours a day, much like Waffle House. While my fifty-cents-an-hour wage remained the same and I still washed pots by hand, the restaurant owned a dishwashing machine for glasses and plates. I continued working there until I obtained my bachelor's degree.

The benefit of working at a restaurant is that they feed you. Since my finances were limited, I ate throughout my eight-hour shift, which allowed me not to eat anything during the next sixteen hours. A great way to save money!

My heavy workload presented a challenge to learning English. Without a strong command of the English language, I wouldn't pass my classes. If I didn't pass my classes, I'd lose my student visa and be forced to return to Cuba. The stress was significant.

By my sophomore year, I felt more confident speaking English, so I began speaking at different Rotary Clubs in the Austin area, trying to build support for the Cuban revolution. At that time, I still assumed that Castro led the insurgence with noble intentions and that he presented the only solution for getting rid of Batista.

Most Americans felt that same sentiment, fomented by a series of articles written by *New York Times* reporter Herbert Matthews. When Batista claimed his troops had killed Castro during the 26th of July Movement's landing, Matthews found him ensconced in the Sierra Maestra mountains of eastern Cuba. His series of interviews for the newspaper painted Castro as a folk hero.

As late as July 1959, Matthews stood by his defense of Castro. "This is not a Communist Revolution in any sense of the term. Fidel Castro is not only not a Communist, he is decidedly anti-Communist."[1]

Other media personalities joined in the chorus. Pulitzer Prize–

winning journalist Walter Lippmann advised, "It would be a great mistake even to intimate that Castro's Cuba has any real prospect of becoming a Soviet satellite."[2] *Newsweek* gushed, "Castro is honest, and an honest government is something unique in Cuba. Castro is not himself even remotely a Communist."[3] *Look* magazine promised, "We can thank our lucky stars Castro is no Communist."[4]

* * *

On January 1, 1959, Fidel Castro called for a nationwide strike that overthrew the Batista regime. With a force of only eight hundred guerrillas, he defeated Batista's thirty-thousand-man army. Initially, the US government and the American people applauded the change, heralding the victory of democracy over repression.

As I mentioned earlier, I returned to Cuba at the end of the summer in 1959 and was shocked by the country's left turn. Very quickly, Castro began acting like a communist dictator. He refused to organize free elections. Like his predecessor, he killed his political enemies and filled the jails and prisons with critics, anticommunist leaders, and other opponents from the Batista government. He placed the press under strict censorship and confiscated foreign-owned land, often without compensation, and gave it to his cronies.

Then, Castro established diplomatic relations with the Soviet Union, who in return provided the country with economic and military aid. By 1961, the United States had closed their embassy in Havana, severing diplomatic ties with their neighbor only ninety miles to the south. The embarrassing Bay of Pigs fiasco that April hammered the final nail in the coffin in the relationship between the United States and Cuba. Later that year, Castro clarified his intentions in a televised address: "I am a Marxist-Leninist and shall be one until the end of my life."[5]

The US government was duped. The American people were duped. I was duped. When people ask me why I supported Castro in overthrowing the Cuban government, I readily admit that I didn't realize he was a communist. I also (wrongly) believed he was the best alternative to the corrupt government at the time.

So what prompted Castro's "sudden" allegiance to Communism?

Without a doubt, the American government's support of Batista's regime played a factor. As the Cold War escalated, the anticommunist Batista seemed like the best alternative at the time—the same way I felt about Castro. The Cuban dictator granted American companies generous favors, which enabled them to take advantage of the people. For example, the ITT Corporation, an American telephone company, gave Batista a golden telephone as a way of saying thank you for the "excessive telephone rate increase" that he approved at the prompting of the US government.[6]

> The US government was duped. The American people were duped. I was duped.

Most telling of all, emboldened by US backing, Batista had murdered twenty thousand Cubans in only seven years,[7] a greater proportion per capita of the Cuban population than the number of Americans who died in both world wars. In only seven years, the Cuban dictator destroyed every individual liberty and transformed democratic Cuba into a police state. As tensions increased between Batista and the 26th of July Movement, the American government beefed up their support of the Cuban strongman. In many ways, America helped nudge Castro toward the Soviet Union.

But Castro's leanings toward Communism go back much further than the 1950s. First of all, Fidel didn't introduce Communism to the island. Communism and the Communist Party in Cuba, the *Partido Comunista de Cuba*, date back to 1925, a year before he was born. In 1943, while the United States, Britain, and the Soviet Union were locked in combat with Germany, the Supreme Soviet of the USSR assembled to devise a plan to suppress the United States' rising international popularity due to its heroic deeds in the war.

The Soviet leaders discussed the importance of undermining

the United States and approved several strategies. One such strategy was to foster groups of youth, intellectuals, and artists in every country of the Western Hemisphere who adopted their communist ideals. So, later that year, Andrei Gromyko arrived in Havana to begin his tenure as ambassador from the USSR.

You may remember his name for his service to the Soviet Union as their minister of foreign affairs from 1957 to 1988. His duties included the implementation of Moscow's new strategy. Gumer Bashirov joined him in Cuba as his agent in charge of recruiting youth for the communist-oriented groups.

As tensions increased between Batista and the 26th of July Movement, the American government beefed up their support of the Cuban strongman. In many ways, America helped nudge Castro toward the Soviet Union.

Every youth who participated in these groups received a monthly stipend. One name on Bashirov's list: seventeen-year-old Fidel Castro.

In a 1997 paper he wrote for the Institute for US–Cuba Relations, titled "When Castro Became a Communist," Salvador Diaz-Verson described his years living in Cuba as a journalist and Cuba's chief of military intelligence from 1948 until 1952. In the late 1950s, Diaz-Verson began collecting information about Castro's background. He wrote:

Every youth who participated in these groups received a monthly stipend. One name on Bashirov's list: seventeen-year-old Fidel Castro.

> We knew and had the proof that Fidel Castro was one of Moscow's agents. We had been

able to gather photographs, documents and reports indicating he was an agent for the Soviet Union although he was not a regular member of the Communist Party.[8]

Three weeks after coming to power in 1959, Castro's soldiers entered Diaz-Verson's home in the Vedado neighborhood of Havana and confiscated all of his secret files, labeled "A-943." Diaz-Verson presented his 1997 paper to report on his forty-year project of recompiling his evidence.

By 1948 Havana served as the primary hub for Soviet activities in Latin America. The Pan-American Conference was scheduled to be held that spring in Bogotá, Colombia, to adopt resolutions protesting communist operations in the Western Hemisphere. Under the leadership of US secretary of state George Marshall, the leaders from countries in North, South, and Central America were going to organize a deliberately anticommunist council called the Organization of American States.

Concerned about the potential consequences of the conference, Diaz-Verson reported that Frances Demont, the treasurer of the Soviet-backed "World Federation of Democratic Youth," flew to Havana with seventy thousand dollars (the equivalent of almost seven hundred thousand in 2015 dollars) in her suitcase to use for propaganda at the conference.

Two months later, twenty-one-year-old Fidel Castro flew to Bogotá implement their plan. He and his comrade Alfredo Guevara (no relation to Che Guevara) were commissioned to attack priests and nuns and to stir up unrest among the youth to disrupt the conference. They also helped organize a counter-conference called the Latin American Youth Congress.

Adding insult to injury, the extremely popular, left-leaning Colombian presidential candidate, Jorge Gaitán—whom Castro admired and met with two days earlier—was assassinated by Juan Roa Sierra one week into the five-week Pan-American Conference. The propaganda, protests, and assassination sent Bogotá into pandemonium. Rioting broke out in the city, effectively destroying the downtown area, with many of the rioters assuming their conservative president, Mariano

Pérez, was behind it. Historians believe this experience influenced Castro in utilizing anger as a means to stir up the masses.

Six hundred people died and 450 were hospitalized as a result of *el Bogotazo.*[9] As the riots calmed down, Castro and Guevara sought asylum in the Cuban embassy, eventually returning to Havana and reporting to Bashirov. They were congratulated for their good work.

Diaz-Verson believed that when Castro and his men stormed the Moncada garrison in 1953, Castro knew they were outnumbered, but he forged ahead, confident the casualties would help turn the tide of public opinion against Batista's government. Neither I nor the rest of Cuba saw what he was doing because we didn't know he had been steeped in Communist philosophy and equipped with the tools to lead a revolution.

Before coming to power, the man promised to restore the 1940 constitution, lead an honest administration, and restore full civil and political liberties. But his true colors were revealed when he came to power.

In 1960, Castro signed a trade agreement with the Soviet Union, further reinforcing American distrust. That same year he severed ties between Cuba and the United States and then broke diplomatic relations with America in 1961.

When Castro took over Cuba, he immediately started indoctrinating the children, focusing on destroying loyalty to anyone or anything except the government. This included undermining loyalty to God and His precepts as well as loyalty to the family. Children lived in intern schools, where they were brainwashed with Communist ideology. In fact, children were encouraged to report their parents to the authorities if they heard them speaking against the government.

Soldiers would walk into a kindergarten or first grade class and ask the children to close their eyes.

"Ask God to give you candy," the children were told. The children would obey. Then the soldiers would tell them, "Open your eyes. Where is the candy? No candy? Now close your eyes again and pray to Fidel for candy."

While the children's eyes were closed, the soldiers would quietly place candy on the children's desks and ask them to open their eyes.

"Who gave you the candy?"

"You did!" the children would reply.

"True," they replied. "But this candy really comes from Fidel. Did God give you the candy?"

"No!"

"Who gave you the candy?"

"Fidel! Fidel Castro!"

> Children will follow the training they have received in their childhood—whether from a parent, youth leader, teacher, television program, video game, you name it.

I must confess, I couldn't help but think of this sad, cynical brainwashing when, just a few years ago, a YouTube video surfaced showing footage of young schoolchildren being led by their teachers chanting praises to President Obama.[10] A truly dangerous practice.

Adolf Hitler reportedly said, "Give me your children and I will change society in ten years." Parents need to be alert in monitoring the messages their children are fed. Fidel Castro's indoctrination began at seventeen years of age. Scripture tells us "Train up a child in the way he should go, and when he is old he will not depart from it" (Proverbs 22:6). This verse rings true regardless of our morals, beliefs, or politics. Children will follow the training they have received in their childhood—whether from a parent, youth leader, teacher, television program, video game, you name it. We must be vigilant in how our children are trained.

* * *

In August 1959, I returned to Cuba. Saving money from my dishwashing job afforded me enough funds to carpool with some friends to Miami and then catch a flight to Havana. A few weeks later I would fly back to Miami and carpool back to Austin.

My visit gave me the shock of my life. In many ways it looked as if history had repeated itself. The Castro regime had begun to curtail freedom of the press and freedom of expression. Newspapers that dared to speak against the revolution were shut down or their offices were destroyed. Radio and television stations suffered the same fate.

Revolutionary tribunals were set up, and anyone who had been involved in the Batista government was brought before the court and declared guilty without a right to trial. Then they were executed before a firing squad. Castro stated that trials were unnecessary because justice was on their side.

After I departed, the government confiscated businesses, factories, and farms and persecuted the wealthy. A mass exodus of medical doctors, engineers, industrialists, and businesspeople—"oppressors of the people"—emigrated to America. The government awarded their *Miami!!* replacements to people on the basis of "revolutionary merit," without even considering their competence to run these enterprises. As a result, productivity dropped dramatically, causing a severe economic crisis.

Because many of the sugarcane cutters now served in the army, the government began forcing the general population, a good number of them in their sixties, to work the fields as "volunteers" to cut sugarcane. The majority of these people had never used a machete, and as a result could not cut the cane efficiently, causing a great deal of waste. And, of course, due to their limited experience and strength, they labored at a slow pace. Consequently, sugar production declined precipitously, and Cuba went from being the largest sugar producer in the world to supplying a small percentage of the total demand.

Castro confiscated all private clinics and hospitals and instituted socialized medicine. Without competent staff and proper hygiene, infections became common occurrences in these hospitals. Shortages of medical supplies have continued to worsen, and even everyday drugs, such as aspirin, are scarce today.

Although not declared openly, the signs of Communism were becoming obvious. I left Cuba after three weeks, disillusioned and feeling betrayed, never to return again. Unfortunately, I again left my parents and sister behind.

When Castro ordered all teachers to teach Marxism in the public schools, my mother faced a dilemma: would she obey the government and violate her core values or refuse to teach this horrible worldview and surely be arrested? In good conscience she could not teach Marxism, but she also didn't want to be imprisoned.

So what did she do? After careful consideration, she staged an attack of insanity in front of her sixth grade students. One day in the middle of class, she started running up and down the classroom aisles, screaming, pulling her hair, and throwing a huge fit, making a fool of herself in front of her students and other teachers. Then, with the help of an empathetic doctor's evaluation, she received a dismissal as a teacher for mental illness reasons.

Later she told me, "I would rather suffer public humiliation than poison the minds of children with Communist indoctrination."

After I returned to Austin, I contacted every Rotary Club where I had spoken before my trip. I felt a moral obligation to go back and set the record straight. At each Rotary Club, I apologized for misleading them. At one club, someone asked me, "Why did you change your mind?"

"I was deceived," I replied, "as were many other people in Cuba. I believed the rhetoric, but now I see that the actions do not match the rhetoric."

Salvador Diaz-Verson, who witnessed Castro's communist policies in action, had this to say about the man:

> He is the most repugnant and cynical traitor that the history of the Americas has recorded because he has sold his country, his family, and his fellow Cubans to an international enslaving power which has already erased from Cuba all vestiges of freedom, dignity and sovereignty, converting a rich and joyful country into a miserable and terrorized piece of land.[11]

This same Castro, who for years promised his own version of "hope and change,"[12] told his fellow Cubans that the rich were evil, that they oppressed the poor, and that the country needed to "redistribute the wealth."

gosh'.
Beep
Stuff!!'?!
We DeT IT, Sir!!!

* * *

When Barack Obama ran for president promising "hope" and "change," I couldn't rid my mind of Castro making the very same promises. Hope and change, but change to what? Throughout his presidency, he has accused the rich of oppressing the poor and worked to redistribute the wealth by taxing businesspeople who supply jobs to the poor. His version of social justice is nothing more than collectivism and creating a society dependent upon the government, as espoused by Karl Marx.

Then he scolded business owners across the country by telling them, "If you've got a business—you didn't build that. Somebody else made that happen." And who is that "somebody"? The government.

a lie!
a truve!

"Who gave you that candy? Fidel gave you that candy!"

My front-row seat to watching "change" in Cuba and the reliance on the government helps me see its subtle appearance in American society today.

In the next chapter, I'll give you a front-row perspective on Communism and its insidious tentacles that reach into our democracy.

4

DOES COMMUNISM WORK?

How do you tell a Communist? Well, it's someone who reads Marx and Lenin. And how do you tell an anti-Communist? It's someone who understands Marx and Lenin.

—RONALD REAGAN

Capitalism and communism stand at opposite poles. Their essential difference is this: The communist, seeing the rich man and his fine home, says: "No man should have so much." The capitalist, seeing the same thing, says: "All men should have as much."

—PHELPS ADAMS

Seattle businessman Dan Price instituted dramatic changes in his company, Gravity Payments, with the noblest of intentions.[1] After his city raised the minimum wage to $15 per hour, Price decided to go one step—okay, one BIG step—further by raising the salary of every employee in his credit card processing company to $70,000 a year. You read that right. All 120 employees would earn the same salary: receptionists, data entry clerks, customer service representatives, even himself (a $930,000 a year pay cut). Before the announcement, the average salary at his company was $48,000 a year.

Overnight, liberal pundits and media outlets across the country heralded the man as a modern-day hero. "Income inequality has been racing in the wrong direction," Price told the *New York Times*. "I want to fight for the idea that if someone is intelligent, hard-working and does a good job, then they are entitled to live a middle-class lifestyle."

Initially, the decision attracted new clients, outnumbering departing clients who disagreed with his decision. To accommodate the sudden upsurge of new business, Price hired a dozen more employees, expenses—at $70,000 a year—that he hadn't anticipated.

Then two of his most valued employees quit, claiming unfairness for doubling the pay of some new hires while giving little or no new raises to longer-tenured staff members. Entrepreneurs in the Seattle business community were angry at Price as well, for "mak[ing] them look stingy in front of their own employees."

One long-term employee, Grant Moran, complained, "Now the people who were just clocking in and out were making the same as me. It shackles high performers to less motivated team members."

Most concerning of all, his brother and cofounder, Lucas Price, filed a lawsuit, telling the *Times*, "Dan has taken millions of dollars out of the company for himself while denying me the benefits of the ownership of my shares, and otherwise favoring his own interests as the majority shareholder over my interests."

With profits directed to salaries, Dan confessed that very few funds are available for him to buy out his brother, pay the legal expenses, or make any long-term capital improvements.

"What's their incentive to hustle if you pay them so much?" departing employees asked Gravity sales director Leah Brajcich.

Like Marxism, Price's decision was rooted in unattainable ideals. All begin with the humanistic assumption that people are inherently good and that, left to our own devices, all of us will naturally work hard and for the betterment of others.

"All you need is love," John Lennon famously claimed.[2] If we just love each other and share everything equally with everybody, the world will be a better place. And while everyone needs love, without a doubt, no one can claim to love with a perfect love—apart from the love of the Father, Son, and Holy Spirit.

The apostle Paul lamented in Romans 3:10–12, "There is none righteous, no, not one; there is none who understands; there is none who seeks after God. They have all turned aside; they have together become unprofitable; there is none who does good, no, not one."

Dan Price, unfortunately, modeled his company on the unattainable ideals of Marxism. Now he may be forced to shut it down.

* * *

On January 1, 1959, the day Fidel Castro overthrew the Batista regime, the new Cuban dictator stood in the main square of Santiago de Cuba and addressed the jubilant crowd: "The revolution begins now," he said. "This time, luckily for Cuba, the revolution will truly come into being. It will not be like 1895, when the North Americans came and took over. . . . For the first time the republic will really be entirely free."[3]

While Castro enforced the Marxist ideal, Cuba never fulfilled it.

As I explained in the previous chapter, Castro accused the wealthy of oppressing the people, so he confiscated their businesses, factories, and farms, eliminating the ownership of private property. All in the name of redistributing the wealth. The government then became the de facto owner of all confiscated businesses. Let freedom ring!

> A great misconception about Communism is that everyone is "equal" under that system. Nothing could be further from the truth.

Homes abandoned by those fortunate enough to escape the island were made into multiple family dwellings, with two or three families living in the same home.

A great misconception about Communism is that everyone is "equal" under that system. Nothing could be further from the truth. Every Communist country, including Cuba, is composed of three distinct classes:

1. The Communist Party. Leaders of the party are the ruling class. They *gre!!* control the government and all the wealth, most of which they confiscated from the population. While they don't publicize it, Communist leaders tend to enrich themselves at their people's expense because few controls *wow!!* hold them accountable. Their stranglehold on the press prevents corruption from being exposed or differing opinions from being aired.

In 2014, Transparency International released their Corruptions Index, which measures perceived levels of public sector corruption worldwide. North Korea, one of the last bastions of hard-core communism, tied with Somalia for the most corrupt among 175 countries.[4] Before dying in 2011, Kim Jong Il, North Korea's "Supreme Leader," reportedly deposited $4 billion in European banks, according to a 2010 article in the *Telegraph*. The article quotes Ken Kato, the director of Human Rights in Asia, as saying,

> I believe this is the most extensive money-laundering operation in the history of organised crime, yet the final destination of the funds has not been given the proper attention it deserves . . . Somewhere in the world, there are bankers who are earning a large sum of money by concealing and managing Kim Jong-Il's secret funds, and at the same time, almost nine million people in North Korea are suffering from food shortages.[5]

Kim Jong-Un, son of Kim Jong Il, apparently takes after his father. His wealth reportedly hovers around $5 billion,[6] equal to over a *third* of North Korea's $14 billion economy.[7] The young dictator parties with retired basketball player Dennis Rodman on his private island and reportedly spends as much as $30 million a year on alcohol.[8] The United Nations tried to apply sanctions against other countries selling luxury goods to North Korea in order to curtail the $645 million a year Jong-un already spends on bribing government officials.

In a 2014 *Bloomberg* article, Communist China was equally criticized for its corruption—which ranked 100 on Transparency International's list.[9] Citing a survey conducted by Chinese newspaper *People's Daily*, *wow!!*

"Nepotism and corruption are commonplace and meritocracy often absent when selecting cadres . . . When multiple candidates vie for a spot, top party leaders use their influence to ensure those they favor win promotion. Buying and selling positions in the party is also commonplace."[10]

So the Communist Party is the first distinct class, the first among "equals." The second class is the army.

surprise

2. The Army. To maintain a totalitarian government, a strong military is necessary. The army, then, serves at the behest of the Communist Party, enforcing their policies with an iron fist, and bullying the general population.

According to Martin Malia in *The Big Black Book of Communism: Crimes, Terror, Repression*, between 85 and 100 million people died under Communist regimes in the twentieth century.[11] The greatest offenders include the Soviet Union under Joseph Stalin, the People's Republic of China under Mao Zedong, and Cambodia under the Khmer Rouge. Obviously a single leader couldn't accomplish these atrocities. They were carried out in large part by the military.

The army also controls the black market, which is one of their greatest sources of income.

The third distinct class is, finally, the people.

3. The People. I suppose you could say that equality exists among the people—they all equally starve. Ironically enough, Communism has never been implemented in its purest form. In true Communism, no leader exists because the people govern themselves directly.

The Communism of Castro's dreams through the redistribution of wealth meant the labor force would raise their standard

> Equality exists among the people [in Communist countries]—they all equally starve.

of living *together*. Unfortunately, Castro's dream became a nightmare.

In pre-Castro Cuba, the exchange rate was approximately one US dollar for one Cuban peso, unique in Latin America, with the exception of Panama, which also had a dollar-based economy. Today, the exchange rate is one dollar for about twenty-six pesos.

In 1958 Cuba had positioned itself as one of the five most developed countries in the region; it had the eighth highest average industrial salary in the world (six dollars a day), according to a 1960 International Labor Organization report. Agricultural wages (three dollars a day) were higher than some European countries. In contrast, the average salary in Cuba today is less than a dollar a day (twenty dollars per month).

Cubans have a saying, *Sin azúcar no hay país,* which literally translates to "Without sugar there is no country." The relationship between Cuba and its sugar production reads like a romantic tragedy. Since Castro came to power, however, production has plummeted.

In the 1950s, Cuba exported about 5 million tons of sugar a year, which at the time represented about one-third of the world's sugar exports. By 2010, annual sugar production slowed to barely more than 1 million tons. This is the lowest sugar production Cuba has known since 1908.[12]

Sadly, since the 1990s, reports indicate that more than a hundred Cuban sugar mills have been shut down, and sugar now accounts for about 5 percent of its exports and workforce. Sugar now ranks seventh on the country's list of earners, reportedly behind foreign currency, services, remittances, tourism, nickel, pharmaceuticals, and cigars. As a whole, collective farming has failed miserably. Today, the once-productive country must import up to 80 percent of its food.[13]

Before Castro, Cubans were free to buy whatever they wanted with their money, and goods and food supplies were plentiful. Despite Batista's corruption, which infused nearly every facet of the Cuban economy, the people thrived. Today, purchases are restricted and people cannot buy more than what their *Libreta* (quota booklet) stipulates. As an example, for many years meat rations have been restricted to *one pound per person per month.*[14] Similar restrictions exist for all other food supplies, clothing, shoes, and so forth. Restaurants and hotel resorts are reserved only for tourists, and native Cubans are not allowed inside.

The collapse of Communism in the Soviet Union in the early 1990s devastated Cuba, with net subsidies shrinking to about a third and totaling about $2 billion a year. Patrick Symmes, in a recent article for *Bloomberg,* explained the Cuban dilemma: "Salaries are paid in ordinary pesos, and average just $20 a month, even though the cost of survival runs around $50 a month."[15]

Because of the severe purchasing restrictions, a flourishing black market has emerged, run by corrupt government officials. Cubans fortunate enough to receive dollars from relatives living in the United States can buy food and other supplies through the black market, but at exorbitant prices.

> In Cuba, "salaries are paid in ordinary pesos, and average just $20 a month, even though the cost of survival runs around $50 a month."

Black markets normally barter in bootleg DVDs, prostitution, and drugs. In Cuba the black market involves just about everything. Archibald Ritter, a Canadian economist, studied the various means Cubans utilize to supplement their incomes through the black market. One person sells pasta door-to-door. A bartender working in a bar catering to tourists skims top-shelf rum and replaces it with home brew. And a bicycle repairman sells spare parts on the sly.

Ritter explained to the *Huffington Post*:

> You could probably say that 95 percent or more of the population participates in the underground economy in one way or another. It's tremendously widespread . . . Stealing from the state, for Cubans, is like taking firewood from the forest, or picking blueberries in the wild. It's considered public property that wouldn't otherwise be used productively, so one helps oneself.[16]

While the black market flourishes, the Castro regime keeps careful watch, similar to George Orwell's predictions in his novel *1984*. On every block, government-paid informants spy on their neighbors with the explicit directive to report "counterrevolutionary" activity. Anyone caught criticizing the government can be labeled an enemy of "the revolution" and incarcerated.

These informants also act as the food police, reporting any family possessing more food than what is allowed in the *Libreta*. Violators are labeled "hoarders," which is a punishable offense. Because of the severe food restrictions, people try to get around them in a variety of ways, such as raising chickens inside their homes (also illegal) so they can have eggs, and perhaps use some of those eggs to barter for other food items.

But the breakdown of Cuba's moral fiber isn't limited to rampant stealing and selling goods on the black market. It goes much deeper than that. Shortages of food, clothing, and other items also create an atmosphere for rampant prostitution.

A few years ago, while attending a banquet in Mexico, I sat next to a Mexican engineer who had just returned from a two-week business trip in Havana. He commented that every evening when he returned to his hotel, about a dozen young girls, thirteen or fourteen years old, waited outside the hotel and begged him, "Sir, for a plate of food I will go to bed with you."

"On weekends, there are housewives who shack up with tourists so they can feed their kids during the week—often with the consent of their husbands!"

A year later, I met a university professor in Miami who had just immigrated to the United States from Cuba. I shared with him the Mexican engineer's story and he replied, "Oh, casual prostitution is much worse."

"What is casual prostitution?" I asked.

His answer absolutely shocked me: "On weekends, there are housewives who shack up with tourists so they can feed their kids during the week—often with the consent of their husbands!"

In fact, fashion-conscious young girls will sell their bodies to European tourists for a pair of blue jeans or a pretty blouse.

And what drives this moral bankruptcy? Atheism. Communism is always undergirded by atheism for one simple reason: Communist leaders want the people to look to the government as their god. All Communist, Marxist, or Socialist regimes (different names, but fundamentally the same) desire to exert absolute control over the population and make them totally dependent upon the government. The government employs them, feeds them, clothes them, and tells them what to think and say. In essence, they want the people to treat their government as their god. To accomplish this, all other allegiances must be extinguished.

All Communist, Marxist, or Socialist regimes inevitably gravitate toward godlessness, and will take the necessary steps to eliminate the mention of God in all areas of society, including schools, public gatherings, and media. Furthermore, they will foster ridicule and offensiveness toward anyone who takes an "extreme" or "fanatical" position by espousing any faith at all.

Christians with left-leaning political beliefs fail to realize that they will eventually be forced to silence their beliefs or face ridicule or even persecution. By that point, we will have already forfeited our right to speak.

For the government to play the role of god, they must force the population to stop relying on the God of the Bible. The two religions—and yes, both are religions—cannot coexist. Contrast this with the biblical command: "I am the LORD your God . . . *You shall have no other gods before Me.* (Exodus 20:2–3, emphasis added)

Another obstacle that stands in the way of the government enforcing godlike power over its people is the family. Socialist governments work hard to systematically sabotage the allegiance of their children and youth to the family—and the public school system is their primary tool in this effort.

Yoani Sanchez, in an article for the *World Post* (of all places!), shares her experience growing up in Cuban schools:

> We went to daycare centers just 45 days after we were born; the Pioneer Camps took us in right after we learned our first letters; we went to schools in the countryside as soon as we left childhood, and spent our adolescence in high schools in the middle of nowhere. The State believed it could take over the formative role of our parents, thought it could exchange the values we brought from home for the new communist moral code.
>
> They also launched themselves against religion, ignoring that dissimilar creeds transmit a share of the ethic and moral values that molded human civilization and our own national customs. They made us denigrate those who were different, we insulted the presidents of other countries with obscenities, mocked historic figures from the past, stuck our tongues out or blew raspberries when passing a foreign embassy.[17]

In Cuba, schools begin their year by gathering their students at an assembly and chanting, "Pioneers for communism, we will be like Che."[18] What does a five-year-old or seven-year-old know about Che Guevara? Nothing. Free universal education in Cuba, which the country touts with pride, begins with indoctrinating their children in communist ideology—even before the students can understand it.

Just as Castro demanded that his Marxist ideology be taught in the schools, so today, the US government is doing more and more to stipulate what can—and cannot—be taught. Our government mandates that teachers affirm alternative, nonbiblical lifestyles, teach evolution as incontrovertible "fact," and mock the notion that God created the heavens and earth. Furthermore, they fully support teachers who teach that moral absolutes do not exist, promote situational ethics and relativism, and encourage their students to think for themselves and rebel against the "outdated ideas" of their parents. Most universities, which receive enormous support from our taxes, have become communist-espousing, anti-Christian seedbeds.

We'll look more closely at how government wants to mandate anti-Christian education in chapter 12 when we discuss Common Core.

> Just as Castro demanded that his Marxist ideology be taught in the schools, so today, the US government is doing more to stipulate what can—and cannot—be taught.

The most *in*tolerant people in America espouse political correctness and consider themselves tolerant. And who lies behind this? The government—because in Communist ideology, the government wants to be your god, and eliminate any competitors for our allegiance.

So think for a minute. Who or what is the government? The government is composed of people who exercise control over the daily affairs of their constituents. Ultimately a Communist government will gravitate toward totalitarianism, with one person who ultimately tells everyone else what to think and do.

The gospel of socialism tells us, "Government is your god." Note the contrast with the preamble of the US Declaration of Independence:

> We hold these truths to be self-evident, that all men are created equal, that they are endowed *by their Creator* with certain unalienable Rights, that among these are Life, Liberty and the pursuit of Happiness. (Emphasis added)

But if your rights come from government, and not from God, then it follows that government can take them away!

* * *

With the collapse of the Cuban economy, the Soviet Union began subsidizing the island, and in return Cuba became their partner in exporting

Communism. Marxist guerrillas were trained in Cuba to further their cause in Bolivia, Angola, Nicaragua, and several other countries. Many of the insurgencies that arose throughout Latin America were launched and/or supported from Cuba. After the collapse of the Soviet Union, Venezuela became Cuba's new benefactor, with dictator Hugo Chávez making frequent visits to Fidel Castro for advice.

With oil prices dropping almost in half in 2015, Venezuela has suffered economic hardship and can no longer support their comrade. So who now will bail out Cuba's failed Communist system? President Barack Obama, who is in the process of restoring and normalizing relations with Cuba. If President Obama succeeds in allowing billions of US dollars to flow to Castro, it will prove to be totally disastrous, for several reasons:

1. Cuba has served as the primary exporter of Communism and insurrection for decades. In 1975 and 1988, Cuba sent troops to Angola to support the Communist cause. By the end of 1975, Cuban troops in Angola numbered twenty-five thousand.

Closer to home, Castro supported terrorist insurgencies such as FARC in Colombia (1964–present) and the Sandinistas in Nicaragua (1979–1990). He also played the role of a catalyst in the civil war in El Salvador (1979–1992). Cuba's history of support for insurgents looks like the Terrorist Hall of Fame. The list contains but is not limited to:

- the Macheteros in Puerto Rico

- the Black Panthers and the Black Liberation Army in America

- the Irish Republican Army in Ireland

- the Basque terrorist/separatists in Spain

- Fatah and the PLO in the Middle East

As recently as 2013, Cuba was caught exporting terrorism. On July 15, 2013, the North Korean ship *Chong Chon Gang*, en route from

Havana to North Korea, was stopped and inspected in the Panama Canal after irregularities were identified with its Automatic Identification System. The search yielded 240 metric tons of Cuban-made weapons, radar/control systems for missile launching, two aircraft missile systems, fifteen plane engines, twelve motors, and live munitions.[19]

2. Normalizing relations with Cuba could jeopardize the US presence at the Guantánamo Bay Naval Base. In 1962, US Intelligence discovered that Soviet missiles had been deployed to Cuba. This led to the two-week Cuban missile crisis, compelling President John F. Kennedy to impose a naval blockade of the island and insist that the USSR remove their missiles. If you were alive back then, you remember those tense days, when many Americans, glued to their television sets, feared that we were on the brink of a nuclear war with the Soviet empire. Everyone breathed an overwhelming sigh of relief when, seemingly at the last minute, Soviet leader Nikita Khrushchev blinked and agreed to remove the missiles.

Our naval base at Guantánamo Bay in Cuba played a major role in facing down the Soviets. Had we given up our foothold on the island, the Soviet Union would have had an undisputed presence in the Western Hemisphere and a major thoroughfare for exporting Communism.

Now, emboldened by President Obama's lack of resolve, Cuban dictator Raul Castro insists that the United States return the Guantánamo base to Cuba—and Obama seems complicit with Raul's wishes. The president continues to empty the base of its inhabitants by releasing dangerous terrorists incarcerated there, many of whom end up joining (or rejoining) ISIS or other terrorist organizations. He seems intent on fulfilling his promise to empty Gitmo before he leaves office. Can the United States afford to relinquish Guantánamo base and its presence in Cuba with a communist regime just ninety miles from our shores? Wouldn't that put America at risk?

3. Normalizing relations will do nothing to help the people. Liberals and progressives claim that normalizing relations with Cuba will help the Cuban people. Nothing could be further from the truth. In December 2014, the Cuban government announced new measures permitting Cubans to work for foreign companies. But first, the Cuban government would pocket *92 percent of the total wages,* leaving the employee only 8 percent. Furthermore, the government would charge the corporation 20 percent of the employee's salary as a finder's fee. Lastly, employees would also lose 9.09 percent of their salaries for "vacation time."[20]

> Can the United States afford to relinquish Guantánamo base and its presence in Cuba with a Communist regime just ninety miles from our shores?

From all appearances, normalizing relations would suit the Cuban government just fine!

* * *

How well does Communism work?

In 2010, just before the release of the first volume of his memoirs *The Strategic Victory,* Fidel Castro confessed to an American reporter, "The Cuban model doesn't even work for us anymore."[21] In 2011, he retired from public life, leaving his brother Raul to lead. Since then, Raul has introduced limited economic reforms that included government layoffs and increased toleration of private enterprise.

Does Communism work? Not in Cuba and certainly not in the United States!

5

ACHIEVING THE AMERICAN DREAM

The American dream is that dream of a land in which life should be better and richer and fuller for everyone, with opportunity for each according to ability or achievement.

—JAMES TRUSLOW ADAMS, *THE EPIC OF AMERICA*

Not all dreamers are winners, but all winners are dreamers. Your dream is the key to your future. The Bible says that, "without a vision (dream), a people perish." You need a dream, if you're going to succeed in anything you do."

—MARK GORMAN

When I set foot on American soil for the first time, I had no money and spoke no English . . . but I did have a dream. When I was growing up, Horatio Alger's books, filled with rags-to-riches stories, inspired me to accomplish great things. If those people did it, why couldn't I do it as well?

Winston Churchill's famous quote "Never, never, never give up" also gave me great inspiration. Years ago, I rephrased his quote in my own words:

> When you fall flat on your face, you have two choices: You can stay down, feeling sorry for yourself, or you can wipe your bloody nose and get up with twice the determination.

I resolved that I would always choose the second option and get up with twice the determination—and that attitude has served me well throughout my life. I may stumble over and over, but I will get up again, and again, and again!

> I may stumble over and over, but I will get up again, and again, and again!

Scripture reinforces the importance of never giving up:

Tribulation produces perseverance; and perseverance, character; and character, hope. (Romans 5:3–4)

Let perseverance finish its work so that you may be mature and complete, not lacking anything. (James 1:4 NIV)

* * *

Even though my first job as a dishwasher looked to many like menial labor, I determined to be the best dishwasher I could be. That attitude did not go unnoticed at the Toddle House, and as my English skills improved, my manager moved me behind the counter, where I began taking orders from customers. My pay jumped to sixty cents an hour, and best of all, I no longer needed to immerse my hands in scalding water!

In addition to my full load of classes at the university, my sophomore year I started grading freshman chemistry homework to earn a few extra dollars. As my only form of entertainment, nine of my friends and I would pile into a car and go to a drive-in movie on Saturday nights. Admission was a dollar per car, so our cost was only ten cents a person. After finding our spot, we pulled four folding chairs out of the trunk and spread out.

At that time, six or seven students at the school were from Cuba on the same student visa as I was, so we enjoyed spending time together. However, because I wanted to learn English as quickly as possible, I also spent time with Americans.

During my sophomore year in college, one afternoon the manager at Toddle House asked me, "When do you want to start cooking?"

"Whenever you say." I knew I could make more money as a cook.

"How about tomorrow?" His answer caught me by surprise, but I was ready for the change.

The Toddle House served approximately 150 orders of eggs between 7:00 and 9:00 a.m., and since I was going to be cooking in front of the customers, I needed to learn how to crack the eggs into the skillet with one hand and flip the eggs using the other. After accepting my promotion, I left the restaurant and went directly to the grocery store and bought a few dozen eggs. When I arrived at my apartment, I began cracking the eggs with one hand. In no time, my arms and the floor were covered with eggs.

Finally, after two dozen eggs I learned how to crack them open without breaking the yolk. Then I needed another dozen eggs to learn how to flip them directly in the skillet, not without several accidents when I scattered eggs everywhere. After conquering the challenge, I felt ready to cook three hundred eggs the next morning! I worked every day with a smile on my face and a great feeling of satisfaction.

After working as a cook for about a year, the branch manager of the four restaurants in the Austin area asked to speak with me.

"Rafael, I can't tell you how pleased I am with your hard work. You've demonstrated the skills to manage a Toddle House of your own someday. So we want to offer you a career with our company. We'd like to move you to an assistant manager position."

"Thank you very much, sir," I replied. The thought of increasing my pay sounded very tempting.

He continued: "But I'm offering you this position under one condition. I need you to quit school."

"But sir," I said, "I already work full-time and go to school full-time. I can handle both."

"I know you can," he answered. "But I cannot afford to spend a year training you as a manager to see you leave the restaurant after you graduate."

While the higher salary sounded enticing, I wasn't willing to forfeit my education and give up the dream of starting my own business.

"Thank you so much for the honor of offering me the position. But I want to stay in school and graduate—so I must decline." I continued working at Toddle House until I obtained my bachelor's degree and enrolled in postgraduate courses.

Initially I pursued a degree in chemical engineering, but, because I've always been a lousy artist, I kept postponing my drafting class, which was a freshman course. Finally, as I entered my junior year, my advisor said, "You either register for drafting or I am going to throw you out of school." So I registered for drafting, but I really struggled in the class and flunked it. My advisor refused to negotiate an exchange of classes, so I changed my major to mathematics, with a minor in chemical engineering.

After graduating with my undergraduate degree, I decided to begin taking graduate courses in mathematics.

The summer of 1961, I worked the graveyard shift (11:00 p.m. to 7:00 a.m.) and then ran two blocks in my soiled cooking uniform to the math building for back-to-back graduate math classes. Most people would struggle staying awake in a *math* class after working all night, but I found the classes invigorating.

My first class, taught by the department chairman, began at 7:00 a.m. (as I said, I *ran* to class!). My next class was taught by a professor emeritus from the school. After a few days, the professor emeritus pulled the department chairman aside.

"Don't you find it embarrassing to have a graduate math student stink up the whole class with his cooking uniform? Why don't we offer him a teaching position so he doesn't need to work in that restaurant?"

So, I have the distinction of being offered a teaching job at the University of Texas without ever applying for it! My career with the Toddle House soon came to an end.

Although my work schedule and studies kept me busy, my family a thousand miles away was constantly on my mind. In the face of

I have the distinction of being offered a teaching job at the University of Texas without ever applying for it!

an ever-escalating Cold War, the US and Cuban governments still allowed Cubans in America to communicate with their families through phone calls and letters. My parents mentioned that the basics were in short supply at home, so I always taped razor blades in my letters for my father so he could shave. One time I even wrapped some coffee in tinfoil and mailed it home.

While I was still in school, the university purchased their first computer, an IBM 650, and offered an intensive two-week programming class in which I eagerly enrolled. Computers back then differed tremendously from the PCs we use today. The rotating drum memory of that old IBM was two thousand *words*. Into that limited memory we crammed the operating system, software program, and all necessary data. Laptop computers today easily fit multiple gigabytes of memory and terabytes of hard drive data into storage. Most programmers today do not realize how easy their job is compared to our challenges fifty years ago!

The IBM 650 was a vacuum tube machine (before the age of transistors) and ran extremely hot, requiring a great deal of air-conditioning to keep it cool. The refrigerator-size CPU (central processing unit) had a hood on top and an extractor fan to remove the hot air. All input and output into the computer was done with punch cards. Because of its limited memory, if you generated an array of data, you punched that data on cards and inputted it again when needed.

This new skill gave me the opportunity to offer my computing programming services on a consulting basis to university professors and graduate students involved in different research projects. This provided additional income to my teaching job in the math department.

In the spring of 1962, IBM came to the UT campus to recruit new employees—so I decided to check them out. As I entered their temporary office, the receptionist handed me a test, and said, "Don't worry if you can't finish the test. It's designed with more questions than you can complete in the time allotted."

To my pleasant surprise, the vast majority of questions on the test were algebra problems. After teaching algebra at the university for a year, I had mastered the material. As a result, I completed the test with time to spare!

Less than a week later, I interviewed with an IBM executive who hired me on the spot as a computer programmer. My job with the Scientific Department of the Service Bureau Corporation, a wholly owned subsidiary of IBM, paid $450 per month. They wanted me to report to work within a week, so a friend helped me replace the brake shoes on my old, beat-up Chevrolet and I drove up to Dallas early in the morning with my sister, Sonia, who had escaped from Cuba a few months before and received political asylum in the United States. We stopped at a service station, I put on my only suit, and Sonia dropped me off at SBC while she drove around close to the office, looking for a furnished apartment to rent.

While I was in school, I met another student, a young woman named Julia. We started dating, and soon we were married and had an adorable baby daughter named Miriam. Julia and Miriam stayed in Austin so my wife could finish the semester. Then they would join me in Dallas.

My parents finally immigrated to the United States at the end of 1967, but it wasn't easy. The process lasted five years, costing thousands of dollars. Sonia deserves the credit for bringing them here because she dutifully filled out reams of paperwork. When my parents

When my parents finally received permission to leave the island, the Cuban government confiscated everything—all but the clothes on their backs.

finally received permission to leave the island, the Cuban government confiscated everything—all but the clothes on their backs.

Because of the travel restrictions between the United States and Cuba, my parents couldn't come directly to our country only ninety miles to the north. They flew to Mexico and then immigrated to the States.

At my new job, I wore the same suit every day for two weeks until I received my first paycheck and could afford to buy a second suit. In those days, IBM enforced a very strict dress code. Men wore suits—black, navy blue, or dark gray. Socks and tie had to match, not contrast, my suit. Beards and mustaches were prohibited. Anyone who drank alcohol during lunch was subject to dismissal.

After a couple of weeks on the job, my manager came to me and said, "Rafael, you are doing such a great job that we are going to give you a parking spot in the basement of the garage." That's where all of the company executives parked.

While initially flattered, I also understood his motives. My old "beater" car I parked right in front of the office sported a huge dent in the trunk and a coat hanger for an antenna. It was a mess.

I looked at my boss and started laughing. "You just don't want me to park my beat-up car in front of the office!" But I said yes to the parking spot. I was the only peon among all the chiefs with a reserved parking spot in the basement!

Before I left the university, several people warned me that since I was a foreigner, I would encounter discrimination in the workplace and would struggle getting ahead. But when I was a boy, my parents had taught me a very wise Spanish proverb: "To stupid words, deaf ears." Very early in life I decided I wouldn't take nonsense to heart. So I considered any negative comments as an encouragement to excel in all my endeavors. The way to overcome any potential discrimination was simply to be so much better than anyone else competing for the job that I would be the obvious choice.

Again, Scripture extols the value of hard work, not just for minorities and people vulnerable to discrimination, but for everyone. "And whatever you do, do it heartily, as to the Lord and not to men" (Colossians 3:23). That way of thinking served me well.

Within a year and a half, IBM transferred me to Houston to work as an analyst in helping them build a petroleum applications department. My sister, Sonia, remained in Dallas, where she continues to live today, and I moved to Houston with Julia and, by now, my *two* daughters, Miriam and Roxana.

I started developing materials and programs for my department and hired several people. When IBM began formalizing the department, I figured they would name me department manager, but instead they just changed the existing title of programming manager to manager of programming and applications.

When I learned about their decision, I walked into the branch manager's office and asked him, "Why didn't you make me the department manager? I earned that job!"

> The way to overcome any potential discrimination is simply to be so much better than anyone else competing for the job.

"Yes," he replied, "but he is already a manager. If we changed your title to department manager, we'd have to give you a raise, and we don't have the budget to do it."

I decided to force their hand. "Then give me the job without the raise."

"That's impossible," he said. "Salaries are dependent upon the title."

I walked back to my office and called Merle, a friend from college, who had a software consulting company in Washington, DC. On the phone he offered me an opportunity to open an office for him in Houston and gave me nearly a 50 percent salary increase.

Obviously I accepted his offer.

So I wrote a letter of resignation and handed it to my branch manager, telling him that I had been given a job offer with a huge salary increase.

"Fine. We'll match your salary offer," he answered. I was shocked.

"If you're suddenly willing to give me a 50 percent raise, does that mean you have been exploiting me all along?"

He didn't know what to say.

Soon I was escorted back to my office, where I gathered my belongings, and accompanied to the door, where I was given my final check and turned in my keys.

I ran the consulting office in Houston with seven to eight employees until the Washington office was forced to close, as well as ours. But through a personnel placement consultant that I had employed on several occasions, a company in New Orleans hired me to be their manager of scientific applications. My new company was developing a seismic data processing software system, and despite never studying geophysics, I understood the mathematics behind it.

About this time, my marriage began falling apart. I can't speak for my former wife, but I was immature at the time and unprepared to be married. To cope with the stress at work and home, I began drinking heavily. To my great regret our marriage did not survive. Julia and the kids moved back to Austin, where she returned to school to earn her PhD, and we divorced.

While in New Orleans, I met a young woman who had moved there to work as the manager of software operating systems for the same company. She was a brilliant mathematician and an expert in operating systems. Eleanor and I fell in love and eventually married.

At the beginning of 1968, a start-up company in Calgary, Alberta, hired Eleanor and me to help them develop a new seismic system and start a data processing company servicing the geophysical industry.

Our son, Ted, was born in Calgary on December 22, 1970. My parents were elated that a boy would carry the family name. Just a few days after Ted was born, they came to Calgary from Dallas, Texas, where they were living with my sister, Sonia. My parents stayed with us until the end of the summer.

Within a year we left the start-up company and launched our own seismic data processing company, R. B. Cruz and Associates, Ltd. We sold that company in early 1975 and moved to Houston to start Explorer Seismic Services, a new seismic data processing company.

Explorer Seismic was fairly successful, and at one point we employed twenty-five workers. We made a decent amount of money, and invested practically all of our profits into real estate, owning several commercial and residential lots, an apartment building, and two office buildings, which held our offices and computer center. We were highly leveraged, purchasing real estate with only 10 percent down, thinking that if the market rose 10 percent, we would double our money.

An old Yiddish saying comes to mind as I think back to those days: "Man plans and God laughs."

In the mid-eighties, the OPEC countries opened the valves to their oil wells and flooded the market, causing oil to drop from thirty-five dollars per barrel to seven dollars per barrel. Several of my clients—independent oil companies—went out of business. Unfortunately, they owed us hundreds of thousands of dollars, and business almost dried up, causing us to lose about fifty thousand dollars per month.

We assumed the downturn was temporary and struggled through the lean times, hoping for a change that never came. Finally we ran out of cash and were forced to lay off our employees. Gathering all of our staff in our conference room and telling them we could not pay them was emotionally devastating. Everyone was crying, including Eleanor and me. These people had been doing a wonderful job, and we were a team, but the well had run dry.

Six employees decided to stay with us. When we told them we had no money to pay them, they responded, "We can't get another job, so we'll ride this together."

In such difficult times, the loyalty of those employees greatly blessed us. They became family to Eleanor and me. When a small job came through, we split the income in equal portions. Unfortunately, the minuscule revenue meant I couldn't service my debt. Finally, after seven months, the mortgage companies foreclosed on all our real estate and we lost everything, and soon thereafter we even lost our home.

About a year before the oil crash, a client of ours offered to buy our company. We had formulated a seven-year growth plan, oil was thirty-five dollars a barrel, and the industry consensus was that by the next year it would be fifty dollars a barrel and we would make millions. So I rejected his offer. I didn't even pray about it because I thought I knew better. A year later we lost everything and were totally broke.

After the dust settled from this difficult experience, I asked God why He had allowed this to happen to me.

I sent you a rescue boat, I heard him say in my spirit.

You probably know the story of the man who encountered a flood. As the waters began to rise, he climbed on the roof of his house. A person in a boat came by, offering to transport him to safety.

"No," he said. "God will rescue me."

A little later, a helicopter flew by and the helicopter pilot offered to help the man.

"No thanks," the man replied. "God will rescue me."

Finally, the floodwaters rose so high that the man was carried off the roof and he drowned.

When the man arrived at the pearly gates, he asked God, "Why didn't You rescue me?"

God told the man, "I sent you a boat and a helicopter, and you rejected them." God had sent me a rescue boat with the client's offer to buy our company, but in my arrogance I rejected it!

But God has continued to be faithful. He will never leave me nor forsake me. Looking back on those lean times, I'm reminded of a beautiful testimonial in Psalm 37:25. "I have been young, and now am old; yet I have not seen the righteous forsaken, nor his descendants begging bread."

And really, all of us are in need of being rescued. Some see their need, but many don't. God throws us a lifeline, but many ignore it, thinking they have time.

In the next chapter, I'm going to share with you the story of my rescue. Hopefully, by the end of the chapter, you'll share the same story.

6

HOW TO FIND TRUE FREEDOM

Therefore whoever hears these sayings of Mine, and does them, I will liken
him to a wise man who built his house on the rock: and the rain descended,
the floods came, and the winds blew and beat on that house; and it did not
fall, for it was founded on the rock.

—JESUS, MATTHEW 7:24–25

For no other foundation can anyone lay than that which is laid, which is
Jesus Christ.

—1 CORINTHIANS 3:11

A husband and wife working together in a profitable business. A
baby boy bringing the happy couple together.

Sounds like the picture-perfect marriage, right?

Wrong.

In the mid-1970s, the oil industry in Calgary was a fast-paced
life. As the owner of a small geophysical company in a hub of the oil
industry, I not only supervised all of our operations, but I also served
as the company's lone salesman—and the local bar served as my remote
office. There, I met prospects and clients for lunch and a few drinks.
Then I met other prospects and clients for dinner . . . and more drinks.
Often until midnight.

Deep down, I knew something was wrong, but I didn't have the
time, emotional energy, or willingness to explore it. Instead I worked

harder and drank more. My long work hours and heavy drinking soon began affecting my second marriage, as they had my first.

My alcohol abuse was a natural by-product of working in the oil industry. Or so I thought. The cost of doing business in a rough-and-tumble industry that exacted a heavy toll on my marriage and relationship with my son. My work habits and heavy drinking drove a wedge between me and the family, which resulted in my decision to leave Eleanor and Ted in Calgary and find other clients in Houston. Initially, I assumed I needed to break free from my family, but my need for freedom ran much deeper.

Before meeting Darrell and Betty Lassonde, as far as I know, I had never even interacted with a Christian. I knew virtually nothing about the Christian faith, and quite honestly, I didn't care. My parents baptized me in the Catholic Church when I was a baby in Cuba, but I had no personal relationship with Jesus. I felt no need for God. "Religion is a product of ignorance," I explained to anyone who mentioned spiritual matters in my presence.

Here's the extent of my indifference toward the Christian faith: Despite knowing he was a follower of Christ, I once invited Darrell to dinner—forgetting to mention that the "restaurant" was actually a strip club. The thought never occurred to me that men existed who didn't frequent them. I just assumed he would enjoy going there.

Darrell greeted me at my table and sat down. He acted kind of strange because he pretty much focused his eyes on me or the table, and he was quieter than usual.

"Are you okay, Darrell?" I asked.

"Sure. I . . . uh . . . I have lot of work I need to get done at the office, so I can't stick around very long."

We discussed the items on my agenda while we ate a quick dinner, and then he and I left as soon as the bill was paid. To his credit, Darrell never shamed me, nor did he ever condemn me.

A week later we engaged in another awkward conversation. This time we met at a real restaurant, where the workers actually wore clothes.

"Hey, Rafael, Betty and I wanted to extend an invitation for you to join us at our house this Monday night for a Bible study."

"I don't know, my friend," I said. "I'm not very religious—and besides I'll probably be busy."

"I understand, Rafael," Darrell reassured me. "But I promise you the evening won't be a waste of your time. I'll tell you what—why don't you join us for dinner, and then you can decide whether or not to stick around for the meeting."

"Sounds reasonable. I'll see you then."

Frankly, I accepted their invitation because I was lonely and had nothing better to do. Eleanor and Ted were in Calgary, and I was renting a small apartment in Houston. I don't remember what we ate for dinner or the topic of our Bible study that night, but I'll never forget the people in the group. They totally unnerved me.

At the end of the evening, Bob Abrams, the leader of the Bible study, asked everyone to share their prayer requests. They all faced problems, but in spite of their problems, everyone—except me—exuded a peace that didn't make sense. One woman in particular mentioned that her son often beat her to get money for drugs, and yet she emanated that same peace as the rest of the people. My life was spinning out of control, yet they seemed to face their challenges with serene hope. As the people prayed for each other, I did my best to swallow the lump in my throat.

I wanted what they had but felt no need for their Jesus.

At the end of the meeting, Darrell's wife, Betty, handed me a little booklet entitled "The Four Spiritual Laws."

"I'd like you to read this," she said. "And can you come back next Monday?"

"I don't have any plans, so yes, that sounds good."

The minute I walked through the door the next Monday, Betty asked me, "Did you read the booklet? What did you think about it?"

"What the booklet says I need to do sounds too easy," I said. "It can't be that easy!"

Instead of answering me directly, she offered me another invitation.

"Our pastor is going to be at our home tomorrow night at 7:00 p.m.; could you come?"

"Sure. Why not?" I replied. "I have many questions for him."

The moment I'd started reading the pamphlet from Betty, I had begun tabulating a mental list of questions. Talking to Pastor Gaylen Wiley from Clay Road Baptist Church was the perfect opportunity to prove to him that Christianity was built on a foundation of hearsay and mistruths.

At the same time, two emotions shook me: first, the unnerving feeling that the Bible study participants had something I wanted, which they called "the peace that passes all understanding" (see Philippians 4:7); second, the overwhelming guilt of being separated from my four-year-old son. To assuage my guilt throughout that time, every two or three days I mailed him a coloring book or storybook. My heart ached.

The next evening, I pelted Pastor Gaylen with questions for four hours. He answered them clearly and calmly, but none of them satisfied me. As a scientist, I needed all the answers before I could make any kind of decision to become a Christian.

Bless his heart; he refused to give up. I wanted to argue historical facts and the existence of God. He wanted to explore my need for Jesus and my inability to save myself and proceeded to share with me the same material I had read in "The Four Spiritual Laws."

The more he probed the issues of my heart, the more I pushed him away.

As the evening came to a close, I lobbed one final shot.

"What about that man up on the mountains of Tibet who has never heard about Jesus?"

The pastor, very wisely, chose not to chase that rabbit, or we would have argued for another two hours and wandered away from the clear message he had shared with me.

"To tell you the truth," he responded, "I don't know about that man up in the mountains of Tibet who has never heard about Jesus. *But you have heard about Jesus; what is your excuse?*"

His statement hit me like a sledgehammer. The eyes of my understanding were suddenly opened, and I fell on my knees and surrendered my life to Jesus.

Darrell and Betty gave me a Bible that night, and I began devouring the Scriptures. The following week Pastor Gaylen baptized me; then I flew back to Calgary to ask Eleanor for forgiveness and to come back with me to Houston. She was understandably skeptical about my conversion, uncertain about whether or not to believe me. But for the sake of Ted, she decided to give me another chance. We sold our company in Calgary, moved to Houston, and bought a house on the north side of the city. Ted, only four at the time, was extremely happy that we were back together again.

Pastor Gaylen encouraged me to begin reading the Bible in the gospel of John. In the second chapter I read that Jesus turned the water into wine. "If it's good enough for Jesus, it's good enough for me," I said to myself. That gave me a good excuse to continue drinking, although now I tried to do it in moderation, because I wanted to maintain a certain "Christian" image.

> "To tell you the truth, I don't know about that man up in the mountains of Tibet who has never heard about Jesus. *But you have heard about Jesus; what is your excuse?*"

A month after surrendering my life to Jesus, Eleanor, Ted, and I flew to Acapulco to celebrate being reunited. While sitting on the beach behind our hotel, I ordered a beer, and later a second. Halfway through the second beer, all of a sudden it tasted terrible. Nothing was wrong with the beer—I had already consumed half of it. Instead, God simply changed my taste for beer and removed from me any desire for alcohol! When we returned home, the first thing I did was open every bottle of liquor and pour it down the drain.

* * *

In 1951, Bill Bright quit his studies at Fuller Seminary in order to focus his energies on a Bible study he had started at UCLA. Bright's Bible study morphed into the largest ministry in the world, called Campus Crusade for Christ, a college-based outreach, which in 2011 numbered twenty-five thousand staff people in 191 countries.[1] In 2012, the organization shortened its name to Cru. In 2014, *Forbes* ranked it nineteenth on their list of the largest charities in the United States, with a total revenue of $544 million.[2]

Quite the visionary, Bill Bright produced the *Jesus* film, a feature-length movie about the life of Christ. Since its release in 1979, the film has been seen by more than 5.1 billion people speaking 800 different languages in 234 countries.[3]

In an article on Bright, pastor Rick Warren said of him, "Within evangelical circles he is paired with Billy Graham as the two most influential Christian leaders of the past fifty years."[4]

But Bill Bright is perhaps best known for writing a short booklet that has become the most widely distributed pamphlet in history. At last count, it has been printed in at least two hundred languages and read by an estimated two and a half billion people. The name of this pamphlet?

"The Four Spiritual Laws."[5]

I count my life as one of the billions it has impacted. If you aren't familiar with it, I'd like to introduce it to you right now (with some personal insights along the way):

Our everyday lives are governed by a set of physical laws. Newton's law of universal gravitation explains why we don't float off into outer space. Kepler's three laws of planetary motion explain how the earth orbits the sun, which in turn gives us four seasons *every* year. Archimedes's buoyancy principle explains why we can float on the water.

You can depend on these physical laws to work every day. Isaac Newton, Johannes Kepler, and Archimedes didn't mandate their respective laws; they discovered them. So they're considered *laws* because they explain how nature works.

In the same way, the Four Spiritual Laws explains who God is and how he works—regardless of circumstances or our feelings about him.[6]

SPIRITUAL LAW #1: God loves you and offers a wonderful plan for your life. Many people who believe in God view Him as a faraway deity with an angry demeanor. He's just looking for a reason to punish us for an errant slip of the tongue or a lustful thought.

But God's true nature isn't anger and punishment; it's love. He tells us in Jeremiah 31:3, "I have loved you with an everlasting love; therefore with lovingkindness I have drawn you."

God's first inclination is love, but it's not a touchy-feely kind of love; it's a love that gives itself for the good of others.

For God so loved the world that He gave His only begotten Son, that whoever believes in Him should not perish but have everlasting life. (John 3:16)

> God's true nature isn't anger and punishment; it's love.

Because God loves us, He has planned for us an abounding, or abundant, life. Jesus said, "I have come that they may have life, and that they may have it more abundantly" (John 10:10).

But wait a minute! you might be saying to yourself right now. *I'm certainly not experiencing that abundant life right now.* If so, you can blame that on the next law . . .

SPIRITUAL LAW #2: Man is sinful and separated from God. Therefore, he cannot know and experience God's plan for his life.

We were created to enjoy intimacy with God, to experience a rich relationship with Him. However, through our own choices, we broke that relationship with Him through our sin.

In the beginning of God's story as recorded in the Bible, we read that Adam and Eve enjoyed an unhindered relationship with God. But eventually, God's firstborn children disobeyed Him by eating the forbidden fruit (read Genesis 2–3). They passed on this compulsion to sin to their descendants, every one of us.

The Bible tells us, "All have sinned and fall short of the glory of God" (Romans 3:23).

Before I gave my life to Christ, I had no problem understanding that I was a sinner. For a long time, I lived like the devil and even denied God's existence, saying things like, "Religion is the product of ignorance; eliminate ignorance from the world and religion will go away with it."

Bright's pamphlet explains,

> Man was created to have fellowship with God; but, because of his stubborn self-will, he chose to go his own independent way and fellowship with God was broken. This self-will, characterized by an attitude of active rebellion or passive indifference, is what the Bible calls sin.[7]

Adding insult to injury, our sin condemns us to eternal separation from God. If God is perfect and absent of sin, then He could not allow imperfect, sinful people into His presence as that would jeopardize His perfection.

A holy God cannot commune with sinful man. Unfortunately, a death sentence hangs over the head of every person who sins. Scripture tells us, "The wages of sin is death" (Romans 6:23).

Imagine working for Company XYZ. After two weeks on the job, you look forward to your first paycheck. When you pick it up on your way out of the office for the weekend, you open the envelope to discover that you owe the company an exorbitant sum of money.

This can't be right! you think. You drive back to the office and hunt down the person in charge of payroll.

"Explain how I can owe Company XYZ all this money when they should be paying me?"

"It's the new law of the land," she explains.

The wages we earn for our sin is death. It's the spiritual law of the land.

Spiritual Law #2 describes our fallen condition. All of us sin, and none of us can do enough to bridge the great divide between our fallen condition and a holy God.

Most of us tend to differentiate *good* people from *bad* people. However, according to God's spiritual laws, we all sin, and even the "smallest" sin merits us separation from God for eternity.

In our own strength, we may try to bridge the gap that separates us from God by doing good things: helping people, giving to charity, praying, attending church regularly. But because they reflect *our* insufficient efforts, they fall short. We cannot do enough to reconnect with God.

Like most children in Latin America, I was baptized in the Catholic Church as an infant. A great many families did this, even if they rarely stepped into a church. A baptismal certificate was considered almost like a birth certificate. My parents did not frequent a church, and neither did I. As a teenager, the only reason I visited a church was to meet girls. But that's not enough.

I had no personal relationship with Jesus.

To bridge the divide between ourselves and God, we would need to be as perfect as God—and that's impossible!

This brings us to a great dilemma: the righteousness of God demands that our sin be destroyed, but the love of God longs for eternal communion with us.

The third law explains the only way to bridge this gulf.

SPIRITUAL LAW #3: Jesus Christ is God's only provision for man's sin. Through Him you can know and experience God's love and plan for your life.

God the Father sent His Son, Jesus Christ, to become a man, one of us, to live a perfect and sinless life and become our substitute. When he was crucified on the cross, Jesus bore the judgment that we deserve, so we could be accepted by God.

Most wonderful of all, God did this for us in spite of the fact that we

> When he was crucified on the cross, Jesus bore the judgment that we deserve, so we could be accepted by God.

don't deserve it! "But God demonstrates His own love toward us, in that while we were still sinners, Christ died for us" (Romans 5:8). Jesus died in our place. He paid the death penalty for our sins. But then, the Bible tells us, to assert His power over death, He defeated it by rising from the dead.

Christ died for our sins . . . He was buried . . . He rose again the third day according to the Scriptures . . . He was seen by [Peter], then by the twelve. After that He was seen by over five hundred brethren at once. (1 Corinthians 15:3–6)

Jesus now leads the way to God—the only way to God. Jesus described Himself like this: "I am the way, the truth, and the life. No one comes to the Father except through Me" (John 14:6).

The Bible tells us that only one foundation exists upon which we can build a life full of purpose and fulfillment and be all that God wants us to be: "For no other foundation can anyone lay than that which is laid, which is Jesus Christ" (1 Corinthians 3:11).

God bridged the gulf that separates us from Him by sending His Son, Jesus Christ, to die on the cross in our place to pay the penalty for our sins.

But knowing these three laws isn't enough.

SPIRITUAL LAW #4: We must individually receive Jesus Christ as Savior and Lord; then we can know and experience God's love and plan for our lives.

We cannot earn our ticket to heaven through doing good things; we must receive Christ, like a gift. The Bible says, "But as many as received Him, to them He gave the right to become children of God, to those who believe in His name" (John 1:12).

And how do we receive this gift? Through faith. We read in Ephesians 2:8–9: "For by grace you have been saved through faith, and that not of yourselves; *it is* the gift of God, not of works, lest anyone should boast."

When we receive Christ, we become new people: "Therefore, if anyone is in Christ, he is a new creation; old things have passed away; behold, all things have become new" (2 Corinthians 5:17). This should be good news for everyone. When we receive Christ into our lives, God forgives our sins and never again holds them against us. Then, as if that weren't enough, He goes one step further and makes us entirely new. The old person who lived before Christ no longer exists (you can read more about our new birth in John 3).

While we cannot do anything to earn this gift (remember, it isn't a wage), there is one thing we can do, that we *need* to do: personally invite Him into our lives.

Jesus said, "Behold, I stand at the door and knock. If anyone hears My voice and opens the door, I will come in to him and dine with him, and he with Me" (Revelation 3:20).

Receiving Christ involves turning to God and away from ourselves (that's what "repentance" means) and trusting Christ to come into our lives to forgive our sins and to make us what He wants us to be. Just to agree intellectually that Jesus Christ is the Son of God and that He died on the cross for our sins is not enough. Nor is it enough to have an emotional experience. We receive Jesus Christ by faith, as an act of the will.

When we truly receive Jesus, our lives change from the self-directed life to the Christ-directed life.

> While we cannot do anything to earn God's gift (remember, it isn't a wage), there is one thing we can do, that we *need* to do: personally invite Him into our lives.

The Self-Directed Life. Have you ever noticed that the more we focus our lives on satisfying ourselves, the more miserable we become? The self-directed, self-absorbed life is an insatiable thirst that can never be slaked. This kind of life leaves no room for Christ.

The Christ-Directed Life. When Christ becomes the center of our lives, we yield our wills, our behavior, everything in our lives, to Him. As a result, we fall into harmony with God's plan.

This brings us to the final point: You can receive Christ right now by faith through prayer. Prayer doesn't need to be anything complicated. It's simply talking with God. God knows your heart and is not so concerned with your words as He is with the attitude of your heart.

If you've never prayed the prayer to accept Christ into your life, you can do it right now by praying something like the following:

> Lord Jesus, I need You. Thank You for dying on the cross for my sins.
> I open the door of my life and receive You as my Savior and Lord,
> asking you to forgive me for me for the wrongs I have done. Thank
> You for forgiving my sins and giving me eternal life. Take control of
> my life. Make me the kind of person You want me to be.

If this prayer expresses the desire of your heart, then Christ has come into your life, just as He promised.

* * *

I would love to tell you that my life became perfect the moment I gave my life to Christ, but that was far from the truth. In my immaturity I failed to realize that I had a great responsibility to share the love of Jesus with Eleanor in the way that I should.

Instead, I insisted that the three of us attend worship together on Sunday mornings—but the rest of the week I left Eleanor and Ted at home while I immersed myself in different activities at the church, like men's meetings, visitation, prayer meetings, and so on.

My wife often told me I had just exchanged the bar for the church. Once again, she felt abandoned, but I was too blind to see it. This tension lasted for almost three years, until one day she told me that a couple of weeks earlier she had given her life to Jesus while watching a Christian television program. At the time, I was away "playing church." Our communication had deteriorated so much that she didn't even know how to tell me.

One important lesson I learned after coming to faith in Christ is that my struggle to resist sin continues for the rest of my life. Christians aren't perfect—and I offer myself as a prime example.

Although I had failed so miserably in sharing God's Word with Eleanor, I did read a children's Bible to Ted every night before he went to bed, and when he was eight, Ted also received Jesus Christ as his Lord and Savior while he was at a church youth camp.

I was proud to help lead my son to Christ, and I'm incredibly proud of the man that he has become.

As I reflect on the past decades, two major events in my life grieve me profoundly. The first is that, after twenty-two years of marriage, Eleanor and I divorced in 1997.

The roots of our divorce began in the mid-1980s when the small business that Eleanor and I founded went bankrupt. We had enjoyed some material success running a small seismic data processing company, but when the oil prices cratered in the mid-80s, our business went under. For two years, we poured all of our personal assets into trying to save the company, to no avail. We lost everything, including our home.

We were in dire need of an income, so I began working for a company that required extensive travel. Monday through Friday I worked in Mexico, opening an office, and then I flew home for the weekend. To cut expenses, the company asked me to stay in Mexico for two weeks at a time before coming home for the weekend. As the months wore on, Eleanor once more felt abandoned by me, and this time the damage was permanent.

When our divorce was imminent, Ted, who was in law school

at the time, tried with all his might to bring us to reconcile. But it was not to be. Our divorce was a failure on my part, one I wish I could do over. But I cannot.

Another thing very much I wish I could do differently concerned my eldest daughter, Miriam. In my first marriage, I had two girls, Miriam and Roxana. When their mother and I divorced, Miriam took it very hard. For the next forty years, she was in a state of rebellion, angry at the world.

She struggled with drug and alcohol addiction, and she associated with men who badly mistreated her. In the mid-90s, when Miriam had just been released from prison for repeated minor offenses, Ted and I drove together to the Philadelphia crack house where she was living and tried to get her to turn her life around. We failed.

Miriam continued to make terrible decisions. In January 2011, Miriam died of an accidental prescription drug overdose. There is quite simply no pain that a parent can experience, like losing a child. But, praise God, she received Christ a year before her death!

Roxana, on the other hand, became a successful doctor. A great deal of her practice focuses on those who are less fortunate, and she has a caring heart for others. She is a real blessing to my life.

Miriam's son, Joey, has become a fine young man, despite his mother's challenges. Somehow, he endured her travails and avoided making the same mistakes. Today, he works in a chocolate factory, and he's a responsible, caring young man. I'm very proud of my grandson.

But I so very much wish I could relive those chapters and somehow not destroy my marriage, and that I could pull my daughter back from the brink of destruction. I know that God forgives me, but both are burdens I must carry every day.

* * *

In late 1979, I was asked to participate on the State Board of the Religious Roundtable, a Judeo-Christian organization that mobilized millions of Christians across America to help elect Ronald Reagan. So throughout 1980, when Ted was nine, our dinner conversation centered on politics from a biblical perspective and why we needed to get rid of this leftist, progressive president named Jimmy Carter and replace him with a constitutional conservative like Ronald Reagan. Ted was mesmerized and inspired as he listened to Ronald Reagan on television. My son received a dose of constitutionally conservative politics from a biblical worldview every day for a year when he was just nine! *abuse.. crap!! bee3y..*

When Ted was eleven, he went on a mission trip to Honduras, and while there, he was able to put his Christian witness to a test. I remember when he came back from that trip; he could not contain his excitement. While there, he had shared the gospel with the former mayor of Tegucigalpa, the capital of Honduras, and this man, a political leader, prayed with Ted to receive Jesus Christ as his Lord and Savior.

That same year we saw the hand of the Lord manifested in our lives in another way. One Sunday afternoon while on vacation in Cancún, Ted and a friend and I walked to a beach to look at some big breakers. Eleanor remained at the condo. *nice ite!!! 1982 } 15 yrs.. 1997 } → pre Divorce*

We ended up at a deserted beach behind a hotel that was under construction. Since it was Sunday, there weren't any workers around, just a few people on the beach of a hotel about two hundred yards away. The boys swam while I sat on the beach, reading a book.

All of a sudden, I heard the boys cry out. I looked up and saw that they had stepped into a hole in the sand, and they could not stand up. I jumped into the water and swam to where they were. Then I grabbed one boy with each hand while I tried to tread water (I couldn't stand up either).

Then, out of nowhere, four lifeguards with full gear swam out to us and brought us ashore. What a providential experience! I still ask myself, *Could they have been angels?*

America faces a similar peril. We're treading water and in danger of drowning—but if we reach out and grab hold of our certain rescue, we will be saved.

In the next chapter I will describe the solid foundation—the only foundation—that will rescue America from destruction. *our Jesus!!!*

7

BUILDING UPON THE SOLID FOUNDATION

I will never forget Your precepts, for by them You have given me life.

—PSALM 119:93

I believe the Bible is the best gift God has ever given to man. All the good from The Savior of the world is communicated to us through this Book.

—ABRAHAM LINCOLN

The Synagogue Church of All Nations has played a significant role in Nigeria's spiritual landscape. Its pastor, T. B. Joshua, has received numerous awards, including recognition as one of Africa's fifty most influential people.[1] The church attracts as many as fifteen thousand in attendance every Sunday,[2] and people from around the African continent have traveled to hear him preach in Lagos.

To accommodate their many visitors, the church decided to build a guesthouse. But in 2014, the multistory guesthouse collapsed, killing 116 people—most of them foreigners. Structural and geotechnical engineers examined the building and announced their findings:

> Based on all the tests and the calculations, we discovered that from inception, the building failed because the base that was supposed to take the load was grossly inadequate. The minimum base that will be required should have been 4.5 metres by 4.5 metres but what we had there was 2.2 metres by 2.2 metres.[3]

The foundation of the guesthouse was approximately 25 percent of the size it needed to be to support the building's weight and multiple stories. As a result, the building collapsed and lives were lost.

Dimensions and the quality of a foundation determine the size of the structure that can safely be constructed on top of it. A larger, higher-quality foundation can accommodate a bigger and sturdier building. A smaller, inferior-quality foundation can withstand little or no stress.

Our Founding Fathers built America on a high-quality foundation, but over time, we have allowed its integrity to be compromised. Without restoring it to its previous condition, it will crumble and our nation will collapse from the foundation's inability to support the structure (I address the shaky foundation in the next chapter).

In Psalm 11:3, King David rightly asks, "If the foundations are destroyed, what can the righteous do?" And what *can* the righteous do? Nothing. Lacking a solid foundation, even the righteous are rendered virtually powerless.

> Our Founding Fathers built America on a high-quality foundation, but over time, we have allowed its integrity to be compromised. Without restoring it to its previous condition, it will crumble and our nation will collapse.

Solid foundations are never created on a whim. They begin with soil tests, painstaking planning, quality materials; you get the point. In the same way, a vibrant, godly country must be built, step-by-step, precept-by-precept, on spiritual foundation. A precept is a commandment or statute that the people in a country obey.

* * *

The following illustration shows how the Christian life is built upon the foundation of Jesus Christ. This is most easily understood by reading from the bottom up.

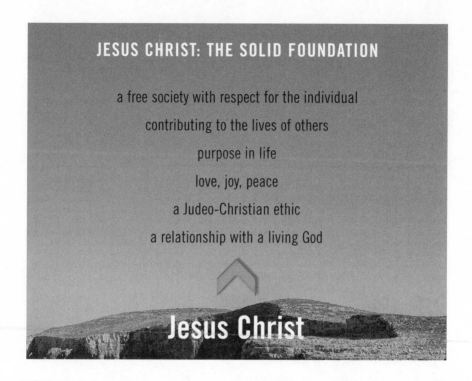

JESUS CHRIST: THE SOLID FOUNDATION

a free society with respect for the individual

contributing to the lives of others

purpose in life

love, joy, peace

a Judeo-Christian ethic

a relationship with a living God

Jesus Christ

In the previous chapter we discussed how we begin a relationship with Jesus Christ when we surrender our lives to Him as our Lord and Savior, so I won't probe any further into the first step.

A JUDEO-CHRISTIAN ETHIC. The telltale sign of engaging God in a personal relationship is the desire to be like Him, to live like Him and reflect His character and values. Then as we study God's Word, we walk in obedience to His Word and His precepts. This next step to which I refer can be considered not only a Christian ethic, but a Jewish ethic as well. After all, the Jewish Bible—which Christians call the Old Testament—counts as about 60 percent of the Protestant and Catholic Bibles. We share a common heritage and many mutual beliefs, and we worship the same God.

The foundational Judeo-Christian ethic for Jews and Christians appears in Exodus 20:3–17. Biblical scholars have classified this passage, often called the Decalogue or Ten Commandments, into two categories. The first four commandments deal with our relationship with God:

1. You shall have no other gods before Me.

2. You shall not make for yourself a carved image . . . you shall not bow down to them nor serve them.

3. You shall not take the name of the LORD your God in vain

4. Remember the Sabbath day, to keep it holy.

The next six commandments deal with our relationship to one another:

5. Honor your father and your mother.

6. You shall not murder.

7. You shall not commit adultery.

8. You shall not steal.

9. You shall not bear false witness against your neighbor.

10. You shall not covet . . . anything that is your neighbor's.

Dennis Prager, the conservative Jewish talk show host, pointed out that the Ten Commandments created universal human rights, women's equality, the end to slavery, and parliamentary democracy. In his explanation of the Ten Commandments, Prager commented:

> These commandments are as relevant today as when they were given over 3,000 years ago. In fact, they're so relevant that the Ten Commandments are all that is necessary to make a good world, a world free of tyranny and cruelty . . .
>
> But there is a catch. The Ten Commandments are predicated on the belief that they were given by an Authority higher than any man, any king, or any government. That's why the sentence preceding the Ten Commandments asserts the following: "God spoke all these words."

You see, if the Ten Commandments, as great as they are, were given by any human authority, then any person could say, "Who is this man Moses, who is this king or queen; who is this government to tell me how I should behave? Okay, so why is God indispensable to the Ten Commandments? Because . . . if it isn't God who declares murder wrong, murder isn't wrong.[4]

Prager went on to illustrate that a person can *believe* murder is wrong but cannot *know* murder is wrong without God saying it's wrong. Without God saying it's wrong, all morality is just personal opinion and belief—and many atheist philosophers have acknowledged this. Finally, Prager concluded, "In 3,000 years no one has ever come up with a better system than the God-based Ten Commandments for making a better world. And no one ever will."

In the ancient Near East, kings codified the laws of the land. Their particular god may have whispered into their ears, but the king established the law. In ancient Israel's case, God made it clear that He was their king. Their authority. That's why even today, Jews and Christians answer to a higher authority than the government—and a government that tries to make people reliant upon itself usurps God's authority and undermines the moral fiber of a nation. As I explained in chapter 4, twentieth-century atheistic governments—communist and totalitarian regimes—killed as many as 100 million people.[5]

The Ten Commandments granted human rights that were unparalleled to other nations at that time. Because God directly established them, they model to us the first rule of law, and serve as the basis for individual responsibility, free enterprise, integrity, hard work, and limited

> "In 3,000 years no one has ever come up with a better system than the God-based Ten Commandments for making a better world. And no one ever will."
>
> DENNIS PRAGER

government. They also serve as the foundation for the Declaration of Independence and the Constitution of the United States. Indeed the image of the Ten Commandments appears in forty-three different places in the courtroom of the US Supreme Court building, including the oak doors leaving the courtroom and carved on the frieze above the Justice's left shoulders. John Adams acknowledged their importance: "If 'Thou shalt not covet,' and 'Thou shalt not steal,' were not commandments of Heaven, they must be made inviolable precepts in every society, before it can be civilized or made free."[6]

Furthermore, the first five books of the Old Testament, otherwise known as the Pentateuch or Torah, reaffirmed the importance of human life in an age that devalued it. In Genesis 9:6, God said to Noah, "Whoever sheds man's blood, by man his blood shall be shed; for in the image of God He made man."

> The death penalty doesn't devalue human life; it preserves it.

In the chapter that follows the Decalogue, God expanded on the sixth commandment: "But if a man acts with premeditation against his neighbor, to kill him by treachery, you shall take him from My altar, that he may die" (Exodus 21:14). You could say, then, that the death penalty actually elevates the value of life; basically God was saying that life is so irreplaceably precious that if you take a life, you should pay with your own. The death penalty doesn't devalue human life; it preserves it.

Imagine the implications of taking the Ten Commandments to heart:

- Tax rates would drop because children would take a more active role in caring for their elderly parents, easing the burden of our welfare and social security systems.

- Divorce rates would plummet because husbands and wives would no longer cheat on each other.

- Families would become stronger, circumventing higher rates of violent crime, gang activity, and drug use that are more likely among children who grow up in single-parent families (especially fatherless families).

- Retail store prices would drop because customers would no longer steal.

- Bankruptcies would diminish because people would no longer covet their neighbors' possessions and buy what they can't afford.

When atheists protested Chief Justice Roy Moore's commissioning of the Ten Commandments monument at the Alabama Judicial Building in 2003, I couldn't help but ask, "How can the Ten Commandments hurt our country?"

THE FRUIT OF THE SPIRIT. We cannot understand the Bible unless the Spirit of God dwells in us. We read in 1 Corinthians 2:14, "But the natural man does not receive the things of the Spirit of God, for they are foolishness to him; nor can he know them, because they are spiritually discerned."

The Bible was written by direct revelation from God. In the same manner, the Holy Spirit reveals to us the truths of the Word of God: "But God has revealed them to us through His Spirit. For the Spirit searches all things, yes, the deep things of God. For what man knows the things of a man except the spirit of the man which is in him? Even so no one knows the things of God except the Spirit of God" (1 Corinthians 2:10–11).

And, as we continue to abide in His Word and with Him in prayer, the fruits of the Spirit are manifested in our lives, and others can see the character of Christ in us.

But the fruit of the Spirit is love, joy, peace, longsuffering, kindness, goodness, faithfulness, gentleness, self-control. Against such there is no law. (Galatians 5:22–23)

"Fruit" in this passage obviously isn't like an orange or a peach. Perhaps a better word we could use here is "produce," like the produce a farmer brings to the market. The fruit is the produce, or product, of his labors. The fruit of the Spirit is the produce of the Spirit's work in our lives.

When I attended the Bible study for the first time and encountered the peace, love, and joy evident in the lives of the attenders, I wanted what they had, even though I didn't know what *it* was. God used them to draw me to Him through the manifestation of the fruit of the Spirit in their lives.

And what is the fruit of the Spirit, really? The character of Jesus. To the extent that we yield to Jesus living through us, people encounter HIM! But here's the catch with the fruit of the Spirit: we cannot manufacture it on our own. Each character quality is the fruit of the Spirit's work in our lives. Our relationship with God waters the seed that becomes love, joy, peace, and so on.

Jesus said in John 15:5, "I am the vine, you are the branches. He who abides in Me, and I in him, bears much fruit; for without Me you can do nothing." The word *abide* means "to "remain," "to dwell," or "to live." We get the English word *abode* from the same word. Abiding in Christ doesn't occur in an instant or a rush. Abiding takes time, just like a farmer who waters an apple or orange tree for months before any fruit appears.

Have you ever spent a morning in a coffee shop and then walked out smelling like coffee? The same applies to your relationship with God. Welcome Him into your day, acknowledge His presence in your life, enjoy random moments with Him, converse with Him, and over time you'll become more like Him. You'll emanate what Paul calls the "fragrance of Christ" (see 2 Corinthians 2:15). When the fruit of the Spirit is at work in our lives, we radiate Jesus.

> When the fruit of the Spirit is at work in our lives, we radiate Jesus.

Notice the last line in Galatians 5:23: "Against such there is no law." When the fruit of the Spirit is at work in our lives, the law becomes a minimal factor in how society functions.

PURPOSE IN LIFE. As our internal life begins coming together, we align ourselves with God's purposes and position ourselves for Him to use us. Contrary to popular belief, God doesn't call only particularly "gifted" people; He gives all of us purpose, a direction in life, and the more we trust Him, the more He directs our steps. "Trust in the LORD with all your heart," the Bible tells us, "and lean not on your own understanding; in all your ways acknowledge Him, and He shall direct your paths" (Proverbs 3:5–6). We no longer need to wander aimlessly, going in one direction until we hit a brick wall and then changing direction . . . only to hit another wall. Twice God affirms the consequence of following "our own way," in Proverbs 14:12 and again in Proverbs 16:25: "There is a way that seems right to a man, but its end is the way of death." We were made for another purpose.

However, this purpose has nothing to do with building our empires, expanding our portfolios, or growing our bank accounts. God's purposes for our lives cannot be reduced to making *us* the focus of our pursuits. Jesus said in Matthew 6:33, "But seek first the kingdom of God and His righteousness, and all these things shall be added to you."

Making ourselves the focus of our lives underestimates ourselves and God. His dreams to use us far surpass ours. Instead, God calls us to be salt and light in our world (see Matthew 5:13–15). Jesus said, "Let your light shine before others, that they may see your good deeds and glorify your Father in heaven" (v. 16).

God assures us in Jeremiah 29:11, "'For I know the plans I have for you,' declares the LORD, 'plans to prosper you and not to harm you, plans to give you hope and a future'" (NIV).

So what does all of this look like?

You don't need to be a politician or a pastor for God to use you. God may be calling you to be a politician or a pastor, but neither is a higher calling. Anyone can fulfill God's purposes for their lives.

Henry David Thoreau was correct in saying, "The mass of men lead lives of quiet desperation."[7] People hunger for purpose. It's no coincidence that Pastor Rick Warren's book *The Purpose Driven Life* has sold more than 30 million copies.[8]

On many occasions I have followed my own desires only to fall flat on my face or run into a brick wall. This is a common experience for those who follow their instincts and are often tripped by circumstances in life. Even worse, they encounter situations in which they have no clue how to react or how to get out of the trap in which they find themselves. They feel desperate, without the peace (the fruit of the Spirit) that can come only from God. Paul wrote in Philippians 2:13, "For it is God who works in you both to will and to do for His good pleasure."

CONTRIBUTING TO THE LIVES OF OTHERS. No characteristic describes the Christian life more than living a life of contribution, investing ourselves in the lives of others. You may call it "ministering to others," "offering a helping hand," or a "pat on the back," or a "listening ear," or "sound advice," or "pointing someone in the right direction," or most critically "leading someone to Christ." Regardless, this is the *fruit* of the fruit of the Spirit because we forget about ourselves in order to help those around us.

Whereas, our relationship with God (foundation step #1) deals with loving God, contributing to the lives of others deals with loving people. And what does love look like? Giving ourselves away. Paul wrote, "Bear one another's burdens, and so fulfill the law of Christ" (Galatians 6:2).

Think for a minute. How do we know that love is naturally expressed through giving? John 3:16, the most beloved verse in Scripture, reminds us that God loved the world so much that He did what? He gave.

> God so loved the world that He gave His only begotten Son, that whoever believes in Him should not perish but have everlasting life.

In the Charities Aid Foundation's most recent report on giving, *World Giving Index 2014*, the United States ranked number one in the world (along with Myanmar) in giving. We were the only country to rank in the top ten in all three categories: helping a stranger (1st), volunteering time (joint 5th), and donating money (9th). In fact, the United States ranks number one in giving over the previous five years.[9]

According to a report by Giving USA, Americans donated an estimated $358.38 billion to charity in 2014—the highest total in the report's sixty-year history. Of that total, about a third of it came through religious means ($114.9 billion).[10]

The Barna Group conducted a poll in 2013 on giving in America (money, items, or time). Their findings showed who in the American population gives the most:

Evangelicals were far and away the group most likely to donate money, items or time as a volunteer. More than three-quarters of evangelicals (79%) have donated money in the last year, and 65% and 60% of them have donated items or volunteer time, respectively.[11]

Furthermore, Barna compared the giving habits of atheists and agnostics with those of evangelicals:

Twice as many atheists and agnostics (40%) donated a relatively small amount (under $100), compared to all donating adults (20%). Evangelical Christians are among the faith groups that donate the most: they are much more likely than average (26% compared to the national average of 7%) to have contributed either $2,500–$5,000, or more than $10,000 (6% compared to 1%) last year.[12]

In a separate study, Barna discovered that political liberals are some of the stingiest givers in the country. And Barna isn't alone in his findings. *The Chronicle of Philanthropy* reported in their "How America Gives 2014" study that the seventeen most generous states in the country voted for Mitt Romney in the 2012 election. This study measured giving in terms of "share of income donated to charity." Not surprisingly, twelve of the thirteen stingiest states voted for Obama.[13]

Why are liberals so stingy? They rely on the government to be generous. They pay their taxes, so why should they give? Entrusting the government to give on our behalf results in failed programs, such as Lyndon Johnson's ill-fated Great Society, which encouraged dependency on the government. Perhaps the term *liberal* is a misnomer and is better suited for evangelicals.

These numbers confirm my belief that Christians are the single most generous people group in the history of the world. Through individual Christians and the church, more money, more voluntary hours, more resources have been given, exponentially more, than from any other group.

But giving doesn't mean throwing money at a problem and then expecting the problem to resolve itself. Giving means getting our hands dirty and involving ourselves in others' lives. The predominant characteristic that we need in our fellow citizens, in our elected officials, in every leader, teacher, or manager, and most of all in every Christian who wants to follow the steps of Jesus, is a servant spirit.

> Christians are the single most generous people group in the history of the world.

Jesus told His disciples, "If anyone desires to be first, he shall be last of all and servant of all" (Mark 9:35). And He taught us by example. He healed the sick (Matthew 12:15). He fed the five thousand (Matthew 14:13–21). He washed His disciples' feet and then commanded them to do the same (John 13:1–17). Then the Son of God modeled the full extent of a humble servant by His willingness to go to the cross in our place (read Philippians 2:5–11).

What love! How can we not love Him in return when He loved us first? And how can we not willingly serve others when he willingly served us first?

> For even the Son of Man did not come to be served, but to serve, and to give His life a ransom for many. (Mark 10:45)

> If you want to win someone's heart, give, not with the expectation of receiving anything in return; just give.

When we truly understand the magnitude of God's gift to us in Christ, when we experience the immensity of His love for us, what happens inside of us? It wins our hearts. If you want to win someone's heart, give, not with the expectation of receiving anything in return; just give.

A FREE SOCIETY WITH RESPECT FOR THE INDIVIDUAL. The net result of this Christian lifestyle, where the Holy Spirit guides us, the fruit of the Spirit reflects the character of Christ through us, and we serve others extravagantly, is that we naturally gravitate toward a harmonious relationship with the people around us. As we walk in accordance with God's purpose for our lives, we move toward the fulfillment of His calling for us and we operate with a servant spirit toward others, creating a free society where mutual respect prevails.

It is for freedom that Christ has set us free. Stand firm, then, and do not let yourselves be burdened again by a yoke of slavery. (Galatians 5:1 NIV)

I understand that the total fulfillment of the above description is possible only in a perfect world, but imagine the possibilities if this became the standard the church—and the American people—followed.

Now let's look at the antithesis of this foundation.

8

AMERICA'S SHAKY FOUNDATION

"But everyone who hears these sayings of Mine, and does not do them, will be like a foolish man who built his house on the sand: and the rain descended, the floods came, and the winds blew and beat on that house; and it fell. And great was its fall."

—JESUS, IN MATTHEW 7:26–27

Professing to be wise, they became fools, and changed the glory of the incorruptible God into an image made like corruptible man—and birds and four-footed animals and creeping things.

—ROMANS 1:22–23

In the fall of 1932, America was wallowing in the throes of the Great Depression. Unemployment had peaked earlier that year at 25 percent, a drought was ravaging the heartland, people and businesses were defaulting on loans, and more than five thousand banks had failed.

Spiritually speaking, America was suffering a dry spell as well. The clash between science and faith had pushed people into taking sides in the argument about God's existence. Already, theological liberalism had hijacked America's seminaries, forcing the fundamentalist–modernist debates. With hope in short supply, people were questioning matters of faith—and the seminaries offered few answers.

Raymond Bragg, a Unitarian minister, listened to a lecture by his friend, philosophy professor Roy Wood Sellers, at the University of Chicago. Afterward, Bragg suggested to Sellers that he draft a statement that would transcend and replace the primitive, small-minded religions that still believed in a God.

Within six weeks, Sellers completed his first draft. In early 1933, Bragg and Sellers began circulating the statement among other prominent Unitarian ministers and college professors. Finally, the Humanist Manifesto was distributed at a University of Chicago conference on May 1, with signatories that included philosopher John Dewey and a host of theologically liberal ministers (mostly Unitarian) and theologians.

From the outset, the framers of the Humanist Manifesto admitted their "creed" was a religious movement and the document's fifteen points, based on reason, ethics, and social and economic justice, spelled out their belief system. Since then, two more humanist manifestos have been crafted, in 1973 and 2003.

Today, religious humanists, who believe in the existence of transcendence (a spiritual *force* that doesn't interact with us) are being replaced by secular humanists, who scoff at any possibility of transcendence. Reflecting this progression, the second manifesto explicitly states, "No deity will save us; we must save ourselves. . . . We are responsible for what we are or will be."[1]

The three manifestos have tilled the soil for atheists to emerge. According to a 2012 report by the Pew Research Center, "2.4 percent of American adults say they are atheists when asked about their religious identity, up from 1.6 percent in 2007."[2] While 2.4 percent doesn't seem like a large amount, consider that these numbers reflect 50 percent growth in only five years!

In Hollywood, atheism has become the latest religious trend. Movie stars such as Emma Thompson (*Sense and Sensibility*), Daniel Radcliffe (*Harry Potter*), Ricky Gervais (*The Invention of Lying*), and comedians like Bill Maher not only deny God's existence, but ridicule those who believe in God.

Today, the American Humanist Association, which acts as the

manifestos' guardian, boasts the tagline "Good without a God" on their logo.[3]

* * *

Secular humanism denies the existence of God. It proclaims that because no God exists, we have no moral principles to follow. Karl Marx and Friedrich Engels built their atheistic system of Communism on this premise.

Sadly, many American public schools promote this atheistic philosophy. John Dewey, who signed the 1933 Humanist Manifesto, is one of the founders of the modern American system of education. In a 1983 article for the *Humanist* journal, John Dunphy described the role of the Humanist Manifesto in public education:

> I am convinced that the battle for humankind's future must be waged and won in the public school classroom by teachers that correctly perceive their role as proselytizers of a new faith: a religion of humanity that recognizes and respects the spark of what theologians call divinity in every human being. . . . The classroom must and will become an arena of conflict between the old and new—the rotting corpse of Christianity, together with all its adjacent evils and misery, and the new faith of humanism, resplendent with the promise of a world in which the never-realized Christian ideal of "love thy neighbor" will finally be achieved.[4]

This is a condensed summary of the 1933 Humanist Manifesto (See http://americanhumanist.org/ for the complete manifesto):

1. The universe was not created.

2. Man has emerged as a result of a continuous process (evolved, not created).

3. The mind and body cannot be separated from one another.

4. The individual is largely molded by its culture.

5. Human values are disassociated from the supernatural, and religion must tailor its beliefs to science.

6. Traditional concepts about God and several varieties of "new thought" have passed away.

7. The distinction between the sacred and the secular doesn't exist.

8. Life is only concerned about the here and now.

9. Religious emotions are expressed to promote social well-being.

10. The supernatural does not exist.

11. We solve our crises in life with our minds by measuring their naturalness and probability.

12. Religion should focus on finding satisfaction and joy.

13. All associations and religious institutions exist for the fulfillment of human life.

14. People are most fulfilled through the redistribution of wealth.

15. Humanism seeks to affirm life and pursue the possibilities of life by establishing conditions that are satisfactory (collectivism?).

Because it denies the existence of the supernatural and any sort of afterlife, the Humanist Manifesto concerns itself only with the here and now. As Dennis Prager explained in the previous chapter, if a divine authority doesn't exist, then sin doesn't exist, and we need not fear eternal punishment for our sin. Eat, drink, and be merry, for tomorrow we may die. And that's the end of us.

This change should come as no surprise. Scripture warns us, "Dear friends, remember what the apostles of our Lord Jesus Christ foretold. They said to you, 'In the last times there will be scoffers who will follow their own ungodly desires.' These are the people who divide you, who follow mere natural instincts and do not have the Spirit" (Jude 17–19 NIV).

Secular humanists scoff at any faith and promote following our natural instincts, because nothing exists outside of nature. Secular humanism, then, advocates hedonism, the belief that pleasure and happiness are the goal of life. Me, me, me, and nothing else. "Man is the measure of all things," as Protagoras, the Greek philosopher, suggested.[5] This contradicts the teachings of all the major religions of the world, especially Christianity. Scripture explains our true purpose:

> A society that exists only for self is a description of hell, not heaven.

> Whether you eat or drink, or whatever you do, do all to the glory of God. (1 Corinthians 10:31)

> For of Him and through Him and to Him are all things, to whom be glory forever. (Romans 11:36)

In the beautiful words of the Westminster Shorter Catechism, "Man's chief end is to glorify God, and to enjoy him for ever." A society that exists only for self is a description of hell, not heaven.

* * *

The following illustration depicts how secular humanism undermines the foundation of society. This is most easily understood by reading from the bottom up.

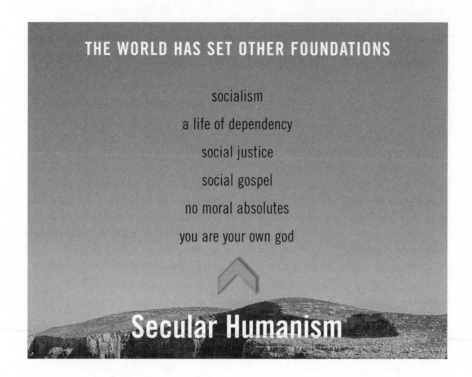

THE WORLD HAS SET OTHER FOUNDATIONS

socialism

a life of dependency

social justice

social gospel

no moral absolutes

you are your own god

Secular Humanism

YOU ARE YOUR OWN GOD. As I already explained, secular humanism denies the existence of God. And if John Calvin was correct in his assertion that "man's nature, so to speak, is a perpetual factory of idols,"[6] then we become the logical choice of our worship.

When a person denies the existence of a divine being greater than himself, his choice relegates him to a life without hope—because this life is all there is. Such an individual strives to achieve all he can in the here and now and joins the "rat race" in search of some temporal significance.

And in those inevitable moments when he encounters circumstances beyond his control, he has nowhere to turn and no one to turn *to*. This becomes very apparent when you walk into the intensive care waiting room at any hospital. There you will see a stark contrast between those who are restless and in despair and do not believe in God, and those with a faith in God, in whose countenances you can see the "peace that surpasses all understanding" that only Jesus Christ can give.

Be anxious for nothing, but in everything by prayer and supplication, with thanksgiving, let your requests be made known to God; and *the peace of God, which surpasses all understanding*, will guard your hearts and minds through Christ Jesus. (Philippians 4:6–7, emphasis added)

NO MORAL ABSOLUTES. Without a divinely established set of standards like the Bible gives us, secular humanists reject the idea of any moral absolutes. Everyone, then, feels entitled to establish his or her own standards by which to live. This has given rise to the attitude "if it feels good, do it," the pursuit of hedonism, immoral or chaotic behavior, greed, and even a life of crime.

Through the years, secular humanists have tried to brainwash schoolchildren with their ungodly philosophies. Outcome-based education (OBE) was introduced in the American public schools at the end of the twentieth century, empowered by Goals 2000 (introduced by George H. W. Bush) and later, No Child Left Behind (introduced by George W. Bush). OBE worked hand in glove with liberals seeking to promote the secular humanist agenda because it replaced objective testing and rote learning with subjective, open-ended essay questions, more problem solving, more analysis, and a greater emphasis on higher-order reasoning. Moving from objective to subjective questions enables educators to couch their teaching in secular humanist philosophy.

OBE guidelines for school districts often include subjective outcomes such as "holistic learning," "openness to change," "positive self-image," and "appreciation of diversity in others [and] appreciation of the global community."[7] What nonsubjective criteria can a teacher use to grade her students' work in these areas? If a student writes from a biblical worldview, what prevents a teacher from grading that child lower out of disagreement with the student's personal beliefs? And how can a teacher assure parents that her personal humanistic beliefs won't infect their lessons? She can't.

For example, Virginia drafted a plan consisting of student outcomes that included environmental stewardship, personal well-being and accomplishment, and interpersonal relationships. Although shelved after the plan was drafted, it illustrates how easily humanistic values can replace education. While noble sounding, personal well-being can easily be taught from a humanistic viewpoint, with the assumption that our value comes from ourselves rather than God. Story problems can present gay marriage as normative. Humanistically educated teachers, who spend more time with students than do students' parents, pass along their values to their unsuspecting pupils. At the same time, this comes at the expense of teaching math and history.

Most concerning of all is the imposition of Common Core into the public school system. While we'll explore this closer in chapter 12, I will say that tying federal funding to its adherence is nothing short of blackmail.

As the secular humanist establishment works overtime to abolish moral absolutes, their definition of sin has logically grown smaller and smaller. Anything goes—except any belief that doesn't agree that "anything goes." Among secular humanists, the greatest sin is to disagree with them and hold to any moral absolutes at all. Standing up and saying, "I disagree" is tantamount to hate speech (a microaggression)—even if the disagreement is based in deeply spiritual reasons.

> With the secular humanist establishment, anything goes—except any belief that doesn't agree that "anything goes."

The hot, burning issue in America right now revolves around the definition of marriage. In 1996, the Defense of Marriage Act (DOMA) was passed by a supermajority in both houses of Congress and signed into law by President Bill Clinton. Section 2 of the DOMA allowed states the right to refuse to recognize same-sex marriages that were granted in other states.

Section 3 of the DOMA explicitly stated:

The word "marriage" means only a legal union between one man and one woman as husband and wife, and the word "spouse" refers only to a person of the opposite sex who is a husband or a wife.[8]

Later, Clinton disavowed himself of his approval and advocated the act's repeal. In 2011, the Obama administration concurred with Clinton and announced that it would no longer defend the law in court. In 2013, the Supreme Court ruled that Section 3 of DOMA—the basic definition of marriage—was somehow unconstitutional, unbeknownst to our Founding Fathers and centuries of Americans.

Just as concerning is the plight of the federal government overruling state governments. Between 1998 and 2012, thirty-one states passed constitutional amendments banning same-sex marriage. During that same period, only two states voted down the amendments (Arizona in 2006 and Minnesota in 2012).

A textbook example is California. In 2000, the California voters approved Proposition 22, affirming marriage as a union between a man and woman by a 61 percent to 39 percent margin. The California Supreme Court struck down the proposition in May 2008.

A mere six months later, in November 2008, the citizens of the Golden State rose up and passed Proposition 8, once again banning same-sex marriage by a 52 to 48 percent margin. As expected, the proposition was challenged in court. The California state attorney general, who is charged with *defending* the laws of the state, refused to defend Proposition 8, so the Alliance Defending Freedom and the ProtectMarriage.com coalition organized to defend the people of California's definition of marriage.

In August 2010, the lawsuit against Proposition 8 was deliberately filed and tried in San Francisco, and, as you can expect, was struck down as unconstitutional. The judge who issued the ruling was in a same-sex relationship and failed to disclose it until after the ruling.

In 2012, the US Court of Appeals for the Ninth Circuit heard the case. The three-judge panel included a judge who had more decisions overturned by the Supreme Court than any other appellate judge in

America—and whose wife also had worked as the executive director of the Southern California ACLU. Not coincidentally, her organization filed a brief urging the court to strike down the proposition. Despite the conflict of interest, the judge refused to recuse himself from the case.

Not surprisingly, the Ninth Circuit upheld the lower court's ruling.

In June 2013, the US Supreme Court dismissed the appeal, basically leaving the lower court's ruling intact, empowering Governor Jerry Brown to order that same-sex marriage ceremonies resume.

Consider this: a handful of federal judges overrode the will of more than 7 million voters in California. Twice. Despite the fact that under the Tenth Amendment, the federal government has no jurisdiction over marriage. The decision belongs to the states.

But most disturbing of all, the recent Supreme Court ruling legalizing homosexual marriage is one of the biggest signs of our country's moral degradation. By purporting to legalize and mandate homosexual marriage, the Supreme Court has given gay couples a "civil right" based on Section 1 of the Fourteenth Amendment of the Constitution:

> All persons born or naturalized in the United States, and subject to the jurisdiction thereof, are citizens of the United States and of the State wherein they reside. No State shall make or enforce any law which shall abridge the privileges or immunities of citizens of the United States; nor shall any State deprive any person of life, liberty, or property, without due process of law; nor deny to any person within its jurisdiction the equal protection of the laws.

While this amendment was originally intended to grant equal rights and protections to former slaves, the Supreme Court's decision, in essence, has decided that it simultaneously—and unbeknownst to every person who voted to ratify it—rendered unconstitutional the marriage laws in every state in the union. This is preposterous. It is not law. It is blatant judicial activism, five unelected lawyers declaring themselves (as Justice Scalia put it in powerful dissent) the "rulers" of 320 million Americans.

And when homosexual marriage becomes a mandatory civil right, the next obvious step is to enforce this civil right in private businesses, Christian organizations, and even churches. You see, the decision in favor of homosexual marriage is really a decision *against* religious freedom.

Even before the Supreme Court decision, the courts and the US government were taking measures to progressively encroach on our religious freedoms.

In 2002, Betty and Richard Odgaard purchased a seventy-seven-year-old Lutheran church building in Grimes, Iowa, and converted it into an art gallery to display Betty's artwork as well as works from other local artists. Their Görtz Haus Gallery also included a bistro, framing shop, and flower and gift shop. To make ends meet, they opened the former sanctuary several times a year for weddings.

However, after years of doing business, the Iowa Civil Rights Commission tried forcing them to close for refusing to host a same-sex wedding, which violated their Mennonite beliefs. The Odgaards had never displayed any animosity toward gays; in fact, they had hired gay employees over the years and willingly served gay customers. But hosting a same-sex wedding—actively participating in celebrating a gay marriage—simply violated their religious beliefs.

The gay couple's complaint stirred up a barrage of negative media exposure, generating hate mail, boycotts, personal attacks, and even death threats. Iowa Civil Rights Commission officials denied them access to the state courts and the state of Iowa refused to dismiss the case—even after the two men admitted that they already had been married for *months* before inquiring about renting the facility.

In the face of years of legal fees and ongoing state pressure, the Odgaards agreed to pay the two men thousands of dollars and stop hosting weddings. Ultimately, the Odgaards were forced to close down the gallery under financial hardship.

"The [gay couple] had a platform to file their case and we didn't get our day in court with a jury of our peers," Richard reflected.[9]

In 2012, Charlie Craig and David Mullins asked Jack Phillips, owner of Masterpiece Cake Shop in Lakewood, Colorado, to create a wedding cake for their same-sex ceremony. Phillips politely explained that he couldn't make a cake to celebrate their wedding for religious reasons, but that he would gladly make another baked item for them. Craig and Mullins immediately left the shop and filed a complaint with the Colorado Civil Rights Commission, which agreed with the couple's complaint.

Later, the Colorado Court of Appeals unanimously decided that the bakery's policy refusing to create wedding cakes for same-sex couples was a "discriminatory and unfair practice."[10] These stories are just scratching the surface, and they will continue to multiply unless the faithful reclaim this country. Take for example:

- Aaron and Melissa Klein, owners of Sweet Cakes by Melissa bakery, whom the state of Oregon fined $135,000 for refusing to bake a wedding cake for a lesbian couple's wedding.

- Atlanta Fire Rescue Department Chief Kelvin Cochran, who distributed a biblically correct but politically incorrect booklet that led the mayor of Atlanta to suspend him for a month without pay, and ultimately fire him.

- Air Force Senior Master Sergeant Phillip Monk, who was relieved of his duties in 2013 for disagreeing with Defense Department policy on same-sex marriage.

Even the erroneous wall our government erected separating church and state (see chapter 9 for more), however, will soon become selectively permeable.

Imagine you're sitting in church one Sunday morning and your pastor announces he's leaving his wife for a man in the congregation. It's only a matter of time before the congregation will have absolutely no biblical recourse but to remove its pastor. But that may well become illegal. In the future, questioning the sexual preferences of any prospective pastor may well become off-limits. If you do, you could be slapped with a civil rights discrimination lawsuit.

After the Supreme Court decision, Rick Scarborough, founder of Vision America, wrote in a column for *Variety*:

> If same-sex marriage becomes a civil right (as it now is), the solicitor general made it clear during oral arguments before the Supreme Court that tax exemption for those who do not comply would be an issue. We are constantly being told that churches will not be forced to conduct such marriages, but churches do a lot of things other than perform marriages: They have food kitchens, rescue missions, schools, day-care centers, hospitals and colleges, all licensed by the state. If their tax exemptions are removed, God's churches won't go away, but much of the good they perform for all Americans will be lost, including benevolence and care extended to homosexuals with AIDS and other illnesses.[11]

If their tax exemptions are removed, God's churches won't go away, but much of the good they perform for all Americans will be lost, including benevolence and care extended to homosexuals with AIDS and other illnesses.

Not only would granting a civil right to gay marriage affect the ministries of churches, synagogues, and mosques, but it could also directly affect the messages that clergy speak to their spiritual communities. Which begs the question: how soon will hate speech—as political liberals define it—become a punishable offense?

While hate speech is not an officially criminally punishable offense at this time, our society is racing that direction. Voicing your opinion in opposition to homosexual behavior can easily generate a vitriolic verbal beat-down that borders on physical assault. Already in some countries, if you say that homosexuality is a sin, you could go to prison and be slapped with a hate speech violation. The Netherlands bans speech that intentionally criticizes people of homosexual orientation with a punishable offense of up to a year in prison.

In 2009, President Obama signed the Matthew Shepard and James Byrd, Jr., Hate Crimes Prevention Act. Matthew Shepard was tortured to death outside of Laramie, Wyoming, in 1998, allegedly because he was gay. James Byrd Jr., an African American man, was murdered in 1998 in Jasper, Texas, by two white supremacists.

Both crimes were horrific, and the murderers deserved the most severe punishments.

But the law enacts stricter punishment on people who commit a crime based on a person's "actual or perceived religion, national origin, gender, sexual orientation, gender identity, or disability of any person." Upon the law's passage, President Obama commented, "After more than a decade, we've passed inclusive hate-crimes legislation to help protect our citizens from violence based on what they look like, who they love, how they pray or who they are."[12]

Criticism of the law was anything but muted. Tim Wildmon, president of the American Family Association, warned, "[The new law] creates a kind of caste system in law enforcement, where the perverse thing is that people who engage in 'nonnormative' sexual behavior will have more legal protection than heterosexuals. This kind of inequality before the law is simply un-American."[13]

Erik Stanley, senior legal counsel for the Alliance Defending Freedom, said, "All violent crimes are hate crimes, and all crime victims deserve equal justice. This law is a grave threat to the First Amendment because it provides special penalties based on what people think, feel, or believe."[14]

People of faith who choose to live according to their consciences are finding themselves on the wrong side of the very country that was founded to provide freedom for people of religious conscience. Ten years or even one year before the Supreme Court's gay ruling, no one would have thought it possible for the deterioration of the moral fiber of America to occur so rapidly.

Janet Porter of Faith2Action wrote, "But this law doesn't just affect pastors; it will criminalize the beliefs of millions of ordinary people who may now be afraid to speak even their "pro-marriage" positions lest it spark a federal hate crime investigation."[15]

Ironically, four members of the US Commission on Civil Rights opposed Obama's Hate Crimes bill, calling it a "menace to civil liberties."[16] The commission argued the law allows federal authorities to level charges against people even if the state court has already cleared them.

> People of faith who choose to live according to their consciences are finding themselves on the wrong side of the very country that was founded to provide freedom for people of religious conscience.

The Alliance Defending Freedom has developed a free, informative manual to help churches, Christian ministries, and Christian schools navigate their way through these uncertain waters. See the resources section on page 234.

The next step is how secular humanism undermines society.

THE SOCIAL GOSPEL. Unfortunately, too many churches have adopted secular humanist concepts in the attempt to "attract the world." Pastors stop preaching or teaching about controversial issues, such as gender identity, homosexual marriage, or the sanctity of life, so as not to "offend" anyone who might be suffering or who has suffered the trauma of these feelings and behaviors.

A young man might be attending the church worship service, looking for answers about his identity or seeking prayer to be set free from bondage. Or a young girl may have suffered an abortion. Both of them are likely struggling with an emotional—and spiritual—scar that only the love of Jesus Christ can heal. Sadly, they won't find any help in a church that refuses to address their pain out of fear of offending them.

Some of these churches even avoid talking about sin because it makes people feel uncomfortable. In the book of Jeremiah, God had harsh words for preachers who dilute His Word: "From the least to the greatest, all are greedy for gain; prophets and priests alike, all practice deceit. They dress the wound of my people as though it were not serious. 'Peace, peace,' they say, when there is no peace" (Jeremiah 6:13–14 NIV).

Over time, people who attend churches that preach the social gospel realize the message they hear week after week is no different from the articles they read in the daily newspaper or the statements they hear on the talk shows they watch on late-night television. Churches like this cease to impact their society. Because these churches stand for everything, they ultimately stand for nothing and peddle a shallow Christianity that attracts those who want little to do with the Jesus of the Bible.

> Churches that stand for everything ultimately stand for nothing and peddle a shallow Christianity that attracts those who want little to do with the Jesus of the Bible.

In the attempt to break free from the doldrums of the social gospel, people jump to action by embodying acts of so-called social justice.

SOCIAL JUSTICE. Recently, this philosophy has become popular—and why wouldn't it? "Social justice" sounds so good. Who wouldn't be in favor of "social justice"? But we need to define the term. What does "social justice" really mean, and from where does that terminology come?

The original concept of social justice comes from Karl Marx (see "Ten Planks of the Communist Manifesto" in appendix 1). Social justice is the equivalent of collectivism, or economic redistribution. It gives priority to the rights of the group and denies individual responsibility (which is what the Bible advocates).

Friedrich Hayek, a 1974 Nobel Prize winner in economics and author of the *Road to Serfdom* said, "I have come to feel strongly that the greatest service I can still render to my fellow men would be that I could make the speakers and writers among them thoroughly ashamed ever again to employ the term 'social justice.'"[17]

Hayek objected to the concept of social justice because he saw that the redistribution of income would come at the expense of freedom. And who enforces this? The federal government.

Compare this with President Obama's remark made in the context of his belief that wealthy citizens should pay higher taxes to serve the public good (read: redistribution of income):

"no, "Progressive Tax- ation "

> There are a lot of wealthy, successful Americans who agree with me—because they want to give something back. They know they didn't—look, if you've been successful, you didn't get there on your own. . . . If you were successful, somebody along the line gave you some help. There was a great teacher somewhere in your life. Somebody helped to create this unbelievable American system that we have that allowed you to thrive. Somebody invested in roads and bridges. *If you've got a business—you didn't build that.* Somebody else made that happen.[18]

If business owners didn't build their own businesses, then who did? If the government giveth, then the government hath every right to take away (see Job 1:21 KJV). Obama has used the concept of social justice to divide people into a series of smaller groups, and make each of these groups feel like "victims" who are "trapped" in their position within society and unable to help themselves. This is fundamentally what was behind his statement: "You didn't build that."

For this reason, Hayek further commented, "I am certain . . . that nothing has done so much to destroy the juridical safeguards of individual freedom as the striving after this mirage of social justice."[19]

One of the most insidious consequences of social justice is that it destroys "the dream." It gives people the feeling that they're running in a circular treadmill with no way to escape. The "American dream" looks like an impossibility, and if the government is going to level the playing field anyway, why even try? Complacency and conformism become the norm, and people just try to live within the system.

Now, let's analyze this situation for a moment. These people are influenced by secular humanism, and if they don't believe in God, they cannot rely on God. Individual responsibility has been destroyed by the collectivistic concept of social justice, so they no longer feel a sense of self-reliance. If they cannot rely on God and lack self-reliance, the only option they have left is to rely upon the "almighty government."

When you believe that you are your own god, you sacrifice your moral absolutes (or you have no moral absolutes), which leads you down the slippery slope of the social gospel and into social justice. This inevitably leads you into a dependent lifestyle.

A LIFE OF DEPENDENCY. The American dream has been destroyed, so you become a member of a "dependent society" that is enslaved by government handouts. The Obama administration has perpetuated this condition by providing long-term and, in many instances, permanent government assistance. This includes unemployment compensation for up to ninety-nine weeks without any requirements to even look for a job, and beyond that period, hundreds of thousands applying and obtaining "permanent disability" benefits. It makes us question how many of those are really disabled.

To further perpetuate this dependency, many of these people, when we add unemployment checks, food stamps, and housing assistance, earn a higher income than if they worked. So they have no incentive to even look for a job!

The way to reverse this destructive situation is to reawaken the American dream. The greatness of America has always been based on the proposition that with hard work and perseverance we can all achieve our dreams, even in the face of adversity. Proverbs 24:16 tells us, "A righteous man may fall seven times and rise again."

We all stumble and fall. That's life! But when you fall, you have two options: you can either stay down on the ground, feeling sorry for yourself, or you can get up with twice the determination and continue moving forward. I encourage you to choose the second option. You haven't given in to defeat until you choose to stay down and stop trying. Again quoting Winston Churchill, "Never, never, never give up!"

Finally, this path leads to outright socialism.

SOCIALISM. As this dependent society continues to grow, its citizens become controlled more and more by a totalitarian government that exerts complete control over the people. The government then uses handouts to buy their votes so it can remain in power. This goes right along with what Karl Marx envisioned in his Communist Manifesto.

Friedrich Hayek spoke of "the mirage of social justice" in *Law, Legislation and Liberty*: "While an equality of rights under a limited government is possible and an essential condition of individual freedom," he wrote, "a claim for equality of material position can be met only by a government with totalitarian powers."[20]

If you want to look at the shaky foundation of a nation that embodies this progression, look at 2015 Greece.

In a seemingly absurd joke, Greece, the birthplace of democracy, bankrupted itself and is nearly toppling the European Union because its financial infrastructure couldn't handle its socialist-inspired programs. Greece's socialist catastrophe provides us with an example of what can happen if we continue to follow in its footsteps.

If the foundations are destroyed, what can the righteous do? Not much. Fortunately the foundations have not been fully destroyed yet—but we must act now before the damage gets any worse.

In this next chapter, I will share with you America's only hope for changing directions and rebuilding our foundations.

9

IT'S TIME TO AWAKEN THE SLEEPING GIANT

Let no one deceive you with empty words. . . . And have no fellowship with the unfruitful works of darkness, but rather expose them.

—EPHESIANS 5:6, 11

Church isn't where you meet. Church isn't a building. Church is what you do. Church is who you are. Church is the human outworking of the person of Jesus Christ. Let's not go to Church, let's be the Church.

—BRIDGET WILLARD

As Hitler grew in power and influence in the 1930s, German pastors and theologians faced one of two options: either conform to Hitler's anti-Semitic demands and accede to the belief that country takes precedence over the individual, or leave the country. And many left. Karl Barth, the famous neo-orthodox theologian and professor, served as the principal writer of the 1934 Barmen Declaration, which rejected the influence of Nazism and allegiance to Hitler in the German church. The next year Barth was forced to resign his position at the University of Bonn because he refused to swear an oath to Hitler. Rather than fight, Barth returned to his native Switzerland and his teaching position at the University of Basel.

At the same time, a twenty-six-year-old German pastor named Dietrich Bonhoeffer, twenty years Barth's junior, gave a radio address on German radio, titled "The Younger Generation's Altered Concept of Leadership." During the broadcast, Bonhoeffer explained, "If he [a leader] allows himself to surrender to the wishes of his followers, who would always make him their idol then the image of the Leader will pass over into the image of the 'mis-leader.'"[1] Before he could finish his speech, the authorities stopped the broadcast.

Bonhoeffer continually poked an irritating finger at the conscience of the nation. Nazi authorities wanted to eliminate him, but his rise in prominence meant killing him would exact a high price. As the German government increasingly turned up the heat on the Jews, minorities, and any opposition, Bonhoeffer knew that remaining in his homeland could cost him his life.

So, like Karl Barth four years earlier, Bonhoeffer fled the country for the United States, where theologian Reinhold Niebuhr welcomed him with open arms and a position teaching with him at Union Seminary in New York. As soon as he arrived, though, he regretted his decision. He wrote to Niebuhr:

> I have come to the conclusion that I made a mistake in coming to America. I must live through this difficult period in our national history with the people of Germany. I will have no right to participate in the reconstruction of Christian life in Germany after the war if I do not share the trials of this time with my people . . . . Christians in Germany will have to face the terrible alternative of either willing the defeat of their nation in order that Christian civilization may survive or willing the victory of their nation and thereby destroying civilization, I know which of these alternatives I must choose but I cannot make that choice from security.[2]

Bonhoeffer bravely returned to Germany and continued leading the Christian resistance against Hitler's totalitarian regime. He helped lead a failed effort to stop the Holocaust by killing Adolf Hitler. As a result, he was imprisoned, and, less than a month before Germany's surrender to the Allied forces in the spring of 1945, Bonhoeffer was hanged at the Flossenburg concentration camp.

Dietrich Bonhoeffer wasn't the first pastor to lead the church in civil disobedience against the state. Jesus opposed the religious establishment in Jerusalem, and it too cost Him His life. Ten of Jesus' twelve original disciples died for their faith as well. Throughout Christian history, courageous heroes such as Polycarp, Justin Martyr, Origen, Jan Huss, and others have boldly proclaimed the gospel and paid for it with their lives.

* * *

Unfortunately, in spite of America's rapid deterioration occurring before our eyes, the American church has largely remained silent for quite some time, and offered a series of excuses for their silence. Chief among their excuses is, "I don't want to say anything because of the separation of church and state."

Interestingly enough, although many people think otherwise, the concept of separation of church and state is found nowhere in either the Declaration of Independence or the Constitution of the United States of America.

To understand this clearly, we need to go back four centuries to the time of the first settlers in America. If you lived in England in the early 1600s and were not a member of the Church of England, you would be considered a heretic and subject to persecution. So the early settlers immigrated to the New World in order to freely worship the Lord their God. What a remarkable heritage of religious freedom this exceptional country gives us! The only country on the face of the earth founded on the Word of God!

As this new constitutional representative republic stretched its wings following the Revolutionary War, citizens of the thirteen colonies wondered if their new

> The concept of separation of church and state is found nowhere in either the Declaration of Independence or the Constitution of the United States of America.

government would impose a state religion upon them like the one their forefathers suffered in England. The Danbury Baptist Association from Connecticut expressed this concern to President Thomas Jefferson, who replied in a letter to appease their fears.[3] Let's look at three portions of that letter from Jefferson:

> Believing with you that religion is a matter which lies solely between Man & his God, that he owes account to none other for his faith or his worship . . .

Here Jefferson states clearly that our relationship with God is personal, between us and Him, and that no one has the right to interfere with that relationship. We do not need to give an explanation about our beliefs to anyone. Jefferson's letter continues:

> . . . that their legislature should "make no law respecting an establishment of religion or prohibiting the free exercise thereof" . . .

Right here, Jefferson is quoting directly from the First Amendment of the Constitution:

> Congress shall make no law respecting an establishment of religion [the Establishment Clause] or prohibiting the free exercise thereof [the Free Exercise Clause] . . .

Jefferson concludes this sentence:

> . . . thus building a wall of separation between Church & State.

When reading all three statements in context, it is absolutely obvious that Jefferson was only referring to *a one-way wall:* A one-way wall to prevent government from imposing a state religion upon the people. A one-way wall to prevent government from interfering with our free exercise of religion.

In no way, shape, or form was Jefferson implying that the church should be restricted from exerting an influence upon society. On the contrary, the Bible tells us that we are the *salt of the earth* and *light of the world* (see Matthew 5:13, 14). Doesn't that suggest that our influence should touch every area of society—our families, the media, sports, arts and entertainment, education, business, and government? Jesus said, "Let your light shine before men" (v. 15). Clearly, our faith, while personal, should not be kept to ourselves.

> Declare His glory among the nations, His wonders among all peoples. (Psalm 96:3)

> For there is no distinction between Jew and Greek, for the same Lord over all is rich to all who call upon Him. For "whoever calls on the name of the Lord shall be saved." How then shall they call on Him in whom they have not believed? And how shall they believe in Him of whom they have not heard? And how shall they hear without a preacher? And how shall they preach unless they are sent? As it is written: "How beautiful are the feet of those who preach the gospel of peace, who bring glad tidings of good things!" (Romans 10:12–15)

* * *

The Founding Fathers were so unconcerned about the church impinging upon the people and the government that the House and the Senate *approved* weekly worship services to be held in the US Capitol building in 1800 (shortly after Congress moved into the building). This continued until Ulysses Grant's presidency in 1870.

Does this sound like the modern concept of separation of church and state?

Don't be overly astonished, because worship services actually began in the Capitol building five years earlier. The July 2, 1795, edition of Boston's *Federal Orrery* newspaper reported, "City of Washington, June 19. It is with much pleasure that we discover the rising consequence of our infant city. Public worship is now regularly administered at the Capitol, every Sunday morning, at 11 o'clock by the Reverend Mr. Ralph."[4]

Jefferson personally approved the use of the building while serving as vice president of the United States and acting president of the Senate.

He then attended weekly worship there throughout his presidency. Not coincidentally, Jefferson attended worship at the Capitol just *two days* before writing his letter containing the much-misconstrued reference to "separation between church and state."

* * *

From 1800 to 1807, interdenominational services were held in what is now the old Senate Chamber while the House Chamber, now called Statuary Hall, was being built. When construction on the House Chamber was finished in 1807, church services were moved there until 1857 when Congress outgrew the room and a new chamber was built. Throughout this time, as many as four different churches conducted worship services at the Capitol on Sundays.

On Sunday, December 13, 1857, the first official event held at the current House Chamber was a church worship service with more than two thousand people crowded into the room to hear a sermon delivered by Episcopal bishop George David Cummins. No one knows why the practice stopped in 1870. Author and historian David Barton has noted that John Quincy Adams lamented the lack of churches in Washington, DC's early years.[5] Perhaps by 1870 the city had grown sufficiently and an ample number of church buildings had been constructed.

Then, after an absence of 144 years, regular interdenominational Christian church services resumed in the US Capitol on Wednesday evening, July 30, 2014, for members of Congress, staff, and their invited guests. These weekly Wednesday evening services, called "the Jefferson Gathering," in honor of President Thomas Jefferson, were launched under the direction of Dr. Jim Garlow and Skyline Church of San Diego, California. The convening pastor is Rev. Dan Cummins, the cousin of Bishop George David Cummins, who years earlier had preached the first sermon in the present House chamber.

The "Jefferson Gathering," which has experienced robust attendance from members of Congress, is the outgrowth of "Washington—a Man of Prayer," an event founded by Cummins and his wife, JoAnn, with the sanction of House Speaker John Boehner. The annual event, held in Statuary Hall, commemorates the first inauguration of President George Washington who after being sworn in proceeded to St. Paul's Chapel where, in one of his first acts as president, he offered a prayer of dedication to God on America's behalf.[6]

So if Thomas Jefferson and the presidents who followed him sanctioned the cooperation between church and state, then what caused the subsequent divide?

In 1954, a first-term, thirty-year-old Democratic senator from Texas, named Lyndon B. Johnson, introduced an amendment to the 501(c)(3) code. It stated: "501(c)(3) organizations are absolutely prohibited from directly or indirectly participating in, or intervening in, any political campaign on behalf of (or in opposition to) any candidate for elective public office."[7] Before the Johnson Amendment, clergy, churches, and nonprofit organizations intermingled freely in politics. (In chapter 10, I'll show the extent to which pastors participated in the American Revolution.)

So what motivated Johnson to change the course of American politics after two hundred years?

Oilman H. L. Hunt created a nonprofit organization called Facts Forum in 1951, and publishing mogul Frank Gannett had created the Committee for Constitutional Government in 1935. Both men were vehemently anticommunist, and through their organizations, both financially supported Johnson's 1954 opponent in the Democratic primary, named Dudley Dougherty. The two benefactors believed Johnson was soft on Communism and began distributing thousands of pieces of literature in opposition to the senator. In the effort to arrest the momentum, Johnson buried his amendment in a pending Senate tax overhaul bill, which President Eisenhower signed into law.[8]

Erik Stanley, senior legal counsel for the Alliance Defending Freedom (ADF), points out that "there were no committee hearings, no legislative analysis, and no attempt to understand the effect this bill might have on the constitutional right of churches and pastors. Johnson's chief aid at the time, a man named George Reedy . . . later

[handwritten note: → not 501-C-3 Tax exempts?]

stated that Johnson never had churches in mind."[9]

In their "Pulpit Freedom Sunday" handout, the ADF explains some of the key reasons why the amendment is unconstitutional:

> The amendment violates the Establishment Clause by requiring the government to excessively and pervasively monitor the speech of churches to ensure they are not transgressing the restriction in the amendment. The amendment allows the government to determine when truly religious speech becomes impermissibly "political." The government has no business making such decisions. *[handwritten note: F.U. !!!]*
>
> The amendment violates the Free Speech Clause because it requires the government to discriminate against speech based solely on the content of the speech. In other words, some speech is allowed, but other speech is not. The Supreme Court has invalidated this type of speech discrimination for decades.[10]

Stanley quotes one legal scholar as saying the Johnson Amendment "is not rooted in constitutional provisions for separation of church and state." But Johnson didn't even have churches in his sights; he was simply using his political power to stem the influence of two right-wing organizations. Johnson defeated Dougherty in the primary and was reelected as senator, eventually becoming the president of the United States in 1963.

In April 2014, when Houston's activist lesbian Mayor Annise Parker proposed that the City Council adopt a "non-discrimination ordinance" (NDO), or "SOGI" (sexual-orientation, gender identity) ordinance, hundreds of pastors stood together and spoke with one *[handwritten note: gee!!]* voice to oppose it.

While those efforts succeeded in making the vote much closer than the mayor anticipated, it still passed. Our choice was simple, but not easy—call for a referendum or quit protesting. The pastors' coalition immediately rolled out a petition drive for a referendum that would require the city council to either repeal the ordinance or place it before a vote of the people. We collected almost twice the signatures required and the city secretary did confirm that the minimum had been met, but the mayor stepped in with her city attorney and declared half the petition sheets invalid on technical grounds. Our choice was simple, but not easy—file a lawsuit or quit protesting.

We filed a lawsuit on July 9, which launched an epic legal battle pitting the legal department of the fourth largest city in America and three of the largest law firms in Texas against a single attorney representing the pastors' coalition.

In September 2014, the City subpoenaed five pastors who were not plaintiffs in the lawsuit for seventeen different categories of information including sermons, literature, texts, e-mails—literally "all communications with your congregation" regarding the ordinance, the mayor, even homosexuality as a topic! Little did they know what they were setting into motion.

Alliance Defending Freedom agreed to represent the five, and filed a motion to quash the subpoenas as violations of First Amendment–protected rights.

The five who now faced the threat of a felony if they did not comply were as follows:

Dr. Hernan Castano – Senior Pastor of Iglesia Rios de Aceite, who as a child had emigrated with his family from the communist insurgencies and drug wars of South America to come to the United States for freedom and opportunity; has pastored over thirty years.

Rev. Magda Hermida – Founder of Magda Hermida Ministries with national influence and reach in the Hispanic community; she and her husband Jose escaped from Castro's communist Cuba in the late 1960s to come to the United States for freedom and opportunity.

Dr. Khanh Huynh – Senior Pastor of Vietnamese Baptist Church; one of the original Vietnamese "Boat People" who survived fleeing the communist purge of South Vietnam in the 1970s to come to the United States for freedom and opportunity; has pastored over thirty years.

Dr. Steve Riggle – Senior Pastor of Grace Community Church, President of Grace International; he and his wife Becky survived being shot and stabbed multiple times as young pastors while visiting a prison in the Philippines; founded Grace, which grew into a megachurch.

Rev. Dave Welch – Founder and President, U.S. Pastor Council. His first ancestor came to America in 1683 with William Penn to serve in leadership of the Quaker Church in Pennsylvania; has family who have served in US military, beginning with the American Revolution.

The "Houston Five" were not the type to be intimidated easily. We had stood together as part of the pastors' coalition against the tyranny of the mayor's LGBT ordinance that allowed men who simply claimed that they "expressed" themselves as female to enter women's restrooms as well as added fines and criminal punishment if a business declined to provide service for a same-sex ceremony. We stood together against the subpoenas with a common commitment that we were not going to yield constitutional rights even if it meant jail.

Several weeks of intense national pressure followed in what the *Washington Times* called a "national uproar," including a letter from the Civil Rights Division of the US Justice Department to Mayor Parker stating she had overstepped the law. At first the mayor declared: "If pastors engage in politics, their sermons are fair game" in an infamous tweet, however on October 26 she was finally forced to withdraw the subpoenas. Too little, too late; the curtain was pulled back again exposing the utter disregard LGBT activists like Parker have for the Constitution or the rule of law.

The shock factor of this "new frontier" that launched an assault against religious freedom brought an unbelievable outpouring of calls, e-mails, and letters from people and pastors from all over the nation. It ignited a firestorm of action from evangelical Christians to get out and vote in the November 2014 General Election and served as one more "wake-up call" that aggression against the foundations of this nation that our Founding Fathers recognized as "the Laws of Nature and of Nature's God" is escalating before our eyes.

Family Research Council president Tony Perkins responded with this statement:

> While we are encouraged by this evidence that the Mayor is responding to pressure and withdrawing her unconstitutional subpoenas, this is about far more than subpoenas. As we have stated since the beginning of this intrusion into the private affairs of Houston churches; this is not about subpoenas, this is not about sermons, it is not even about biblical teaching on sexual immorality, it is about political intimidation and the bullying by Mayor Parker that continues.[11]

The net effect of the Johnson Amendment has silenced the church and curtailed her influence on our country. The churches' fear of losing their tax-exempt status has contributed to the slow deterioration of America's shaky foundation. But get this: since the passage of the Johnson Amendment sixty years ago, not one church has lost its tax-exempt status or been punished for politically charged sermons delivered from the pulpit. Pastors and churches *must not* allow threats against free speech to intimidate them into being silent.

In an effort to counter the effect of the Johnson Amendment, the ADF has been promoting "Pulpit Freedom Sunday" since 2008, encouraging pastors on a given Sunday in October to preach a sermon on politics, record it, and send it to the IRS, challenging them to sue the churches.

According to Greg Scott, a spokesman for the ADF, in 2008 thirty-three pastors preached

> Since the passage of the Johnson Amendment sixty years ago, not one church has lost its tax-exempt status or been punished for politically charged sermons delivered from the pulpit.

sermons from their pulpits about candidates and issues in light of Scripture. By 2014, 1,500 pastors preached on political issues and 240 pastors signed a statement calling for the repeal of the Johnson Amendment.[12] In all, 3,800 pastors have either preached a sermon or signed a statement challenging the Johnson Amendment. Again, to date, *Fear!!* the IRS has not sued even one of these churches.

* * *

In one of his first acts as president, George Washington publicly prayed for America. And for hundreds of years, prayer to the God of the Bible has played a public and prominent role in our country.

In Scripture, God Himself, through the apostle Paul, issued a call to action for every church to pray for their country and their leaders.

> Therefore I exhort first of all that supplications, prayers, intercessions, and giving of thanks be made for all men, for kings and all who are in authority, that we may lead a quiet and peaceable life in all godliness and reverence. For this is good and acceptable in the sight of God our Savior, who desires all men to be saved and to come to the knowledge of the truth. (1 Timothy 2:1–4)

The officials we elect act as gatekeepers in our country. According to 1 Timothy, our prayers for our leaders lead to godliness and reverence, and ultimately open the way for God's truth to be made known—and the world to be saved.

Furthermore, the transformation and healing of our nation doesn't begin with secular governmental officials making a change; it begins with God's people repenting of their sins and calling on His name. In Second Chronicles 7:14, God says, "If My people who are called by My name will humble themselves, and pray and seek My face, and turn from their wicked ways, then I will hear from heaven, and will forgive their sin and heal their land."

This command was written to God's covenant people, not to the secular culture. Only after *we* pray will we hear from heaven, receive forgiveness for our sin, and experience healing in our land.

Simultaneously, we live our faith openly, taking to heart the apostle Paul's words that we are "ambassadors for Christ" (2 Corinthians 5:20). We are God's representatives here on earth, God's feet and hands, and His mouthpiece.

Jesus provides a good model for all of us:

> Now in the morning, having risen a long while before daylight, He went out and departed to a solitary place; and there He prayed. And Simon and those who were with Him searched for Him. When they found Him, they said to Him, "Everyone is looking for You." But He said to them, "Let us go into the next towns, that I may preach there also, because for this purpose I have come forth. (Mark 1:35–38)

Notice the rhythm to Jesus' ministry. Repeatedly in Scripture, we see examples of Jesus spending time in prayer with His heavenly Father and then ministering to the people. So we seek God's power and direction in prayer, but then we put our renewed faith into action. God didn't call His church to sit inside the four walls of the sanctuary, singing "Hallelujah." He calls us to prayer *and* action.

Along with prayer and action, we must also feed our souls with the sustenance of God's Word. Jesus said in Matthew 4:4, "'Man shall not live by bread alone, but by every word that proceeds from the mouth of God.'"

Reading Scripture from cover to cover in a year was common practice among our Founding Fathers. John Quincy Adams once commented, "I have myself for many years made it a practice to read the Bible once every year."[13]

Abraham Lincoln noted, "[The Bible] is the best gift God has given to man. All the good the Saviour gave to the world was communicated through this book. But for it, we could not know right from wrong."[14]

The Word of God was utilized to its fullest extent in the early days of America. Primary education of upper-class students in colonial days included reading, writing, math, poetry, and prayer. The three most widely used books in the classroom were the Bible, a primer, and a hornbook (a wooden paddle with lessons tacked on and covered by a transparent piece of material).

"Rightly dividing the word of truth" (2 Timothy 2:15) was a valued skill among pastors (and still should be). So the first universities in America were founded upon the "word of truth" and charged with equipping pastors to lead their congregations. In fact, many of the first universities actually began as colleges (like modern-day seminaries) commissioned to equip pastors for ministry and mission work among the Indians:

HARVARD (1638). America's first university was started by Puritans only eighteen years after the pilgrims set foot on Plymouth Rock. Their Rules and Precepts adopted in 1646 included the following:

Let every Student . . . consider well the maine end of his life and studies is, to know God and Jesus Christ which is eternal life [John 17:3] and therefore to lay Christ in the bottome as the only foundation of all sound knowledge and learning.[15]

YALE (1701). Our nation's third university was created to train *63 yrs. later* Congregational ministers and lay leaders in Connecticut. Ten Congregational pastors, in fact, pooled their books to form the school's first library.[16]

PRINCETON (1746). Originally called the College of New Jersey, *45 yrs. later* Princeton began in part as a result of the Great Awakening, a spiritual revival that swept across colonial America in the 1730s and '40s.[17] Jonathan Edwards, perhaps America's greatest theologian, served as school president in 1758.[18] Originally founded to train Presbyterian ministers, the school remained solidly evangelical until the turn of the twentieth century.

COLUMBIA UNIVERSITY (1754). Originally named "The King's College," the school began as a branch of the *Society for the Propagation of the Gospel in Foreign Parts* for the Church of England.[19]

Other colonial colleges (founded before the American Revolution) that began as pastors' colleges or included pastors' colleges in their charter:

College of William and Mary (1693), Church of England[20]

Brown University (1764), Baptist[21]

Rutgers University (1766), Dutch Reformed[22]

Dartmouth College (1769), Congregationalist[23]

* * *

In light of the deep Christian foundation of our country, it comes as no surprise that prayer and God's Word played a prominent role in our everyday lives. Families gathered in prayer and Bible reading at the beginning or end of their day. Since our inception, public schools in America regularly started the day with prayer and employed the Bible as their textbook. It was an integral part of the school day.

Then, in 1962, the Supreme Court issued a decision (*Engel v. Vitale*) banning state-sponsored prayer from public schools. A year later (in *Abington School District v. Schempp*), the Supreme Court removed the Bible from schools . . . and the church remained silent.

Their excuse? "It's a political issue."

How can prayer and Bible reading be considered political issues? But that is exactly what the church deemed them!

David Barton with WallBuilders points out that after 1962:[24]

- birth rates for unwed girls (ten to fourteen) rose 553 percent

- sexually transmitted diseases for high school students increased 225 percent

- sexual activity among teens under seventeen increased 271 percent

- violent crimes have increased 794 percent

Consider the economic impact of our decisions. Between 1962—the year prayer was removed from the schools—and 2014, the top four bureaus in the US Department of Justice spent $622.2 billion fighting crime.[25] These numbers, which come from a report released by the Marshall Project, a nonprofit, nonpartisan news organization, included the FBI, the US Attorneys and the Marshals Service, the Bureau of Prisons, and Office of Justice programs. Add the tax money spent on state and local crime enforcement agencies and the marginal cost of removing prayer and Bible study from our schools has been enormous.

America also leads the world in television watching. I mention this because television has replaced the Bible in teaching morality to our children. According to a 2009 Nielson Newswire, on average, American children ages two to five spend thirty-two hours a week in front of their TVs—watching television, DVDs, DVR, and videos, and using game consoles. Kids ages six to eleven spend about twenty-eight hours a week in front of the TV.[26] Teens spend about twenty hours a week watching television. Sadly, study after study has confirmed that illicit sexual behavior and violence increase among children who watch television regularly.[27]

Apart from the removal of prayer and the Bible from the public school, other factors have contributed toward America's downward slide. Here are just a few.

ABORTION

In 1973, nine unelected justices of the Supreme Court decided that a baby in the womb did not have that unalienable right to life as stated in the Declaration of Independence.

> We hold these truths to be self-evident, that all men are created equal, that they are endowed by their Creator with certain unalienable Rights, that among these are Life, Liberty and the pursuit of Happiness.

Again, the church remained largely silent and offered the same excuse: "It's a political issue."

The website Numberofabortions.com tabulates the number of abortions performed in America and worldwide with a real-time abortion counter. As of this writing, 58,218,677 babies have been aborted in the United States since 1973. That's more than the 2014 population of New York, Illinois, Pennsylvania, and Ohio *combined*. Think of the lives lost—countless pastors, business leaders, inventors, poets, senators, members of Congress, maybe even a president. On average, a million babies a year are murdered through abortion.

We, as the church of Jesus Christ, need to fall on our knees in corporate repentance for the sin of abortion. The blood of more than 58 million babies cries out to God like the blood of Abel (see Genesis 4:10; Matthew 23:35).

> Since 1973, as of this writing, 58,218,677 babies have been aborted in the United States. That's more than the 2014 population of New York, Illinois, Pennsylvania, and Ohio *combined*.

THE REDEFINITION OF TRADITIONAL MARRIAGE. Because we explored this in the previous chapter, I won't delve any deeper into the topic here, but when the Supreme Court redefined marriage in the summer of 2015, the church became surprisingly silent. It felt as though we gave up the fight.

How long will we remain silent? More important, how will we answer to God for our silence?

Dietrich Bonhoeffer is believed to have said, "Silence in the face of evil is itself evil: God will not hold us guiltless. Not to speak is to speak. Not to act is to act."

Martin Niemöller, another pastor and a friend of Bonhoeffer's in Nazi Germany, said,

First they came for the Socialists, and I did not speak out—because I was not a Socialist. Then they came for the Trade Unionists, and I did not speak out—because I was not a Trade Unionist. Then they came for the Jews, and I did not speak out—because I was not a Jew. Then they came for me—and there was no one left to speak for me.[28]

If we remain silent, Scripture will bear witness against us:

He who justifies the wicked, and he who condemns the just, both of them alike are an abomination to the LORD. (Proverbs 17:15)

Are we justifying the wicked by remaining silent? Silence is not an option.

"But," argue some well-meaning pastors, "God has called me to share the *gospel*." And they use that as an excuse to avoid getting involved in the civic arena. Thus they remain totally silent about everything that affects the society of which we are a part.

I answer those pastors with a question: "And what is the gospel?" It is much more than just John 3:16. Let's see what the apostle Paul had to say about it:

Therefore I testify to you this day that I am innocent of the blood of all men. For I have not shunned to declare to you *the whole counsel of God.* (Acts 20:26–27, emphasis added)

The "whole counsel of God" begins with Genesis 1:1 and continues to the end of Scripture, Revelation 22:21. The whole Bible, cover to cover—and the Bible addresses every issue affecting our civic society.

In a 2014 interview on American Family Radio's program *Today's Issues*, George Barna shared about a research project his organization was conducting concerning pastors and their beliefs. Specifically, he wanted to know how Scripture speaks to societal, moral, and political issues in their sermons. "What we're finding," he said, "is that when we ask them about all the key issues of the day, [90 percent of them are] telling us, *Yes, the Bible speaks to every one of these issues.* Then we ask them: *Well, are you teaching your people what the Bible says about those issues?*—and the numbers drop . . . to less than 10 percent of pastors who say they will speak to it."[29]

If we remain silent, Jesus will bear witness against us. It was He who said, "You are the light of the world" (Matthew 5:14).

All too often, though, we gather at our churches and point our little flashlights on one another. But light is worthless unless you point it at the darkness! Jesus said, "No one, when he has lit a lamp, puts it in a secret place or under a basket, but on a lampstand, that those who come in may see the light" (Luke 11:33).

We need to stop simply playing church inside the four walls and take the church out to the marketplace.

Remember, too, that Jesus also said, "You are the salt of the earth" (Matthew 5:13). Salt acts as a preservative (beef jerky, for instance), but for salt to preserve anything, it must be applied to whatever you want to preserve.

The time has come to preserve the sanctity of life . . .

The time has come to preserve the sanctity of the traditional family. . .

The time has come to preserve the virtue and purity of our teenagers. . .

We need to be light and salt to a world in darkness!

But the most common excuse Christians use to justify their staying out of politics is this: "Politics is a dirty business; I don't want any part of it!" Many people of faith use this to totally disengage from civic society, laying any responsibility they might have at someone else's feet. Where have we seen *that* before? On the night before Jesus was nailed to a cross, when He stood before His accusers and Pontius Pilate. Pilate had the power to release Jesus, but instead we read that "he took water and washed his hands in front of the crowd. 'I am innocent of this man's blood,' he said. 'It is your responsibility!'" (Matthew 27:24 NIV).

God help us if we follow Pilate's example and wash our hands of the fate of our nation.

We desperately need men and women of righteousness to change the direction of our country. "When the righteous are in authority," the

Bible tells us, "the people rejoice; but when a wicked man rules, the people groan" (Proverbs 29:2).

It should come as no surprise that when the wicked are in authority, they legislate their wicked brand of morality. But fortunately, the opposite is true of the righteous. When I say, "the righteous," I'm not referring to self-righteous people; I'm referring to people who rely on the righteousness of Jesus Christ and act in accordance with God's precepts, with the foundations upon which this great country of ours was built.

How many times have you heard someone say, "Politics can't legislate morality"? Give me a break! Politics legislates morality all the time. If it didn't, we wouldn't need the judicial system. We wouldn't exact punishment on people who kill or steal or rape. We also wouldn't need any laws because all of our laws assume a semblance of morality.

People of principle must vote for people of principle so we can become a principled nation. Unfortunately, Christians seem overly reluctant to vote.

Today, there are roughly 90 million evangelical Christians in America, roughly 30 percent of our population.[30] And, of those, in 2012, 54 million evangelical Christians stayed home and didn't vote.

54 million.

So, if "the righteous" are not voting, not even running for office, then what is left? "The wicked"—those who reject biblical precepts and foundations—will be voting for those who adhere to their same way of thinking. And the fault belongs to us for opting out of the process. If you don't vote, you have no right to complain . . . and you are part of the problem!

> People of principle must vote for people of principle so we can become a principled nation.

* * *

Many Christians wonder what criteria they should use when going to the polls to vote. The Bible offers us some guidance.

In Exodus 18, Jethro visited his son-in-law Moses in the wilderness after leading the people of Israel across the Red Sea. The day after his arrival, Jethro noticed Moses was stressed, trying to govern the entire nation by himself. So Jethro asked Moses, "What is this thing that you are doing for the people? Why do you alone sit, and all the people stand before you from morning until evening?"

Moses answered, "Because the people come to me to inquire of God."

Knowing that his son-in-law was carrying a heavy load, Jethro replied, "The thing that you do is not good. Both you and these people who are with you will surely wear yourselves out. For this thing is too much for you; you are not able to perform it by yourself" (vv. 14–18).

And then in Exodus 18:21, Jethro offered this godly counsel: "Moreover you shall *select* from all the people *able men, such as fear God, men of truth, hating covetousness*" (emphasis added).

Note that Jethro didn't say *"Let God appoint,"* but *"you shall select"* (or "elect") from among the people, and then He gave four qualifications for those that should be elected:

. . . able men . . .

This simply means electing candidates who are capable of doing the job and qualified to perform the task. Don't take their word for it; look at their experience, education, and job performance.

. . . such as fear God . . .

When you fear God, you obey God's precepts, and you walk in accordance with a Judeo-Christian ethic. This means a moral code of behavior, and it also means honesty, integrity, hard work, individual responsibility, the rule of law, and even free enterprise and limited government.

. . . men of truth . . .

Aren't you tired of politicians who lie? They tell you one lie to cover up another, whether it is about the Fast and Furious gunrunning operation, or the terrorist attack in Benghazi, or the IRS targeting conservatives, or the NSA's invasion of privacy, or missing e-mails and documents, or donations from foreign governments. Some people tell lie upon lie upon lie.

The reason so many Americans have a distaste for politics is because they're tired of candidates running for public office making promises they will never keep, and then, after they're elected, doing exactly the opposite. However, you can greatly minimize that risk by following this simple rule: Don't listen to their *rhetoric*, but rather, look at their *record*. Don't listen to *what they say*, but instead look at *what they do* and have done.

Jesus put it this way: "You will know them by their fruits" (Matthew 7:16). It's about time we did some fruit inspecting!

... hating covetousness ...

Interestingly enough, covetousness in government is not primarily about money, but rather about power and control. Politicians covet power, and they covet the control that power gives them over "We the people."

That is why we have elected politicians who have served in Washington, DC, for thirty years, and they want to stay there for another twenty. They do not want to give up that power.

> Don't listen to their *rhetoric*, but rather, look at their *record*. Don't listen to *what they say*, but instead look at *what they do* and have done.

Jethro further instructed Moses:

> ... and place such over them to be rulers of thousands, rulers of hundreds, rulers of fifties, and rulers of tens. (Exodus 18:21)

So the order of authority goes as follows: Moses, rulers of thousands, rulers of hundreds, rulers of fifty, rulers of tens. This is equivalent to federal government, state government, county government, local government—and *all* of them elected by the people based on their godly character.

Finally, Jethro concluded:

> Then it will be that *every great matter* they shall bring to you [i.e., to Moses, or *the federal government*], but *every small matter* they themselves shall judge [i.e., *at the local level*]. (v. 22, emphasis added)

This is the essence of federalism and of limited government—Article 1, Section 8 of the Constitution, and the Ninth and Tenth Amendments.

Article 1, Section 8 is often called the "enumerated powers of Congress." There are eighteen powers listed in this section. If it is not there, Congress has no authority to exercise that power; it is reserved for the states, in accordance with the Ninth and Tenth Amendments.

The Framers of the Constitution looked to this passage of Scripture, Exodus 18:21–22, as a key for establishing the United States of America as a constitutional representative republic, and not a democracy. In a pure democracy the minority has no rights and can be squashed by the majority.

In his presidential farewell address, George Washington said, "Let us with caution indulge the supposition, that morality can be maintained without religion. Whatever may be conceded to the influence of refined education on minds of peculiar structure, reason and experience both forbid us to expect, that national morality can prevail in exclusion of religious principle."[31]

We've looked at God's call to the faithful—the church—to reclaim America. Now let's look at God's call on the men and women who lead them.

10

THE ROLE OF PASTORS IN THE AMERICAN REVOLUTION

I sought for the greatness and genius of America in her commodious harbors and her ample rivers—[and her] fertile fields and boundless forests and . . . her vast world commerce . . . and her matchless Constitution—and it was not there. Not until I went into the churches of America and heard her pulpits flame with righteousness did I understand the secret of her genius and power. America is great because she is good, and if America ever ceases to be good, she will cease to be great.

—ATTRIBUTED TO ALEXIS DE TOCQUEVILLE

The local church is the hope of the world, and its future rests primarily in the hands of its leaders.

—BILL HYBELS

The year 1729 doesn't stand out as noteworthy on the palette of world history. Not like 1492 or 1776, and certainly not like 4 BC, the year many scholars believe Jesus was born. But it was, in fact, significant because that year, a certain preacher—one who would impact the world—assumed the pulpit from his grandfather.

Jonathan Edwards towers above any other theologian in US history. As we've already discussed, he served as an early president of Princeton Seminary. Edwards, however, was anything but an ivory-tower academician.

Jonathan Edwards was a preacher. Upon his grandfather Solomon Stoddard's death, Edwards served as sole pastor in the Northampton, Massachusetts church. He was twenty-six.

Five years later, in 1734, a revival broke out in his church. His fervent preaching on the sovereignty of God, human depravity, hell, and the need to be born again converted many people to the Christian faith both inside and outside the congregation. By 1740, the revival had spread outside his church and began sweeping across New England. According to Ezra Stiles, president of Yale from 1778 to 1795, for the next twenty years, 150 new churches were planted and as many as fifty thousand people were added to membership of New England congregations. Some estimate that at least 7 percent of the New England population entered the church as a result of what we now call the First Great Awakening.[1]

> Seven percent of the New England population entered the church as a result the First Great Awakening.

A similar awakening had broken out in England because of the preaching of George Whitefield and John Wesley. But with the fields white for the harvest across the Atlantic, both men traveled to America. Wesley arrived in 1734 and began an outreach in Georgia. Whitefield joined him in 1738, returned to England, and then joined Edwards in 1740.

While Edwards was the head of the First Great Awakening, Whitefield was the heart. His dynamic preaching and booming voice enabled him to address thousands of people at a time—and eager listeners rode great distances on horseback to hear him. No less than Benjamin Franklin estimated that Whitefield's voice could be heard by up to thirty thousand people at a time.[2] In fact, Franklin became such a deep admirer of Whitefield that he purchased a meetinghouse where Whitefield could preach. It is situated on the present-day campus of the University of Pennsylvania.

Before George Washington rose in prominence, George Whitefield was the most popular figure in America. Although a staunch Calvinist like Edwards (both known for their stoic worship style), Whitefield didn't shy away from the emotionalism that often accompanied his meetings. He worked across denominational lines with ease and brought different groups together to dedicate their lives to serving God, including slaves. At a time when the spiritual vitality in America had ebbed, the First Great Awakening brought a new sense of purpose and identity to her people.

Like New England's, other regions' church rolls soared. In the Mid-Atlantic colonies, the number of churches, especially Presbyterian, multiplied. In the South, the number of Methodist churches expanded, with John and Charles Wesley as the catalysts. Baptist churches began to take root down south as well. By 1760, churches were sorely in need of pastors. To fill the void, schools like Princeton, Rutgers, the University of Pennsylvania, and Brown University worked diligently to train and mobilize pastors to fill the vacant church pulpits and start more churches.

In the South, Baptist and Methodist preachers began converting slaves to Christianity. Stories about the Israelites' oppression at the hands of the Egyptians and their exodus out of Egypt became a source of hope and inspiration to the captive slaves. Because whites insisted on worshipping in segregated congregations, opportunities opened for blacks to lead congregations of their own, especially in the Baptist church.

In the 1780s, a slave named Andrew Bryan was arrested and whipped in Savannah, Georgia, for preaching to a small group of slaves. In spite of their persecution, the small group flourished and ten years later became the First African Baptist Church of Savannah. It later spawned two more churches, also led by black pastors.

As the Great Awakening grew to maturity in the 1760s, so did the self-awareness and self-identity of the American people. While pastors were preaching "freedom" and "liberty" (both biblical terms) from the pulpits, King George III and the British Parliament in England began leveling oppressive taxes on the colonies. This prompted Rev. Jonathan

Mayhew in Boston in 1765 to object from the pulpit, decrying their "taxation without representation."

The colonies protested, arguing that they had no representatives in Parliament yet they were subjected to unfair taxes. Nevertheless, Parliament asserted, in the Declaratory Act of 1766, their sovereignty over the colonies "in all cases whatsoever." To a country in the midst of spiritual renewal, a distant monarch declaring sovereignty over them—instead of God—was heresy. *Freedom* and *liberty* became both religious and political terms.

When British troops fired on the people of Boston in the massacre of 1770, ministers such as Rev. John Lathrop, Charles Chauncey, and Samuel Cooke publicly denounced the abuse of power and vilified the troops' actions from the pulpit. Tensions heightened, especially in Boston. British troops tightened the noose around the necks of the Bostonians, and they responded by dumping tea into the harbor.

Harry S. Stout, the Jonathan Edwards professor of American religious history at Yale University, commented on the social landscape at the time:

> Who will you turn to now for direction? There are no presidents or vice-presidents, no supreme court justices or public defenders to call on. There are a handful of young, radical lawyers, like the Adams cousins, John and Samuel, but they're largely concentrated in cities, while you and most of your friends live in the country. In many colonies, including Massachusetts, there are not even elected governors or councilors—they have all been appointed by the British crown and are answerable to it.
>
> Where you turn is where you have habitually turned for over a century: to the prophets of your society, your ministers. . . .
>
> Colonial congregations heard sermons more than any other form of oratory. The colonial sermon was prophet, newspaper, video, Internet, community college, and social therapist all wrapped in one.[3]

Stout went on to explain that "the American Revolution was first and foremost a religious event." By the mid-1770s, the number of clergymen had grown to more than six hundred ministers throughout New England. Liberals, conservatives, Congregationalists, and Presbyterians—many unified through the Great Awakening—stood together in resistance to the British authorities.[4]

The First Great Awakening undoubtedly provided the spark that ignited the American Revolution. And I am not alone in this belief, nor is Professor Stout. In 1842, minister and historian Joseph Tracey wrote an influential book titled *The Great Awakening*, which actually gave the movement its name. He, as well, believed the First Great Awakening ushered in the American Revolution.

* * *

Secular historians who minimize the First Great Awakening's influence on the American Revolution and our Founding Fathers commit a disservice to every American.

> "The colonial sermon was prophet, newspaper, video, Internet, community college, and social therapist all wrapped in one."
>
> —HARRY STOUT, AUTHOR OF *THE NEW ENGLAND SOUL: PREACHING AND RELIGIOUS CULTURE IN COLONIAL NEW ENGLAND*

Pastors of local churches played pivotal roles in mobilizing and leading the nation in their insurrection against England. And from their pulpits, many of these fiery preachers aired their communal grievances.

Pastor Jonas Clark, a Harvard graduate, for example, pastored the Church of Christ in Lexington, Massachusetts, from 1755 to 1805. The greens outside his church became the flash point of the Revolutionary War.

As the British marched toward Lexington in April 1775, Colonel Paul Revere warned the people of the British troops' arrival (historians doubt he actually yelled, "The British are coming!"). Revere's destination was Reverend Clark's house, where Samuel Adams and John Hancock were hiding. Hancock was a cousin of Reverend Clark, and for fifty-four years their grandfather had pastored the church where Clark now served. British general Thomas Gage had offered a pardon to any patriots—except Adams and Hancock—who would step forward and lay down their weapons. When they heard of the troops' imminent arrival, Hancock and Adams quickly escaped to Burlington to avoid capture.

On the dawn of April 19, more than seven hundred British troops assumed their position in the field adjacent to the church. Across the green, seventy-seven minutemen looked into the eyes of their seemingly insurmountable enemy. To ensure no one abandoned the militia, Captain John Parker threatened that every deserter would be shot.

The fighting began, and when the smoke cleared, eight militiamen were dead and nine were wounded. Only one Redcoat was injured. The American patriots retreated and the Redcoats marched seven miles toward Concord in search of military supplies. After a few skirmishes along the way, the Redcoats prepared to return to Boston. Little did they realize that two thousand militiamen had mobilized while the British were searching for supplies.

Minutemen began positioning themselves behind trees, barns, and houses along the eighteen-mile trek leading to Boston. As they fired on the unsuspecting Redcoats, the enemy troops began shedding their weapons, clothing, and equipment in order to pick up the pace and get back to Boston.

In the end, 250 Redcoats were killed or wounded, compared to 90 minutemen. The ill-equipped, undertrained Revolutionary troops proved they could stand up to one of the most powerful armies in the world.

Seven of the eight men who died in the Battle of Lexington were members of Reverend Clark's church. Historian James Adams commented that "the patriotic preaching of the Reverend Jonas Clark primed those guns."[5] Another historian, Joel Headley, wrote, "The teachings of the pulpit of Lexington caused the first blow to be struck

you are The next emor. Rev. Hero, heh?? you are above The elected!!! a Pastor!!!.

for American Independence."[6]

After their surprising victory, Reverend Clark preached a sermon to commemorate the battle, titled, "The fate of blood-thirsty oppressors and God's tender care of his distressed people." If that isn't incendiary enough, consider his subtitle: "To commemorate the MURDER, BLOOD-SHED and Commencement of Hostilities, between Great-Britain and America, in that Town, by a Brigade of Troops of George III, under Command of Lieutenant-Colonel SMITH, on the Nineteenth of April, 1775."

Apparently, Reverend Clark wasn't one to mince words. (To read excerpts from his sermon, see appendix 3, "Jonas Clark Sermon.")

As tensions between the colonies and the British Empire increased, John Adams commented on the abundance of patriotic preachers: "[The clergy] engage with a fervor that will produce wonderful effects. Those . . . of every denomination . . . thunder and lighten every Sabbath."[7]

Weeks later, at the Battle of Bunker Hill, ministers again marched into battle. When Rev. David Grosvenor learned that the battle had begun, he left the pulpit, rifle in hand, and marched to the battlefield. Other pastor-soldiers in the Continental Army included Rev. John Craighead. One Sunday, he preached "in glowing terms, Jesus Christ, the only hope of salvation, and after the delivery of his sacred message, in eloquent and patriotic strains exhorted the youth of his congregation to rise up and join the noble band, then engaged under the immortal Washington, in struggling to free our beloved country from British oppression."[8]

Other valiant ministers who served their flocks and their fellow American citizens included these:

REV. JOHN BLAIR SMITH, a Presbyterian minister, who led a contingent of about sixty-five students in 1777 to defend Williamsburg, Virginia, from the Redcoats.

REV. JAMES HALL, who pastored the congregations in Fourth Creek, Concord, and Bethany, North Carolina. When he heard that General

Cornwallis and his British forces had overtaken South Carolina, Hall mobilized a militia to defend their colony. His speech so emboldened the troops that they asked him to lead their contingent. So in 1779, he led the expedition into South Carolina, serving as the troops' commander and chaplain.

REV. WILLIAM GRAHAM, who in 1781 learned that General Banastre Tarleton and his British Rangers were in hot pursuit of Governor Thomas Jefferson and the Virginia legislature. To counter the troops, Graham called a militia and gallantly defended their leaders from the enemy.

To say the least, these brave men preached and lived their faith without apology.

Here are other historians' observations regarding the involvement of the clergy in the American Revolution:[9]

> As a body of men, the clergy were pre-eminent in their attachment to liberty. The pulpits of the land rang with the notes of freedom. (*American Quarterly Register*, 1833)

> If Christian ministers had not preached and prayed, there might have been no revolution as yet—or had it broken out, it might have been crushed. (*Bibliotheca Sacra*, 1856)

> The ministers of the Revolution were, like their Puritan predecessors, bold and fearless in the cause of their country. No class of men contributed more to carry forward the Revolution and to achieve our independence than did the ministers . . . [B]y their prayers, patriotic sermons, and services [they] rendered the highest assistance to the civil government, the army, and the country. (B. F. Morris, 1864)

Countless pastors also enlisted in the Continental Army and fought at the forefront in battle after battle for independence. Many of the British blamed the "Black Robe Regiment," a sarcastic reference to the clergy who wore long black robes, for their defeat in America.

The first battle for independence, the Battle of Lexington, was fought April 19, 1775, right outside of Jonas Clark's church, and he and the men of his congregation joined the militia fighting next to his church under the command of Captain—and Reverend—Theodore Parker. The second battle, at Concord, was also fought outside of the church that was pastored by Rev. Joseph Emerson (grandfather of Ralph Waldo Emerson).

Throughout the war, more than a hundred ministers served as Continental Army chaplains, and to a lesser extent, Anglican ministers who joined the British army. As it had fifteen years earlier, this left many congregations with empty pulpits.

In July 1775, the Continental Congress called for a day of prayer and fasting in light of the escalating tensions. Ministers who were still serving in churches utilized the opportunity to preach about the colonial cause.

A statue of Rev. Peter Muhlenberg stands in front of the Woodstock, Virginia, courthouse. Underneath his black robe you can see the uniform of a colonel in the Continental Army. On January 21, 1776, the Lutheran pastor preached from Ecclesiastes 3. He began, "To everything there is a season . . ." and concluded with verse 8, "a time of war, and a time of peace." Then he removed his black robe, revealing his colonel's uniform.[10]

"This is a time for war," he said. Looking at his congregation, he continued. "How many of you men will follow me to go fight for our independence?" Three hundred men left with him that Sunday to join the Revolutionary War. By the end of the war, Muhlenberg had risen to the rank of major general. A hero to his native Philadelphia, he spent the remainder of his career in local and national politics. A statue of him also stands in Statuary Hall.

The British troops treated clergy of the Black Robe Regiment with particular brutality because of their influence on the American people.

Even modern historians agree about the ministers' impact on the American Revolution and formulation of the Declaration of Independence. The late Alice M. Baldwin, former dean of the Woman's

College of Duke University, in her book *The New England Clergy and the American Revolution*, commented, "There is not a right asserted in the Declaration of Independence which had not been discussed by the New England clergy before 1763." She also asserted that "the Constitutional Convention and the written Constitution were the children of the pulpit."[11]

Likewise, by order of the Continental Congress, the lower margin of the original Declaration of Independence included instructions that parish ministers were "required to read the same to their respective congregations, as soon as divine service is ended, in the afternoon, on the first Lord's day after they have received it."[12] Not

> "There is not a right asserted in the Declaration of Independence which had not been discussed by the New England clergy before 1763."
>
> —ALICE MARY BALDWIN

newspapers or town clerks. Ministers. So much for the Johnson Amendment.

Oh, ambition." Fascist pig". Lightweight!

* * *

As the Committee of Five (John Adams, Thomas Jefferson, Benjamin Franklin, Roger Sherman, and Robert Livingston) began working on the draft of the Declaration of Independence, two influences assuredly guided them: first, the many sermons delivered by fiery preachers, which aired grievances of the American citizens; and second, the writings of John Locke, namely, his book *Two Treatises of Government*. In its four hundred pages, Locke referred to the Bible more than fifteen hundred times to demonstrate the way civil government should work. Many of his peers considered him a theologian in his own right.

Imagine the thoughts spinning in the heads of the signers. Writing their names in ink for everyone to see, including the British government, put their lives on the line. If the colonies lost, every signer would be put to death for treason and their families would spend the rest of their lives in poverty. Robert Morris, a wealthy businessman who practically financed the war on his own, would lose everything. But sign they did.

The spiritual lives of the signers cannot—and should not—be ignored. Following are the religious affiliations of the fifty-six men when they signed the historic document:

RELIGIOUS AFFILIATION[13]	NUMBER OF SIGNERS[14]
Anglican/Episcopalian	32
Congregational	13
Presbyterian	12
Quaker	2
Unitarian	2
Catholic	1

Among the signers, three men were ministers, most notably, Rev. John Witherspoon. A native of Scotland, Witherspoon grew up with a healthy mistrust of the British government. After a classic Scottish Presbyterian education, he pastored two churches in his homeland before being invited to serve as president and head professor at the College of New Jersey (present-day Princeton) at age forty-five in 1768. Under his leadership, the small school flourished and became a training center for future judges, Supreme Court justices, senators, congressmen, and members of the presidential cabinet and Continental Congress.

As the British authorities tightened their grip on the colonists, Witherspoon dedicated his loyalties in support of the Revolution. In 1776 he was elected to the Continental Congress and was appointed their chaplain by Congress president John Hancock. During his political career, Witherspoon served on more than one hundred committees and helped draft the Articles of Confederation. When he died in 1794, he was one of the most respected men in America.

Robert Treat Paine worked as a Congregationalist minister before becoming a lawyer and entering politics. He also served as a military chaplain before the Revolution. Similarly, Lyman Hall was educated as a Congregationalist minister before delving into a career in medicine and later politics.

But to say *only* three ministers signed the Declaration of Independence understates the meaning of the word *minister*. David Barton of WallBuilders explains:

> There are many others who should also be noted for their ministry work, including Francis Hopkinson, a church music director and choir leader who edited a famous American hymnbook; Roger Sherman, who wrote the doctrinal creed for his denomination in Connecticut; Benjamin Rush, who started Sunday School in America and founded the country's first Bible Society; James Wilson, who had been trained as a clergyman in Scotland but became an attorney, teaching students the Biblical basis of civil law; and many others. In fact, at least 29 of the signers had been trained in schools whose primary purpose was the preparation of ministers . . . They attended universities and seminaries of learning such as Harvard, Yale, William and Mary, Princeton, Cambridge, and Westminster.[15]

"At least 29 of the signers [of the Declaration of Independence] had been trained in schools whose primary purpose was the preparation of ministers."

—DAVID BARTON, WALLBUILDERS

Eleven years after the signing of the Declaration of Independence, the Articles of Confederation's shortcomings had become apparent, so a Constitutional Convention was called to create a new governmental system. James Madison provided the blueprint and George Washington was elected president of the convention.

Five weeks into the proceedings, the convention was in disarray. Disputes about the election of senators, defining proportional representation, the division of executive powers, electing a president, and the abolition of slave trade were a few contentious issues that jeopardized the possibility of a new constitution. Then, on June 28, 1787, Benjamin Franklin stood up to address George Washington and his colleagues. Please read this carefully:

Mr. President:

The small progress we have made after 4 or five weeks . . . our different sentiments on almost every question, several of the last producing as many noes as ays, is methinks a melancholy proof of the imperfection of the Human Understanding . . .

In this situation of this Assembly groping as it were in the dark to find political truth, and scarce able to distinguish it when to us, how has it happened, Sir, that we have not hitherto once thought of humbly applying to the Father of lights to illuminate our understandings? In the beginning of the contest with G. Britain, when we were sensible of danger we had daily prayer in this room for the Divine Protection. Our prayers, sir, were heard, and they were graciously answered. All of us who were engaged in the struggle must have observed frequent instances of a Superintending providence in our favor. To that kind providence we owe this happy opportunity of consulting in peace on the means of establishing our future national felicity. And have we now forgotten that powerful friend? Or do we imagine that we no longer need His assistance.

I have lived, Sir, a long time and the longer I live, the more convincing proofs I see of this truth—that God governs in the affairs of men. And if a sparrow cannot fall to the ground without his notice, is it probable that an empire can rise without his aid? We have been assured, Sir, in the sacred writings that "except the Lord build they labor in vain that build it." I firmly believe this; and I also believe that without his concurring aid we shall succeed in this political building no better than the Builders of Babel: We shall be divided by our little partial local interests; our projects will be confounded, and we ourselves shall be become a reproach and a bye word down to future age. And what is worse, mankind may hereafter this unfortunate instance, despair of establishing Governments by Human Wisdom, and leave it to chance, war, and conquest.

I therefore beg leave to move—that henceforth prayers imploring the assistance of Heaven, and its blessings on our deliberations, be held in this Assembly every morning before we proceed to business, and that one or more of the Clergy of this City be requested to officiate in that service.

Despite his reputation as a devout deist, in no way are these the words of a deist! His comment that "God governs in the affairs of men" tells us that he believed in a God who interacts with mankind.

After Franklin's call to daily prayer, a new spirit of harmony emerged among the Framers, and that September, they gave us the greatest document that has ever been written, outside of the Bible: the Constitution of the United States of America. The next year the document was ratified.[16]

Godly men wrote the Constitution for a godly nation. John Adams wrote, "The Constitution was made only for a moral and religious people. It is wholly inadequate for the government of any other."

I believe without a shadow of a doubt that the reason the Declaration of Independence and the Constitution of the United States have lasted over two centuries is that they were divinely inspired and then written by men who had spent time on their knees. These were men of God seeking revelation from God, and that's what He gave them. Of course, these two documents aren't equivalent to the Word of God, but God certainly directed the men who crafted them.

For millennia, the model that man created for government has always been the same: "Authority flows from God, to the government, to the people," as my friend Bill Federer has said many times.

In 1 Samuel 8, the Israelites asked the prophet Samuel to give them a king so they could be like the other nations. Disappointed, Samuel sought the Lord in prayer and God answered back: "They have not rejected you, but they have rejected Me" (v. 7).

The people of Israel wanted to place themselves under that same man-made model, "Authority flows from God, to the government, to the people." If you want to see how many problems that caused them, read 1 and 2 Kings and 1 and 2 Chronicles in your Bible. Ultimately, they ended up in slavery in Babylon for seventy years. Kings and tyrants use this man-made model to justify their oppression of the people, reasoning, "I have the right to oppress you because my authority comes from God."

But when the Framers were on their knees, seeking revelation from God, he answered their prayers and gave them divine revelation, and a totally different model. No longer was it "Authority flows from God, to the government, to the people," but rather, "Authority flows from God, *to the people*, to the government." (Again, these are the words of Bill Federer.)

It is not coincidental that the first three words in the Constitution are "We the People." All the God-given authority in the Constitution is given to "We the people." And with that authority comes an awesome responsibility for us to elect righteous leaders.

* * *

The First Great Awakening began in the 1730s and lasted into the late 1740s or early 1750s. The Second Great Awakening began around 1790 and ended in the early 1840s. This second great move of God started when Timothy Dwight, the president of Yale University, began leading the school's chapel services. Revival broke out at the school in 1802, which led to a third of the students giving their lives to Christ.

The fire of revival spread to other college campuses, prompting college graduates to enter pastoral ministry and foreign mission work. Quickly, this move of God gravitated toward the western borders of the American frontier among people of low income and little education.

Hooper! Kentucky, Tennessee, and southern Ohio became fertile soil for revival preachers to reap a spiritual harvest. During this time, highly emotional worship services were commonplace. Some denominations objected to the emotionalism, but Baptist and Methodist preachers used it to their advantage, spurring tremendous growth.

In 1816, the American Bible Society (ABS) was formed to make the Bible available to new converts and people around the world. Presidents of the ABS included Elias Boudinot, the former president of the Continental Congress, and John Jay, the first chief justice of the US Supreme Court.

Denominational lines faded as traveling preachers with no affiliation gathered the people in rural areas. Remember that without television or movie theaters or radio stations or the Internet, dynamic preachers were the best show in town. The abolition and temperance movements also gained traction during this time as people sought to live holy lives in response to their desire to follow Jesus.

Lyman Beecher, James McGready, and Peter Cartwright served as key figures in the revival, but Charles Grandison Finney left the biggest imprint on the movement. Called "the Father of Modern Revivalism," Finney hit his stride preaching in upstate New York and Manhattan from 1825 to 1835. Then he taught at Oberlin College, where he later served as its president from 1851 to 1866.

In 1873, toward the end of his life, Finney wrote a magazine article titled "The Decay of Conscience." In it he wrote:

> Brethren, our preaching will bear its legitimate fruits. If immorality prevails in the land, the fault is ours in a great degree.

Finney was holding preachers, or pastors, responsible for the lack of moral values in society! Through his years as a preacher, professor, and college president, he had come to realize that moves of God needed leaders—that America needed leaders—and that it was the pastors who should be those leaders.

When our pastors cease being the conscience of the nation, our

me?? Yup! M.E.!!!

nation ceases having a conscience.

Finney continued:

> When our pastors cease being the conscience of the nation, our nation ceases having a conscience.

> If there is a decay of conscience, the pulpit is responsible for it.

The decay of conscience (difficulty knowing right from wrong) occurs when people no longer take responsibility for their actions. Add to that a government that fosters collectivism (giving the group priority over the individual) and the people become conditioned to live as victims. Paul wrote in Romans 10:14, "How then shall they call on Him in whom they have not believed? And how shall they believe in Him of whom they have not heard? And how shall they hear without a preacher?" Pastors must not shy away from preaching about sin. Without it, we have no need for Jesus.

> If the public press lacks moral discrimination, the pulpit is responsible for it.

Today much of the conventional media have become a propaganda machine for the Obama administration, with no regard for truth. They just promote the liberal talking points, with Hollywood mocking biblical values and Christians in general. Pastors must not allow a presidential administration—or Hollywood—to control the conversation. And the best way to control the conversation is to share God's love and win the hearts of the people who oppose us.

> If the church is degenerate and worldly, the pulpit is responsible for it.

As discussed earlier, many churches in America are preaching a "social gospel," diluting the Word of God to accommodate homosexual marriage, cohabitation, abortion, and so forth. These churches are trying to look more like the world in order to attract the world. The problem is that when the worldly come, they find nothing different, because we talk and act just like they do . . . and those churches lose their impact upon society.

If the world loses its interest in religion, the pulpit is responsible for it.

We have seen the results of secular humanism in the schools brainwashing our children, especially at the college level, with many professors espousing a blatantly anti-Christian philosophy. Pastors need to equip parents to raise children who love God and hate evil.

If Satan rules in our halls of legislation, the pulpit is responsible for it.

The time has come for pastors to again fearlessly preach toward the political landscape, just like their predecessors centuries ago. If they don't, Satan will rule without opposition in our halls of legislation.

If our politics become so corrupt that the very foundations of our government are ready to fall away, the pulpit is responsible for it.

Notice that Finney did not blame the politicians for the righteousness or unrighteousness in a nation. He blamed the preachers. Why? His last statement gives us a clue:

> The time has come for pastors to again fearlessly preach toward the political landscape, just like their predecessors centuries ago.

Let us not ignore this fact, my dear brethren; but let us lay it to heart, and be thoroughly awake to our responsibility in respect to the morals of this nation.

One of the biggest lies that people of faith have swallowed is that "politics cannot legislate morality." That is a lie! Politics legislates morality all the time! Was politics legislating morality when the Supreme Court banned prayer and Bible reading from schools? When it legalized abortion? When homosexual marriage became the law of the land? Wasn't that legislating morality? Of course it was!

Let's look again at Proverbs 29:2: "When the righteous are in authority, the people rejoice; but when a wicked man rules, the people groan." If the "wicked" are in charge of government, they will legislate their wicked brand of morality.

Before you dismiss Finney's words, rationalizing that you are not a preacher, you should realize that *all of us have some kind of pulpit.* For you, it may be where you work. It may be your school. It may be among your extended family or in your neighborhood, but we all have a pulpit. Of course, the pastor has a greater responsibility. Jesus said, "For everyone to whom much is given, from him much will be required" (Luke 12:48). But we are responsible too. We have a responsibility to be light to those who are in darkness. And we have a responsibility to elect righteous leaders, those who will legislate *true* morality.

Instead of trying to be politically correct, let us be biblically correct, because when we meet our Lord face-to-face, we want to hear Him say, "Well done, good and faithful servant!"

11

FIVE DANGERS IF AMERICA DOESN'T CHANGE COURSE

Therefore if the Son makes you free, you shall be free indeed. —JOHN 8:36

Train up a child in the way he should go, And when he is old he will not depart from it.

—PROVERBS 22:6

On January 13, 2012, Captain Francesco Schettino was commanding the helm of the cruise ship *Costa Concordia* off the coast of the island Isola del Giglio in Italy. Normally, the ship remained five miles offshore, but that day, the ship's maître d'hôtel asked the captain, who hailed from the island, to perform a "sail-past." A sail-past is a salute to a crewmember's family or friends that is performed by steering a ship close to shore.

Schettino agreed, and then turned off the alarm system for the ship's computer navigation system so he could navigate by sight. Realizing that the ship was about to hit the reef, he ordered an abrupt turn, but it was too late. The ship's hull ran into the rocks, listed, and then lay down in the water. Thirty-two of the 4,252 people on board perished. Captain Schettino was found guilty of manslaughter of the thirty-two passengers and sentenced to sixteen years in prison.

America, too, is headed straight toward a perilous reef. If we don't make an immediate change of course, the dream of our Founding

Fathers and many conservative Americans today will perish.

In this chapter, I will describe five dangers, five monumental changes that will take place in our country and jeopardize our freedoms, unless we do something.

DANGER #1: *FREEDOM OF RELIGION* COULD BECOME *FREEDOM OF WORSHIP*.

While "freedom of religion" and "freedom of worship" sound alike, they differ a great deal. Let's review what the First Amendment of the Constitution says about religion:

> Congress shall make no law respecting an establishment of religion, or prohibiting the free exercise thereof.

Nowhere in the US Constitution or its twenty-seven amendments does the word *worship* appear. So what's the big deal?

In an alarming online article on Catholic Online, dated July 19, 2010, Fr. Randy Sly exposed President Obama's change in terminology (which actually began during Bill Clinton's presidency). The Obama administration now equates the "freedom of worship" with the "freedom of religion."[1] In fact, the federal government now uses the term "freedom of worship" instead of the constitutional "freedom of religion" in its mandatory test for immigrants who want to become US citizens.[2]

What's the difference between the two? Ashley E. Samuelson, in a 2010 article for *First Things*, explained:

> If we don't make an immediate change of course, the dream of our Founding Fathers and many conservative Americans today will perish.

> To anyone who closely follows prominent discussion of religious freedom in the diplomatic and political arena, this linguistic shift is troubling.

The reason is simple. Any person of faith knows that religious exercise is about a lot more than freedom of worship. It's about the right to dress according to one's religious dictates, to preach openly, to evangelize, to engage in the public square. Everyone knows that religious Jews keep kosher, religious Quakers don't go to war, and religious Muslim women wear headscarves, yet "freedom of worship" would protect none of these acts of faith.

Those who limit religious practice to the cathedral and the home are the same people who want to strip the public square of any religious presence. They work to tear down roadside memorial crosses built to commemorate fallen state troopers in Utah, to strip "Under God" from the Pledge of Allegiance, and they recently stopped a protester from entering an art gallery because she wore a pro-life pin.[3]

They also challenge worship in the home by banning home Bible studies, employing weak excuses such as "Too many cars are parked on the street," or "Zoning ordinances don't allow them," or the people in attendance are "disturbing the peace."

In Cuba and other communist countries, you can talk about religion and share the gospel *inside* a church building, but if you do it *outside* of a church building, you can be arrested. That is freedom of worship as opposed to freedom of religion. Incidentally, the government also places spies in those worship services to monitor what is said.

Is it any coincidence that President Obama appointed extreme homosexual activist and Georgetown University Law School professor Chai Feldblum to the Equal Employment Opportunity Commission? Ms. Feldblum is on record as saying, "We should . . . not tolerate private beliefs about sexual orientation and gender. . . . Protecting one group's identity may, at times, require that we burden others' belief liberty. . . . It is essential that we not privilege moral beliefs that are religiously based over other sincerely held core, moral beliefs."[4]

The shift from the free exercise of religion to the freedom of worship means people can practice their faith only in corporate worship. But if you read this Obama appointee's words closely, she expressly urges that the government should be able to *discriminate* against people with any religious beliefs that differ with her own politically correct beliefs.

This shift is frightening and must be stopped!

DANGER #2: THE GENDER LINES COULD BECOME BLURRED, AND THE FAMILY FUNDAMENTALLY REDEFINED.

Houston mayor Annise Parker's attempt to allow people to choose their public restroom based on their choice of gender identity is just the beginning of a continued blurring of gender lines.

In the same way, the media has celebrated Bruce (who now calls himself "Caitlyn") Jenner's decision to try to transform himself into a woman, with ESPN granting him the Arthur Ashe Award for Courage. Not long after that, the E! network rewarded him with an eight-part, one-hour reality-television series.

Since then, transgender issues have become the newest lifestyle trend in Hollywood. CBS announced that a transgender actress will star in a transgender legal drama series. That same person was named to *People* magazine's 2015 list of the world's most beautiful people. Also, a fourteen-year-old transgender girl was recently given her own show on the TLC network and became one of the faces of a skincare line.

Men becoming women and women becoming men is bad enough. But boys becoming girls and vice versa, before they even exit puberty and fully understand themselves, then holding them up as role models for young people to emulate is ridiculous!

What could possibly be worse?

Recently, the University of Tennessee Office for Diversity and Inclusion asked students to replace gender-specific pronouns, such as *he* or *she*, with genderless pronouns, like *ze*, *hir*, or *hirs*. UT's Pride Center director, Donna Braquet, explained their reasoning: "Transgender people and people who do not identify within the gender binary may use a different name than their legal name and pronouns of their gender identity, rather than the pronouns of the sex they were assigned at birth."[5]

The university also advises students to ask their peers, ["What pronoun do you want me to use for you?" Perhaps a "he" wants to be called "she" or "ze." Imagine trying to remember the different pronouns for every person you know. The task is overwhelming, troubling, and undoubtedly blurs the lines of gender.

When Obama nominated Chai Feldblum to the Equal Employment Opportunity Commission, concerned citizens protested because she had signed the Beyond Marriage statement. This statement calls for an entirely new definition of marriage rights that, in their words, extends to "households in which there is more than one conjugal partner" (in other words, more than two romantic partners). In Ms. Feldblum's opinion, companies and the US government should be forced to extend benefits to people in open marriages.

If we continue down the current path, new draconian regulations, called Sexual Orientation and Gender Identity (SOGI) laws, will affect Americans in multiple ways:

1. *Businesses and business owners will be forced to violate their moral and religious convictions.* As we discussed in chapter 8, everything from mom-and-pop restaurants to large corporations—and those who own them—will be mandated to violate their faith or risk lawsuits and be driven out of business.

2. *Christian-based companies will be unprotected by religious exemptions.* While churches and clergy sometimes receive minimal protections, those same protections typically do not apply to Christian-based companies, such as Christian bookstores, religious publishers, and religious television and radio stations. Much less to the run-of-the mill business, owned by faithful believers. Forced policies to embrace homosexuality will assuredly compromise the values of those companies.

3. *Privacy rights will be sacrificed in order to conform.* If transgendered people can choose which bathroom to use, what prevents sexual predators from entering the bathroom of the opposite sex as well? Men would have the right to walk directly into the women's restroom and gawk (and vice versa), and no one could prevent

it. The laws would also permit them to use the same showers as women and young girls (this is why some critics have dubbed such laws bathroom bills). Imagine the damage it would do to women and young girls. Supporters of these laws ridicule any potential threat, but provide no substantive response to the reality that they would be powerfully enabling those who prey on our children.

When the ship of righteousness departs from the proven route established by Scripture, a crash *will* occur. Soon, every depraved practice will demand equal rights—if we don't change direction.

We need to pray for our children who will be forced to grow up in this mess.

DANGER #3: OUR JUDEO-CHRISTIAN ETHIC COULD BE SUPPLANTED BY A SECULAR HUMANIST WORLDVIEW.

Someday future generations of Americans will look back at our era (if Jesus doesn't return) and ask, "What were you thinking? Why didn't you value human life?"

Fifty-eight million abortions since 1973. School shootings. Inner-city violence. The problem with the violence in our country isn't the result of the proliferation of guns. The problem lies with how little we value human life. After Noah, his wife, his three sons, and their wives stepped off the ark following the global flood, he told them, "Whoever sheds man's blood, by man his blood shall be shed; for in the image of God He made man" (Genesis 9:6).

Before the flood, we read God's reason for sending the "natural" disaster: "The earth also was corrupt before God, and the earth was filled with violence" (Genesis 6:11). So afterward, He told Noah's family (and us), "I made you different from the rest of the animals at creation. I created you in *My* image. Life is precious and people are precious. For this reason, any person who takes the life of another must pay with his life."

Later, when God gave Moses the Ten Commandments, he reserved six of his directives to instruct us how to treat each other. (See Exodus 20:12–17.)

Since evolutionary theory tells us we're nothing more than animals, why should we be surprised when we act like them? But when we realize that God set us apart from the animal kingdom—and that every human being is created in the image of God—we begin behaving differently from animals.

> Since evolutionary theory tells us we're nothing more than animals, why should we be surprised when we act like them?

If we don't change course, the value of human life will become even less. Already, four states (Vermont, Massachusetts, Oregon, and Washington) have legalized physician-assisted suicide. Not surprisingly, they're all blue states.

By keeping our faith to ourselves, we guarantee our grandchildren will grow up in a secular humanist society. The Christian faith is not a personal thing—much to the dismay of every secular humanist. Little do they realize that the future of society and even possibly their lives depend on the Christian faith. Secular humanists weren't the early advocates of abolition; Christians were—both in England and in the United States. And someday, when they're sitting in a nursing home, Christians will be defending their lives against people who see no problem with freeing a bed by taking their lives.

Unless we do nothing.

DANGER #4: GUN CONTROL COULD DISARM THE AVERAGE LAW-ABIDING CITIZEN.
As I explained in chapter 2, tyrants throughout history have removed firearms from their people in order to control them. The freedom to bear arms helps prevent hostile government oppression. The Founding Fathers understood this, which is why the Second Amendment, passed in 1791, reads, "A well regulated Militia, being necessary to the security of a free State, the right of the people to keep and bear Arms, shall not be infringed."

Note that the Second Amendment calls keeping and bearing arms a right that "shall not be infringed." It assumes that *you already have that right*, because it is intrinsic in the "unalienable" right to life with which we have been "endowed by our Creator" (as stated in the Declaration of Independence). If we have a right to life, we also have the right to defend our lives and the lives of our loved ones.

As long as guns are readily available, the possibility of the overthrow of our government by tyrants is minimal. Too many people can defend the country.

But here's an example of the stupidity of gun restrictions: On July 16, 2015, Mohammod Youssuf Abdulazeez opened fire at two different military centers in Chattanooga, Tennessee. Four Marines and one sailor were killed and three more people were wounded. However, the casualties would have been significantly fewer if the employees of the two facilities hadn't been federally prohibited from carrying firearms. Obviously, the sign on the front doors prohibiting the use of firearms did nothing to prevent Abdulazeez from opening fire. All it did was disarm our servicemen and women inside.

If guns are outlawed, as they say, only outlaws will have guns. Pity the single mother who works a second-shift job and drives late at night to her home in a high-crime neighborhood. If guns are outlawed, she'll have absolutely no protection against a predator. Pity the store owner who cannot defend himself from criminals trying to rob him. Pity the family rendered powerless to defend themselves from an intruder who breaks in.

Chicago enforces some of the strictest gun control laws in the country. Ironically—and not coincidentally—they also register some of the highest crime rates in the country. Every twenty hours or so, a person in that city is murdered, more than 80 percent of the time by gunshot. After a particularly bloody Independence Day weekend in 2014, Chicago police superintendent Garry McCarthy appealed for even tougher gun control laws.

Detroit, on the other hand, also experienced high crime rates. But instead of asking for stricter gun control, police chief James Craig encouraged the people of Detroit to arm themselves. As the crime rate began to fall in 2014, Craig attributed the lower crime rate to the many citizens taking his advice.

Or take Houston, Texas, for example. Their demographics in many ways mimic Chicago. Between two and three million people. Very diverse. Median income virtually the same. But their gun laws are like night and day. Unlike Chicago, Houstonians can carry concealed weapons. Houston has eighty-four dedicated gun shops and fifteen hundred places where consumers can purchase guns. Chicago? None.

So, following the logic that more guns increases crime, you'd expect the homicide rate to be much higher in Houston, right? Wrong. The number of homicides per 100,000 people in Houston is almost half that of Chicago (9.8 vs. 15.2 in 2013).

Again, take away the guns from law-abiding citizens and only criminals will have guns.

DANGER #5: EDUCATION COULD CHANGE THE LESSONS OF HISTORY.

"History is written by the victors," Winston Churchill reputedly said. This is never more accurate than in the realm of education. The victors in education will determine how we interpret our country's history. They will either revise history and teach that America began as a secular nation, or they will accurately show that America, indeed, began as a Christian nation.

The fight for the minds of our young people is very real. Educators are notorious for leaning left. Far left. And teachers' unions almost exclusively support liberal candidates in every election.

In the past, parents felt empowered to give feedback regarding their children's education. Schools were the product of communities. But today, our educational system is facing an unprecedented assault by progressives as a result of the new Common Core (CC) initiative.

So what is Common Core? According to the people who developed it, CC is "a set of high-quality academic standards in mathematics and English language arts/literacy (ELA)."[6] Sounds pretty innocuous. But in reality, CC delineates the skills every student should possess. On a deeper level, CC takes the responsibility of education from the grassroots level and hands it over to liberal educators, who will determine not only what our students should know, but how it is taught. And as we've discussed, not many good things happen when we give the federal government authority over local and state entities.

) Fox

Because education is not included in Article 1, Section 8 of the Constitution (the enumerated powers of Congress), which serves as the job description of the federal government, it remains within the authority of the states.

> Common Core takes the responsibility of education from the grassroots level and hands it over to liberal educators.

In 2010, President Obama in effect bribed the states with $4.35 billion in grants to adopt Common Core standards by participating in his Race to the Top Fund.[7] At a time when state budgets were struggling for funds in the midst of a faltering economy, many took the bait.

Forty-two states have adopted Common Core.[8] Funded in part by the Bill and Melinda Gates Foundation to the tune of $200 million,[9] CC is a single set of national standards developed by educators under a cloak of confidentiality and without public input. Interestingly enough, the only mathematics and English language arts specialists sitting on the validation committee did *not* approve the standards. A 2014 Gallup poll revealed that 60 percent of Americans are opposed to this initiative.[10]

Here are my concerns about Common Core:

Common Core standards are not grounded in research. Despite claims that their standards are based on international research—scant evidence exists. Two committees composed of 135 people wrote the early childhood standards, without any of them having any experience as

K–3 classroom teachers or early childhood education professionals. Then, when the standards were beginning to be implemented in 2010, five hundred early childhood experts determined the early childhood standards were so inappropriate that they called for their suspension.[11]

Commenting on this in a recent *Washington Post* blog, Carol Burris reported, "Dr. Louisa Moats, one of the few early childhood experts on the team that wrote the literacy standards, is now an outspoken critic because the Common Core standards disregard decades of research on early reading development. . . . Moats describes the Common Core as a 'political (and philosophical) compromise' which reflects contemporary ideas, not reading research."[12]

Despite the claims that Common Core prepares students for career and college, absolutely no evidence exists. Diane Ravitch, a former assistant US secretary of education and research professor of education at New York University, in an article for the *Huffington Post*, wrote, "The biggest fallacy of the Common Core standards is that they have been sold to the nation without any evidence that they will accomplish what their boosters claim."[13]

Already, Indiana, Oklahoma, South Carolina, and Louisiana have exited the standards, and other states are hitting the brakes. Alaska, Nebraska, Texas, and Virginia were smart enough to avoid adopting it in the first place, which leads to the next concern.

Common Core lowers the bar in education. CC boasts that it will prepare students to be "college and career ready."[14] Wait a minute! How can one standardized approach equally prepare one student pursuing a career in auto mechanics or hairstyling and another student pursuing an undergraduate degree and still another student preparing to become a doctor? It's simply impossible. To hit the different groups, the bar must be lowered. And that's already happened.

David Coleman, the lead Common Core Standards writer, was named president of the College Board in 2012. The College Board administers the SAT and PSAT tests. In 2013, the College Board began tailoring the

SAT to conform to CC. Shaan Patel, director of SAT programs for Veritas Prep, told *U.S. News and World Report* in March 2014, "My opinion is this test will be easier than the current SAT and the College Board is betting on more students taking the SAT because of that."[15]

I thought CC claimed to *raise* the bar! Now, for enough students to pass the SAT, the test must be made easier.

In the ongoing competition between the SAT and the ACT for test-takers, Patel added, "It's a good move that it's becoming easier in [a] way, but it's also a very bad move in that I think it's sort of a race to the bottom now." He added that "when and if" the ACT makes its next change, it might lower its standards to remain competitive against the SAT.[16]

What has Common Core produced? A race to the bottom.

A good teacher knows how to adapt the material to the students. In high-performing communities, teachers can make their lesson plans more rigorous. In lower-performing communities, teachers can slow down and simplify. But CC makes no allowance for this. Teachers must teach to

> How can one standardized approach equally prepare one student pursuing a career in auto mechanics and another student preparing to become a doctor? It's simply impossible.

federally established standards, and states are forbidden to change them. In the meantime, CC disempowers good teachers.

Last of all, teachers are now pressured to "teach to the test," rather than "teach to the student." What is the bottom line of education? Not passing a test. The bottom line of education is learning. When educators teach to the test, they sacrifice learning in the process. When educators teach to the test, they treat students as data rather than people.

Common Core creates an opening for liberal educators to promote their liberal agenda. In defending Common Core, educational elitists claim that their initiative only establishes standards and has nothing to do with curriculum. Nothing could be further from the truth.

When introducing CC, Bill Gates explained, "Identifying common standards *is just the starting point.* We'll only know this effort has succeeded when the curriculum and tests are aligned to these standards."[17]

By giving the federal government permission to determine standards that rightfully belong to parents, teachers, and school boards, we are also giving them permission to create the curriculum by which the standards are taught. For this reason, many people are comparing CC to a Trojan horse.

> By giving the federal government permission to determine standards, we are also giving them permission to create the curriculum by which the standards are taught.

Educational elites can now brainwash our students through federally mandated curriculum that extols socialism, globalism, and immorality from a secular humanist worldview. And guess who's developing much of this curriculum? Bill Gates's Microsoft, one of the most politically liberal companies in America.

For example, a test writer can pose manipulative discussion questions in the math curriculum that reflect unbiblical worldviews like same-sex orientation, situational ethics, socialism, "values clarification," anarchy, and atheism. Through curriculum, unbiblical beliefs and behaviors can be normalized and radical agendas can then be pushed on our children.

And while CC limits itself to math and English, you can bet they will expand it into science and history. Already, "disturbing" national sexuality standards have been established.[18]

As I said, history is written by the victors. And if we falter or give up this battle, CC elitists will literally rewrite our history to conform to their secular humanist worldview (much has already been done rewriting history to remove our Judeo-Christian heritage).

David Barton with Wallbuilders points out four ways revisionist historians excise our Christian heritage from American history:

1. PATENT UNTRUTHS. Whenever a historian claims, "America began as a secular country," you're witnessing a patent untruth. Rather than make an untruthful claim about a subject in which most people have a general knowledge, revisionists make claims in areas in which most people lack knowledge.

2. OVERLY BROAD GENERALIZATIONS. Revisionists take the exception and make it the rule. For example, because Thomas Jefferson and Benjamin Franklin accepted certain deist beliefs, historians often ignore the deep spiritual lives of men like Patrick Henry and John Hancock, claiming that Christianity played an insignificant role in the formation of our country.

3. OMISSION. By omitting the context of a story or spiritual nuances of a quote, our students are led to believe a different story or even outcome. For example, take a "revisionist" quote of the 1620 Mayflower Compact: "We whose names are under-written do by these presents solemnly and mutually in the presence of God, and one of another, covenant and combine our selves together into a civil body politick."

Seems pretty innocuous. But here is the true Mayflower Compact quote: "We whose names are under-written having undertaken for the glory of God, and advancement of the Christian faith and honor of our king and country, a voyage to plant the first colonie in the Northern parts of Virginia do by these presents solemnly and mutually in the presence of God, and one of another, covenant and combine ourselves together into a civil body politick" (italics added).

4. A LACK OF PRIMARY SOURCE REFERENCES. Instead of citing "primary-source documents," revisionist historians will cite biased, second-hand resources. Barton explains:

The text *The Search for Christian America* purports to examine the Founding Era and finds a distinct lack of Christian influence. Yet 80 percent of the "historical sources" on which it relies to document its finding were published after 1950! That is, to determine what was occurring in the 1700s, they quote from works printed in the 1900s.[19]

For this reason we cannot be silent and we cannot sit still. We must imitate the Berean believers in Acts 17 who "searched the Scriptures daily *to find out* whether these things were so" (Acts 17:11). We must be mindful of the changes in our culture and be aware of the government's insidious tentacles reaching into our daily lives. In the next two chapters I will submit a strategy for helping America return to her former greatness.

12

RESCUING AMERICA FROM AN AGE OF
LAWLESSNESS

Even so you also outwardly appear righteous to men, but inside you are full
of hypocrisy and lawlessness. . . . And because lawlessness will abound, the
love of many will grow cold.

—JESUS, MATTHEW 23:28 AND 24:12

The problem with socialism is that eventually you run out of other people's
money.

—ATTRIBUTED TO MARGARET THATCHER

When I was a young man in Cuba, I heard a young, charismatic
leader. An activist by trade. He promised hope and change.
The year was 2008, and I was addressing an audience in excess
of ten thousand people at a Tea Party rally in Texas.
"The man promised to redistribute the wealth so that everyone
would have equal opportunities. He promised jobs and universal health
care and a stronger central government that would take care of its people.
He took the responsibility on himself and wouldn't let anyone stand
in the way of accomplishing his goals. But what was the cost? Liberty."

Afterward, journalists from across the country raked me over the
coals. "Comparing Barack Obama to Fidel Castro seems extreme," they
said. "Rafael Cruz is nothing more than a right-wing extremist." Some

True

even called me a fascist. A chicken on a rotisserie would have received better treatment.

In the midst of the criticism, my son, Ted, signed up on one of the blogs using his own name, and he commented, "All of you seem to be hysterical about my dad's speech. I just want to point out one thing: he never once mentioned the name 'Barack Obama.' He simply described what Fidel Castro did. Now what does it say about you that when you hear what Castro did, you immediately assume he's referring to Barack Obama?"

gosh! Princeton! clever! H.S. stuff!

Conservative, liberal, or Tea Partier, all of us can see similarities between the two men, if we can be honest. Granted, enormous differences exist; the United States is not imprisoning and torturing political dissidents. And truthfully, I was talking about both men.

But the point is that in more than one State of the Union address, President Obama has promised, "If Congress doesn't act, I will." That doesn't sound much different from the old, bearded dictator I left behind in Cuba almost sixty years ago— governing by decree, by fiat, just like Fidel Castro.

> Our forefathers laid down their lives to win liberty and freedom for Americans. In turn, too many of us are simply lying down and giving up.

Our forefathers laid down their lives to win liberty and freedom for Americans. In turn, too many of us are simply lying down and giving up. We stand at a critical moment in our nation's history. We now must fight for the future of our children and our children's children. The longer we wait, the greater our struggle will be.

Unfortunately, we don't need to go to Cuba to see the socialist agenda described here. We have seen many of the same tactics used by the Obama regime with exactly the same objective in mind. And as courageous constitutional conservatives, we have an obligation to

open the eyes of Americans whom the left wing has blinded with their *vs fools &*
empty promises. *Tools!!*

Socialism's promises share nothing in common with socialism's results. Take, for example, Venezuela. A recent *Wall Street Journal* article by Maolis Castro and Kejal Vyas reported on the chaos taking place in the South American country. With the collapse of oil prices around the world, Venezuela—which nationalized the oil industry in its country—has lost its main source of income. People living on government handouts have turned into mobs looting local stores and setting fire to government offices.

> When I lost my freedom in Cuba, I had a place to flee; if we lose our freedom here, where do we go?

"What's certain is that we are going very hungry here and the children are suffering a lot," a grandmother said. The *Wall Street Journal* reported on a poll by Venezuelan pollster *Consultores 21* that found 30 percent of Venezuelans eat two meals or fewer a day and about 70 percent of the people had stopped purchasing at least one basic food item because they were either unavailable or too expensive.[1]

That's the kind of *hope* and *change* the American people can do without—but it's the kind of hope and change we can look forward to if we follow the path President Obama has charted for us. *vicious lies*

* * *

As I told my son, Ted, on many occasions, "When I lost my freedom in Cuba, I had a place to flee; if we lose our freedom here, where do we go?"

When we take inventory of the extensive damage the Obama administration has committed against America, we can easily get discouraged and conclude that we are beyond recovery. The prophets of doom and gloom will tell you that the freedoms we knew years ago are a relic that can never be restored:

GAY MARRIAGE. Since we've already explored this, I won't go into detail here. But by enforcing the Supreme Court's lawless ruling, people of faith—not just Christians—are being forced to accept a lifestyle that violates their conscience. If the left wing continues their stranglehold on public policy, the day will soon come when speaking out against gay marriage will be a punishable offense.

OBAMACARE. President Obama and the left-wing Democratic Party have strong-armed Americans into accepting their form of socialized medicine. Giving government greater control over our lives never solved any problem. No one ever accused the government of working efficiently (or effectively). As expected, health care costs have risen.

While trying to sell the American people on the Affordable Care Act, the president promised, "If you like the plan you have, you can keep it. If you like the doctor you have, you can keep your doctor, too. The only change you'll see are falling costs as our reforms take hold."[2] But as expected, this wasn't true. People were forced to leave the plans they loved, plans they *chose* for themselves. Some people's health care plans were changed for them, without their even knowing about it.

When the American people complained, President Obama changed his promise: "If you have or had one of these plans before the Affordable Care Act came into law and you really liked that plan, what we said was you can keep it *if it hasn't changed since the law passed.*"[3] What plan hasn't changed since the president's administration force-fed Obamacare down our throats?

Rather than letting the market (and actuary science) determine premiums, our socialist-minded president through the Affordable Care Act now places limits on how much insurance companies can charge. For example, insurance companies cannot charge more than three times as much for older people as they do for younger people (known as "modified community rating"). So, insurance companies have no choice but to pass the health care costs to younger people in the form of premiums. Consider the contradiction: older people, many of whom spend a lifetime accumulating wealth and can afford the higher premiums, now pay less. Young people, who are at the start of their careers and have far less wealth, are forced to pay more.

So how do young families afford their sky-high health insurance premiums? They're forced into subscribing to policies with enormous deductibles. Health insurance intended to actually help families live healthy lives has turned into a major medical policy only available in cases of emergency. Or they opt out of health insurance altogether and pay a government-assessed penalty that amounts to far less than the premiums.

> Older people, many of whom can afford the higher premiums, now pay less. Young people, who are at the start of their careers and have far less wealth, are forced to pay more.

Most concerning of all, now that the government's hands are in our health care, it can mandate what care we receive. And that every constituent pays for abortion services. Moreover, they're trying to force religious hospitals, charities, and schools to abandon their beliefs in order to provide their employees with insurance that covers abortion-inducing drugs and contraception. *insanity, Catholic mileval anti-Science cultism*

ABUSE OF EXECUTIVE POWER. At last count, the Obama administration has made thirty-two significant unilateral changes to the Affordable Care Act since its launch, according to the Galen Institute.[4] In a recent Op-Ed piece for *Forbes*, M. Northrup Buechner, associate professor of economics at St. John's University, New York, wrote:

> The Constitution authorizes the President to propose and veto legislation. It does not authorize him to change existing laws. The changes President Obama ordered in Obamacare, therefore, are unconstitutional. This means that he does not accept some of the limitations that the Constitution places on his actions. We cannot know at this point

what limitations, if any, he does accept. The main responsibility the Constitution assigns to the President is to faithfully execute the Laws. If the President rejects this job, if instead he decides he can change or ignore laws he does not like, then what?

President Obama has not been shy about pointing out his path. He has repeatedly made clear that he intends to act on his own authority. "I have the power and I will use it in defense of the middle class," he has said. "We're going to do everything we can, wherever we can, with or without Congress." There are a number of names for the system Mr. Obama envisions, but representative government is not one of them.[5]

Furthermore, Buechner points out that President Obama made four recess appointments while the Senate was not in recess. Taking cues from our chief executive, attorney general Eric Holder, charged with enforcing federal laws, announced he would find ways to get around a Supreme Court ruling that struck down a key provision of the Voting Rights Act of 1965.[6]

In 2014, my son Ted was the Ranking Member on the Constitution Subcommittee of the Senate Judiciary Committee; in that capacity, he released a report chronicling *76 lawless acts by the Obama Administration*.[7]

NATIONAL DEBT. By the end of 2015, the US national debt should run in the neighborhood of $21.694 trillion.[8] At the beginning of 2009, as President Obama took office, the national debt was $10.7 trillion.[9] In other words, one presidential administration, over seven years, *doubled* our

> The Obama administration *doubled* our national debt over seven years.

national debt. Obama inherited a shaky economy, and when he steps away from office, he will leave the next president with an even shakier one.

Chevy Bush II Great Depression II

Even the left-leaning *Huffington Post* recently pointed out that between 2000 and 2014, "the U.S. national debt has grown at four times the rate of its national economy." Sheldon Filger, who penned the op-ed piece, admitted that the only way our economy can survive is for the "Federal Reserve [to] maintain artificially low interest rates in perpetuity."[10] In perpetuity? That's impossible!

ISIS AND IRAN. When President Barack Hussein Obama began his first term in January 2009, no one had heard of ISIS apart from the mythological goddess from ancient Egypt. The Islamic State was still in its infancy back then, but since 2013, it has become an international concern. In a 2014 interview with *60 Minutes*, President Obama admitted the United States "underestimated what had been taking place in Syria" that allowed the country to become "ground zero for jihadists around the world."[11] Then, as ISIS began gaining ground in the Middle East, the president confessed that they still hadn't decided on a strategy to stem their growing influence. In the meantime, Christians, Kurds, and Muslims who didn't embrace their radicalism were being slaughtered by the thousands.

Although Obama "underestimated" ISIS, it's abundantly clear that he assumes he isn't underestimating Iran. In 2015, the president negotiated an agreement with Iran, requiring them to promise to reduce their nuclear weapons program in exchange for billions of dollars in relief from international sanctions. First, entering into an agreement like that requires trust—that the United States will follow through on relieving their sanctions, but also that Iran won't secretly build any nuclear warheads. But how can the United States monitor that? In his negotiations, he didn't require that Ayatollah Ali Khamenei recognize Israel's right to exist. Khamenei, incidentally, has made opposition to the United States and Israel a central part of his foreign policy since he rose to power in 1989.

Secretary Kerry and President Obama acquiesced on every point and completely surrendered to Iran. They violated their oaths of office, which require them to protect this country against all enemies, foreign, and domestic. And their excuse was "It is either a deal or war."[12] The opposite is true: this deal all but guarantees war, because it allows Iran to keep their centrifuges and enriched uranium; it allows Iran to continue their nuclear program and ultimately facilitates their building a nuclear bomb.

If Iran builds a nuclear weapon, the chances are far too great that they will use it against Israel ("the Little Satan") or against America ("the Great Satan"). This misguided deal also allows Iran to continue their ICBM (intercontinental ballistic missile) program, which will serve only one purpose: to carry a nuclear warhead across the Atlantic to bomb America. And, amazingly, the deal also trusts Iran *to inspect itself*.

> The billions of dollars released to Iran will assuredly find their way to terrorist organizations throughout the Middle East, making the Obama administration the greatest sponsor of terrorism in the world.

There are no American inspectors or international inspectors; rather, the Obama administration trusts the Ayatollah Khamenei to "self-report."

Moreover, much of the over $100 billion released to Iran will find its way directly to *Hamas, Hezbollah, the Houthis,* and terrorist organizations throughout the Middle East, making the Obama Administration, quite literally, the world's leading financier of radical Islamic terrorism. This is, in a word, insane!

How can we be sure these billions won't be secretly channeled into further nuclear development? We can't, but we do know this: our sanctions up to this point have slowed it down. Furthermore, the United States has been Israel's staunchest ally since the country's formation in 1948. By entering into the deal, we are turning our backs on one of our closest friends.

↳ *lie!*

184

* * *

We cannot afford to throw our arms up in despair and give up. I refuse to believe the negative messages. In fact, I believe that the lawlessness and deterioration in our country can act as a catalyst, a spark, to wake up the sleeping giant, the millions upon millions of hardworking Americans who have been devastated by the socialist policies of the Obama administration. The millions of courageous constitutional conservatives who have seen the Constitution, the rule of law, separation of powers, and our unalienable rights trampled. And the millions of people of faith who have suffered an unprecedented infringement of their religious liberty by an imperial president and an out-of-control activist judiciary. *lie !!*

Our country stands at a precipice, and if another radical Democrat gets elected as chief executive, the future of America as we know it is in jeopardy. We cannot afford four or eight more years of the socialist policies that are destroying America at such a fast pace. If we stop fighting for God's dream for America, the dream will die. Edmund Burke once said, "All tyranny needs to gain a foothold is for people of good conscience to remain silent." We cannot remain silent!

Thomas Jefferson reportedly said, "If a nation expects to be ignorant and free, it expects what never was and never will be." We must engage ourselves in the principles that formed the foundation of what made America great. Read the Declaration of Independence. Know the Constitution. Read the accounts of our Founding Fathers—and avoid the revisionists who seek to erase our Christian presence from the pages of history. God, speaking through the Old Testament prophet Hosea, said, "My people are destroyed for lack of knowledge" (Hosea 4:6).

In 1979, Americans found themselves in a similar condition. The shah of Iran had been

> "If a nation expects to be ignorant and free, it expects what never was and never will be."
>
> —THOMAS JEFFERSON

overthrown and Ayatollah Khomeini had risen to power. In turn, he cut Iran's oil production, which caused gas prices to soar, plunging the American economy into recession. Interest rates shot up to 20 percent and Americans tried to make ends meet under double-digit inflation. And with President Jimmy Carter at the helm, government bureaucracy grew.

On the foreign front, fifty-two American diplomats and citizens were held hostage in Iran. Then, in the spring of 1980, a rescue operation failed, with eight American servicemen and one Iranian citizen losing their lives. The Sandinista National Liberation Front had overthrown the Samoza government in Nicaragua, which added one more country under communist domination.

President Carter and America looked weak, and the rest of the world laughed at us.

But in 1980, the American people had had enough and voted in America's greatest president since Abraham Lincoln, President Ronald Reagan. We did it then, and we can do it again! The failed policies of Jimmy Carter inspired millions of courageous conservatives to go to the polls and bring America back to respectability and greatness.

And we have a great advantage over 1980. In 1980 the Internet didn't exist, nor did e-mail, Facebook, Twitter, bloggers, or conservative radio. All of these tools are at our disposal today. Through them, we can bypass the liberal media and go directly to the American people.

There are more of us than there are of them. The problem has been that the "us" have been asleep at the wheel. Well, the time has come for "us" to wake up! Get active! Let's put our hearts and souls into restoring this great nation of ours to that "shining city on a hill."[13]

But accomplishing this will require all of us, with no one lagging behind. America's future is at stake, the future of our children and our children's children. It is for them that we must fight with all our might. Remember President Ronald Reagan's words from his famous 1961 "Encroaching Control" speech:

> Freedom is never more than one generation away from extinction.
> We didn't pass it on to our children in the bloodstream. The only

way they can inherit the freedom we have known is if we fight for it, protect it, defend it and then hand it to them with the well thought lessons of how they in their lifetime must do the same. And if you and I don't do this, then you and I may well spend our sunset years telling our children and our children's children what it once was like in America when men were free.[14]

I hope you will join me in saying, "I'm not willing to have that conversation with my children and grandchildren. I will fight now, while there is still time." America is worth saving! May we be willing to covenant with one another before God, like the signers of the Declaration of Independence:

"And for the support of this Declaration, with a firm reliance on the protection of divine Providence, we mutually pledge to each other *our Lives, our Fortunes and our sacred Honor.*"

Our lives are under attack from the cradle to the grave. We have already seen how more than 58 million babies have been murdered through abortion since 1973. The elderly, on the other end of the spectrum, aren't much safer. In countries where socialized medicine has been instituted, care for the elderly is severely restricted, with delays for medical procedures ranging, in many instances, from twelve to eighteen months.

What makes us think it will be any different under Obamacare? As a matter of fact, several states have already passed or are in the process of passing euthanasia and assisted-suicide laws. Military veterans have died because of denied or delayed care by our VA hospitals. What a travesty! Men and women who risked their lives to protect our freedoms are being victimized by this failed, unconstitutional medical system called "Obamacare." And in between, our quality of life is eroded by taxation, regulation, and infringement upon our liberty.

Our fortunes? The Obama administration has both hands in your pockets, trying to take every hard-earned dollar you make to give it out in handouts to buy votes. A recent government report tragically estimates that more than 23 percent of Americans live in a family that receives some form of welfare. That's up 17.1 percent over the last year

Cheney's

of ~~Bush's~~ administration. A December 2014 analysis released by the Department of Health and Human Services reported, "About 87 percent of people who selected health insurance plans through HealthCare. gov for coverage beginning Jan. 1, 2015, were determined eligible for financial assistance to lower their monthly premiums, compared to 80 percent of enrollees who selected plans over a similar period last year."[15]

That means 87 percent of Americans can't afford Obamacare!

The problems in America's economy prompted a rebuke from Richard Trumka, president of the AFL-CIO, the nation's largest federation of unions. He threatened to withhold endorsing any Democrat who uses Obama's economic team: "If you get the same economic team, you're going to get the same results," he said. "The same results aren't good enough for working people. For most folks it seems to be an economy of stagnation."[16]

> Eighty-seven percent of Americans can't afford Obamacare!

But remember: they may take our lives, they may take our fortunes—and they are working very hard to do just that—but *no one can take our honor.* You have to surrender that yourself.

I am not willing to do that, and neither should you. I lost my freedom once. I refuse to lose it again.

Recently, I was speaking to a group on the western edge of Miami. The crowd was composed mostly of Cubans, and the weather reminded me of the scorching, humid Cuban days of my childhood. People were sitting at picnic tables and using Styrofoam plates and hats to fan themselves to stay cool.

While I was speaking, a man jumped onstage and grabbed the microphone out of my hands.

"Your son is a fascist! An anti-Latino! A Cruz by chance! I forgive you for giving him your last name, but he doesn't deserve it! I hope this man's son is never president!"

The emcee snatched the mic out of the man's hand and handed it back to me, but not before I could whisper a few words in the man's ear. I was so surprised by the outburst that I didn't know what to say to the crowd. I still don't remember what I said. A few other people had interrupted from the audience as well. When I finished speaking, I stepped off the stage.

Afterward, a reporter with the *National Journal* caught up with me and asked me what I had said to the man. "I told him, 'We still have the freedom in this country to disagree with someone. You couldn't do that in Cuba.'"

And with that freedom we must speak out with boldness and act.

13

A CALL TO ACTION

Therefore, to him who knows to do good and does not do it, to him it is sin.

—JAMES 4:17

All that is necessary for the triumph of evil is that good men do nothing.

—EDMUND BURKE

H e had just preached the greatest sermon of his brief ministry. Crowds had hung on every word and refused to disperse, even in the midst of the unrelenting Middle East sun. With broad brushstrokes, Jesus had painted a portrait of His kingdom, composed of those who are poor in spirit, meek, hungry and thirsty for righteousness, pure in heart, and peacemakers. He'd promised that when they were reviled and persecuted for His sake, they were blessed. He had commissioned them to live as salt and light and to love their enemies. He'd told them to pray and seek first His kingdom. But then He had also warned His listeners about false prophets and trees that bear bad fruit.

Finally, in concluding His sermon, Jesus had compared two men. One man had built his house on the rock. "The rain descended, the floods came, and the winds blew and beat on that house," but the house stood firm because it was founded on the rock.

But the foolish man who had built his house on the sand didn't fare so well. "The rain descended, the floods came, and the winds blew and beat on that house," but the house collapsed. "And great was its fall" (Matthew 7:24–27).

So what made the difference between the wise man and the foolish man? What had the wise man done that the foolish one hadn't? And from what was the right foundation composed?

Many biblically astute people would answer that Jesus is the foundation of this parable at the end of Matthew 6. And while Scripture tells us He's the only foundation for our faith (see 1 Corinthians 3:11), in this, His ministry-defining sermon, the foundation isn't Him. Let's read:

> "But everyone who hears these sayings of Mine, *and does not do them*, will be like a foolish man who built his house on the sand: and the rain descended, the floods came, and the winds blew and beat on that house; and it fell. And great was its fall." (Matthew 7:26–27, emphasis added)

What caused the house to collapse? The foolish man heard Jesus' sayings and didn't do them. He did nothing. He wasn't necessarily a bad person. He just got distracted or lazy or overwhelmed. Whatever it was, his inaction caused the downfall of his house.

If you enjoyed reading this book but then set it aside to go on with your daily life, if it inspired you but didn't motivate you to do something to restore this great country to the vision of its Framers, then I have utterly failed. But the fact is, America is not too far gone. America is worth saving! So as I conclude, I offer you some action steps that, if we all work together, will prevent this country from falling down with a great crash.

> What caused the house to collapse? The foolish man heard Jesus' sayings and didn't do them.

I am your Jesus, your Leader, Persons...!'' Follow me!! Obey me!!!

ACTION STEP #1

MAKE SURE EVERYONE UNDERSTANDS THAT VOTING IS THEIR *CIVIC RESPONSIBILITY*.

We cannot afford to stay at home. If we do, we become part of the problem and have no right to complain. But we must do much more than just register to vote and then go to the polls. We must encourage everyone we can to do the same. This is a continuous effort.

When the Framers gave us this great constitutional representative republic, all authority under the Constitution was placed upon "we the People" and, as mentioned before, with that authority comes an awesome responsibility: to elect righteous leaders. If we fail to do so by not voting, then the consequence is that the wicked will elect the wicked and implement disastrous policies, as we have seen in America since the beginning of the Obama administration. Only by all of us realizing we have a civic duty to be involved in the political process can we restore this wonderful country of ours to the vision that the Framers had for America.

Dr. James McHenry, one of the delegates from Maryland to the Constitutional Convention in 1787, in his notes in the *American Historical Review*, stated that at the conclusion of the convention, a lady by the name of Mrs. Powel asked Benjamin Franklin, "Well, Doctor, what have we got, a republic or a monarchy?" Franklin responded, "A republic, if you can keep it."[1]

> Mrs. Powel: Well, Doctor, what have we got, a republic or a monarchy?
>
> Benjamin Franklin: A republic, if you can keep it.

ACTION STEP #2
STUDY AND THEN SHARE MESSAGES ON BIBLICAL PRINCIPLES RELEVANT TO OUR SOCIETY.

Our churches are partly to blame for the rot that is causing the disintegration of our country. For far too long, churches have avoided discussing moral issues for fear of offending their fellow parishioners and their neighbors. And what good has that done? None!

What many pastors have failed to realize is that God has placed them in a position of leadership over their congregations, who are looking to their pastor, the person they trust the most, for answers about the many challenges they encounter in our society. If the pastor does not provide that leadership role, the people are scattered, "like sheep having no shepherd" (Matthew 9:36). *[handwritten: J. Dobson, Rick Warren, Osteen, Billy Graham, Can,]*

Jesus said, "You are the light of the world. A city that is set on a hill cannot be hidden. Nor do they light a lamp and put it under a basket, but on a lampstand, and it gives light to all who are in the house. *[handwritten: healer spam,]* your light so shine before men, that they may see your good works *[handwritten: and pst]* glorify your Father in heaven" (Matthew 5:14–16). *[handwritten: Popes (2)]*

Society is in a state of moral decay because too many churches have avoided issues like these:

- the sanctity of life *[handwritten: Anti Religious Freedom, Catholic crap!!]*

- the sanctity of the traditional family

- sexual purity before and during marriage *[handwritten: → divorced x2 !!!]*

- individual responsibility and a work ethic

- honesty and integrity

- our responsibility in civic society

But we cannot afford to just rely on the preachers to communicate truth. Every one of us needs to "shout from the housetops," as Jesus commanded (Matthew 10:27 NLT). And don't forget to share that God hasn't given up on our country. It's not too late to return to Him. *[handwritten: Fascist ass!!]*

[handwritten right margin: F.U.!]

193

ACTION STEP #3

ENCOURAGE PASTORS AND PEOPLE OF FAITH TO RUN FOR PUBLIC OFFICE.

We need Christians at every level of elected office: school board, city council, state legislature, and so forth. Remember Proverbs 29:2: "When the righteous are in authority, the people rejoice; but when a wicked man rules, the people groan."

After seeing his pastor barely lose an election for an open seat in the California legislature—despite being massively outspent and shunned by Republican leaders—David Lane created a blueprint that any pastor can follow. Lane and his American Renewal Project are now recruiting one thousand pastors to run for office in 2016.

Lane shared his vision with the *Washington Times*:

> There are 100,000 pastors on my email list, and I started thinking what if the Lord were to call 1,000 pastors in 2016 to run for county commissioner, and city council and school board, and mayor and Congress, and let us say they did only half as good as my pastor did with volunteers—they only had 300 volunteers per campaign. That would be a 300,000 grass-roots precinct-level explosion in the public square. It would change America, and that is what I am up to.[2]

Through the American Renewal Project's "Issachar training," they teach pastors the basics of running a campaign, from building grassroots support to raising money.

In March 1992, my good friend Dr. Rick Scarborough, senior pastor of First Baptist Church in Pearland, Texas, heard from a church member that someone was going to speak on AIDS awareness at a local high school and that he should attend. Because Pearland High School didn't have a large enough meeting room to accommodate all the students at one time, multiple assemblies were scheduled throughout the day. Since Dr. Scarborough was very busy, he sent his associate pastor in his place.

At about 11:30 a.m., the associate pastor returned to the church office and interrupted Dr. Scarborough's busy schedule, urging him to attend the afternoon assembly. Fortunately, he had his Dictaphone with him and was able to record some of the remarks. In his book *Enough Is Enough*, Dr. Scarborough shares what transpired next:

> I listened to a cute, petite, bubbly, twenty-four-year-old coed speak to our students, including my own daughter, Misty, who sat midway in the auditorium. I could not believe my ears. She spoke in the vernacular of her audience, using just enough technical terms to alert everyone that she knew what she was talking about. She proceeded to describe in great detail every form of sexual expression you can imagine. She used humor to diffuse the tension and embarrassment that a mixed crowd of teenagers would feel, as various sexual activities were described. She was careful not to pass moral judgment on any behavior. . .
>
> Predictably, she displayed a condom, today's amoral solution for the host of afflictions that accompany illicit sex. She stretched it, made jokes about the male anatomy, and announced, "Condoms are 94 percent effective in combating AIDS when used correctly." I cannot describe to you how incensed I was as I listened to this young lady. She was giving license to hundreds of students, including two of my own who were in high school at the time, to commit any wicked act they chose. To now add to her shame, her purported fact that condoms were 94 percent safe in preventing AIDS was more than I could take. I had had enough.[3]

When Scarborough questioned her statistics, she quickly dismissed him, but he was greatly blessed when, after the assembly, his daughter threw her arms around his neck and said, "Daddy, I am so proud of you."

Dr. Scarborough knew he needed to do something. He transcribed his recording of the meeting, made copies, and then announced on the large marquee at the front of his church: "Learn what students heard about AIDS this Sunday." When he shared the transcript of the meeting with his congregation, the members of First Baptist Church of Pearland decided enough was enough.

As a result of that morning, three members of his church were elected to city council, and four were elected to the school board. And now the police chief, the city attorney, and the county assistant district attorney are all members of his church, and many other church members began serving as volunteers in various committees throughout the city, county and state.

From there, Dr. Scarborough founded Vision America, whose mission is to "inform, encourage and mobilize pastors and their congregations to be proactive in restoring Judeo-Christian values to the moral and civic framework in their communities, states, and our nation."[4] His website also offers free downloadable resources for getting involved in local politics.

ACTION STEP #4
BE INFORMED.

One of the most idiotic statements I have ever heard is, "It doesn't make a difference who you vote for; just go and vote." That is insane!

Of course it makes a difference who you vote for. Why do you think we have so many rotten politicians in office? Because, unfortunately, too many uninformed voters simply vote for the names they recognize, without any consideration of what those candidates stand for, much less what they have done in the past.

First of all, check the voting record of all elected officials and candidates for public office. Don't just listen to what they say; look at what they have done. Contrary to the old saying that all of us have heard, what you don't know *can* hurt you.

Fortunately, many Christian organizations provide free voters guides, which list the candidates, regardless of party affiliation, and provide an easy-to-read chart of how they have voted on many of the issues affecting our society. Here are some websites that provide voters guides or voting records of our elected officials:

- Vision America (visionamerica.us)

- Liberty Counsel (lc.org)

- Liberty Institute (freevotersguide.com)

- Eagle Forum (eagleforum.org)

- Concerned Women for America (cwfa.org)

ACTION STEP #5

VOTE FOR CANDIDATES WHO UPHOLD AND DEFEND BIBLICAL VALUES.

We cannot leave our principles at the door when we go into the voting booth. Many people vote for a political party because their family has always done it. I see people voting Democrat because their parents and/or grandparents voted Democrat, without realizing the Democratic Party of today is not the same party it was years ago. It has drifted more and more to the left to the point that today its platform promotes an ungodly socialist agenda that is destroying America. And, unfortunately, there are those in the Republican Party who aren't much different.

While voting in the general elections is important, voting in the primary elections is even more important because it gives you the opportunity to select the candidates that best align with biblical and constitutional principles.

> Voting in the primary gives you the opportunity to select the candidates that best align with biblical and constitutional principles.

Make sure you support the candidate that best reflects the fundamental values that made America great:

- a firm adherence to the Constitution

- the rule of law

- limited government

- strong defense and American sovereignty

- the sanctity of life

- biblical definition of marriage

- support for Israel

- free enterprise

- fiscal responsibility

- empowerment for all citizens to achieve the American Dream, unleashing their entrepreneurial and innovative spirit by removing the heavy burden of taxation and regulation

As I mentioned in chapter 9, 54 million evangelical Christians stayed at home in the 2012 election—12 million of whom weren't even registered! Imagine if those people registered and voted according to the principles just stated. How different America would be! Even if 10 or 20 percent of that total voted, it would change the outcome of any election. Just 10 or 20 percent.

Well, it can happen, it must happen, *and it will happen* if millions of courageous conservatives lock arms, shoulder to shoulder, and move forward to reignite the promise of America.

That's what we must do together.

EPILOGUE

If you've read this far, you now understand why, for my entire life, my father has been my hero.

My cousin Bibi (the daughter of my aunt, Tía Sonia) and I have often reflected on what a blessing it is to be the children of those who fled oppression. As children, we would sit at the feet of our grandparents, *Abuelo* and *Abuela*, and hear stories of my dad and my aunt fighting in Cuba.

My father, fighting against Batista, was imprisoned and tortured by Batista's army. My tía Sonia, a few years later, fighting against Castro, was likewise imprisoned and tortured. When you are the children of those who fled oppression and came to America, it makes you appreciate how precious and fragile liberty truly is.

My dad is a freedom fighter. And if we need anything today, it is more freedom fighters.

Our country is in crisis. The challenges we are facing today are not like in the past, and the upcoming 2016 presidential election will not be an election like every other. We are bankrupting our kids and grandkids. Our constitutional rights are under assault from Washington as never before. And America has receded from leadership in the world, making the world a far more dangerous place. Today, our friends and allies no longer trust us, and our enemies no longer fear us.

I am convinced, it is now or never. There comes a point where the hole is too deep, the debt is too great, our liberties are too receded, and there is no going back. I don't think we're there yet . . . but we're close. Very close.

It is a time for truth. It is a time for action.

lie !!!

* * *

In September 2015, I met at the county jail with Kim Davis, the Kentucky clerk jailed for acting according to her faith. She and I embraced, and I thanked her for her courage. I told her that millions were inspired by her stand. That she was being lifted up in prayer by believers across America and across the world. That she may have thought she was alone in that jail cell, but she didn't realize just how crowded it was.

lie !!

A year ago, if I had suggested that a Christian woman would be sent to jail for honoring her faith, that would have been dismissed as crazy. Paranoid, even. But that is where we are.

lie !!

Why was Kim Davis jailed? Two reasons: First, the Supreme Court's fundamentally illegitimate gay marriage opinion. Five unelected lawyers declared themselves, in Justice Scalia's words, the "rulers" of 320 million Americans, insisting that their radical view of marriage—contrary to the biblical definition, to the understanding of marriage that predated America by millennia—would be forced on the rest of us. That was not law. Courts don't make law. And that was not the Constitution. In the penultimate paragraph of his dissent, Justice Scalia predicted that state and local officials would refuse to obey the Court's lawless edict.

lie !

gee !!

fascism !!

Second, a federal district judge and the state of Kentucky both violated Kentucky law. Kentucky, like the federal government and many states, has a Religious Freedom Restoration Act, which protects expressions of faith. It mandates reasonable accommodations for religious faith. Thus, Jehovah's Witnesses are exempted from having to make pledges or oaths, which is contrary to their faith. Amish are exempted from sending their children to mandatory schooling. Christian Scientists are exempted from mandatory medical treatments. Muslim truck drivers are exempted from carrying alcohol. Jews are exempted from being forced to work on the Sabbath. All of that is current law.

And yet, Christians are somehow singled out. Kim Davis, as a Christian, did not want her name to appear on a homosexual marriage license. Under Kentucky law, her faith should have been respected and

lie ! Catholics + "Lite"

+ resign the job !!

lie !

her name removed. Since the state decided to treat the court opinion as law, it would have been a simple matter to comply with Kentucky's RFRA and accommodate Kim's religious convictions. Instead, she was sent to jail, the act of an imperious, arrogant judge wanting to punish a Christian for daring to live according to her faith.

In the aftermath of Ms. Davis's imprisonment, virtually every Democrat—and sadly, more than a few Republicans—said that she should either abandon her faith and issue the same-sex marriage certificates or resign her office. They gravely intoned that her honoring her faith was somehow a profound threat to liberty and the rule of law. What nonsense.

And, it seems, none of those commentators was concerned with the behavior of other government officials (with whom they agreed) defying actual laws. None raised concern about former San Francisco mayor Gavin Newsom *granting* same-sex marriage certificates, when doing so was directly contrary to California law. Nor were they troubled by the current San Francisco mayor's policy—mirrored by Democratic mayors in cities across America—declaring San Francisco to be a "sanctuary city." Thus, San Francisco openly obstructs federal immigration law, in effect inviting violent criminal illegal aliens, such as the career criminal who is accused of murdering Kate Steinle.

Nor do most of the politicians take serious issue with the extraordinary pattern of lawlessness demonstrated by President Obama. Whether it is federal immigration law, or welfare reform law, or even his own Obamacare, the president, repeatedly, has simply refused to follow the law.

None of these commentators who are outraged by Kim Davis has called for the resignation of the San Francisco mayor or of President Obama. How can it be that one Kentucky clerk, honoring her Christian faith, poses a grave threat to the rule of law, but a president who routinely ignores federal law is not a problem at all? The hypocrisy is staggering.

What we are really seeing is an increasing hostility to religious liberty, and to Christians in particular. When Kim and I visited in that

Kentucky jailhouse, I told her she was highlighting the threats to millions, that each of us could be next. Trembling at the impact she was having, she replied, "It is all to the glory of God."

These threats are coming. And not just to Kim Davis. In the summer of 2015, I was honored to host a rally for religious liberty in Iowa. Some twenty-five hundred people came out to attend the rally, and we listened to the stories of heroes who had stood for their faith and been persecuted: Dick and Betty Odgaard, Aaron and Melissa Klein, Chief Kelvin Cochran, Sergeant Phillip Monk, Barronelle Stutzman, Blaine Adamson. Amazing stories. Ordinary people—a florist, a baker, a soldier, a fireman—who stood by biblical values and faced vicious persecution. If you want to be inspired, watch the video of their stories at www. tedcruz.org/Iowareligiouslibertyrally.

They are not alone. Indeed, at the Supreme Court oral argument in the gay marriage case, Justice Alito asked the Justice Department whether, if the Obama administration prevailed, the next step would be for the IRS to deny tax-exempt status to Christian colleges and universities that follow a biblical teaching of marriage. By extension, his question could apply as well to Christian grade schools, Christian charities, or even Christian churches. Chillingly, the Obama solicitor general replied that, yes, that was a real possibility.

These threats are only growing. If we don't stand up and stop them, you and I could be next. Chief Cochran was fired from his job as Atlanta's fire chief because he wrote, in his personal time, a Christian book discussing and analyzing Scripture. Pastors, being punished for preaching the Word of God could well be next.

The Iowa religious liberty rally ended with the story of Naghmeh Abedini, the wife of Pastor Saeed Abedini, an American citizen sentenced to eight years in an Iranian prison for the crime of sharing the gospel. Tragically, the Obama administration's extended negotiations with the Islamic Republic of Iran did nothing to secure Pastor Saeed's release, or that of his fellow American hostages languishing in Iranian prisons. Our commander in chief should be fighting for the release of

American hostages, not appeasing Islamist dictators.

All of us pray fervently for the swift and safe release of all of the hostages. And yet, even in the darkness of an Iranian prison cell, God is sovereign. Since he began his sentence, Pastor Saeed has led dozens of fellow prisoners and even some of his captors to Christ.

leader!!

* * *

As I write this today, I'm campaigning for president. Our campaign is enjoying enormous momentum; I could not be more encouraged.

We need strong leadership. Principled, constitutional leadership.

If I am elected president, let me tell you what I intend to do on the very first day in office:

The first thing I intend to do is rescind every single illegal and unconstitutional action taken by President Obama.

The second thing I intend to do is instruct the Department of Justice to open an investigation into Planned Parenthood and the horrible videos that have emerged and exposed them, and to prosecute any and all criminal violations by that organization. The administration of justice should be blind to party and ideology; the only allegiance of the Department of Justice should be to the laws and Constitution of the United States.

gosh!!
Det Thik Drs.!!

The third thing I intend to do is to instruct the Department of Justice, and the IRS, and every other federal agency, that the persecution of religious liberty ends today. That means that our servicemen and women will be able to pray and worship God, and their commanding officer has nothing to say about it. That means that the Little Sisters of the Poor—a Catholic charity against which the Obama administration is currently litigating to try to force the nuns to pay for abortion-inducing drugs—will have the case against them dismissed.

+ Nurses·
kill 'em!
lie!

The fourth thing I intend to do is to rip to shreds Obama's catastrophic Iranian nuclear deal. The single greatest national security threat facing America is the threat of a nuclear Iran—we should not be sending over $100 billion to a theocratic zealot like the Ayatollah Khamenei,

Jewish sycophant·

who pledges "death to America"—and if I am president, under no circumstances will Iran be allowed to acquire nuclear weapons.

The fifth thing I intend to do is begin the process of moving the American embassy in Israel to Jerusalem, the once and eternal capital of Israel.

All of that is on day one. It is an example of how quickly things can change. The Left, and the media (who are in cahoots), try to convince us that nothing can change. They want us to give up. But strong presidential leadership, backed by the American people, can usher in dramatic change. In the days that follow, as president I intend to do the following:

Go to Congress and repeal every word of Obamacare. In its place, we will pass commonsense health care reform that makes health insurance personal, portable, and affordable, and keeps government from getting between our doctors and us.

Instruct the Department of Education—which should be abolished—that Common Core ends today. Education is too important to be dictated by unelected bureaucrats in Washington; it should be controlled at the state or local level, where we parents have direct control over our children's education.

Expand school choice—the civil rights issue of the twenty-first century—so that every child, regardless of race, ethnicity, income, or zip code, has a right to access an excellent education.

Rebuild our military, and honor the commitments made to our soldiers, sailors, airmen, and marines. Peace through strength should always be our goal, but we must remember that we can't have the first without the second. If we are committed to peace, we need an equally profound commitment to maintaining America's strength.

Reform the VA to give our veterans the right to choose their own doctors at whatever hospital they wish, and protect the right of our servicemen and women to keep and bear arms and protect themselves.

Stand up and defeat radical Islamic terrorism. Confront it by its name. Utterly destroy ISIS, which is the face of evil, crucifying Christians, beheading children, and working to establish an Islamic caliphate to spread their theocratic hate. And as commander in chief, make clear to jihadist militants across the globe, "If you go and join ISIS, if you take up arms and wage jihad against America, trying to kill innocent men and women, you are signing your death warrant."

Finally, finally, finally secure the borders and end sanctuary cities. Put an end to the Obama administration's indefensible practice of releasing violent criminal illegal aliens, and pass Kate's Law, ensuring that fewer violent criminals go free.

Take on the EPA, and the CFPB (Consumer Financial Protection Bureau), and the alphabet soup of federal agencies that are strangling small businesses and killing jobs. Unchain booming economic growth, so that young people coming out of school once again have two, three, four job offers and a brighter economic future.

Unleash an American energy renaissance, allowing America finally to become energy self-sufficient and ushering in millions of high-paying jobs. Stopping the Obama administration's war on coal and crushing regulatory assault will revitalize manufacturing across America, enabling us to bring back millions of jobs from foreign nations like China, based not on low-cost labor, but on abundant God-given low-cost energy.

And work with Congress to pass fundamental tax reform, passing a simple flat tax. Where all Americans can fill out their taxes on a postcard. And when we do that, we should abolish the IRS.

This is a bold, aggressive agenda. And yet it's simple common sense. Return to the free-market values and constitutional liberties that built America. Live within our means. Don't bankrupt our kids and grandkids. Follow the Constitution.

How can we get it done? Ecclesiastes 1:9 tells us "there is nothing new under the sun." And I believe where we are today is very much like the late 1970s.

The same failed economic policies. The same misery, stagnation, and malaise. The same feckless and naïve foreign policy. Indeed, the very same countries—Russia and Iran—openly laughing at and mocking the president of the United States.

Why does that analogy give me so much hope and optimism? Because we know how that story ended. Millions of men and women rose up and became the Reagan Revolution.

And it didn't come from Washington. Washington *despised* Ronald Reagan. (Remember, Reagan had primaried Gerald Ford in 1976. You want to incense the Republican establishment? Come within an inch of defeating the incumbent Republican president in a primary.) It came from the American people—from people just like you and me—and it turned the country around. We went from misery and stagnation to booming economic growth. To millions being lifted from poverty into prosperity and the American dream. We went from our hostages languishing in Iran, to winning the Cold War and tearing the Berlin Wall to the ground.

And the same thing is happening today. When we launched our campaign for president at Liberty University (the largest Christian university in the world), the mainstream media scoffed. The *New York Times* opined, Cruz has almost "no chance" to win because the GOP "despises" him.

I've often joked, "I kinda thought that was the whole point of the campaign!"

If you think Washington is doing great, that we need to keep going in the same direction and just fiddle about the edges, then I ain't your guy. But if you think Washington is profoundly broken, that there is bipartisan corruption of career politicians in *both parties* who get in bed with lobbyists and special interests and who grow and grow government, and that we need to bring power out of Washington and back to *we the people* . . . that is what this campaign is all about.

And the support has been incredible. From the grassroots. From the people.

In the first two quarters of the campaign, out of seventeen Republican candidates for president, our campaign *raised more hard money than that of any other Republican candidate*. Over $14.3 million, from all fifty states. Our average contribution was sixty-eight dollars.

To date, we've received more than 275,000 contributions, from people all over the country going to www.tedcruz.org.

Signing up, volunteering, contributing. As of September 2015, we have financial supporters in over 55 percent of the zip codes in America.

And we're seeing the old Reagan coalition coming together. Conservatives, evangelicals, libertarians, young people, Hispanics, African Americans, women, Reagan Democrats.

No other candidate has the grassroots team we have put together . . . in Iowa, New Hampshire, South Carolina, Nevada, and all across the South—the so-called SEC primary states that are voting on Super Tuesday.

If you agree with my father's message, that our country is in crisis, that we must change direction *now,* then join us. The only force powerful enough to defeat the Washington cartel is *we the people.*

We need revival. We need awakening. And it is happening all across America. If you wonder why our government is daily assaulting life, and marriage, and religious liberty, why we've abandoned Israel and aided and abetted the rise of radical Islamic terrorism (going so far as President Obama's working to send more than $100 billion to Iran's Ayatollah Khamenei), the answer is simple. In 2012, 54 million evangelical Christians stayed home. And millions more Reagan Democrats—blue-collar Catholics—stayed home as well.

If our nation's leaders are elected by unbelievers, is it any wonder that they do not reflect our values?

I tell you this: we will stay home no longer.

If the body of Christ arises, if Christians simply show up and vote biblical values, we can restore our nation.

Imagine, in 2016, if just 44 million evangelicals stayed home. Now, let me be clear: that would be a miserable failure. It would mean we failed to reach and motivate 44 million Christians to take a stand. But even so, if just an additional 10 million evangelicals showed up, the election would be over.

We wouldn't be waiting up at 2 a.m. to see the results in Ohio or

Florida. Instead, they would call the election at 8:45 p.m., because 10 million more Christians showing up is all it takes.

That is our task. To do it together. For pastors to take the lead, to reawaken the Black Robe Regiment and call upon Christians to stand for truth.

It is a time for truth. It is a time for action.

It is our time to preserve the last best hope of mankind, to restore that shining city on a hill that is the United States of America.

From our first days, God's providential blessing has been on our nation, and I'm convinced *God isn't done with America*. Brighter days are still ahead, if only we stand and act in accordance with our faith.

—TED CRUZ

APPENDIX 1

TEN PLANKS OF THE COMMUNIST MANIFESTO

In 1848, German philosophers Karl Marx and Friedrich Engels wrote a political pamphlet they called "The Manifesto of the Communist Party." Better known today as the Communist Manifesto, the document serves as a blueprint for Communism. Over time, political theorists have derived ten objective planks that summarize Marx and Engel's flawed theory and document. Tragically, more than a few of these planks are manifested in today's federal government.

PLANK #1: ABOLITION OF PRIVATE PROPERTY
Did you know the US federal government owns almost 650 million acres of land—about 28 percent of our nation's total surface area? In fact, it owns 85 percent of the state of Nevada. The 2012 Congressional Overview of Federal Land Ownership readily admits:

> 47% of the 11 coterminous western states [is federally owned]. By contrast, the federal government owns only 4% in the other states. This western concentration has contributed to a higher degree of controversy over land ownership and use in that part of the country.[1]

But the government's voracious appetite isn't satisfied. In the 2005 *Kelo v. City of London* ruling, the Supreme Court expanded the interpretation of eminent domain, allowing the government to seize citizens' properties outside traditional depressed areas. Today, property can be seized any time the state deems its use for the public good, including for private shopping malls and sports complexes.

Through Fannie Mae and Freddie Mac, the government also purchases home mortgages on the secondary market and can seize properties when loans become delinquent.

PLANK #2: A HEAVY PROGRESSIVE OR GRADUATED INCOME TAX
When Ronald Reagan was elected president in the taxpayer revolt of 1980, the marginal tax rate had reached 70 percent. By the end of his second term, the top tax rate had plummeted to 28 percent. At the conclusion of President Bill Clinton's presidency, the rates had risen to 39 percent. With the imposition of Obamacare, taxes will only increase.

At the same time, the US corporate tax rate is now the highest in the world at 39.2 percent, higher than France, Denmark, and even Sweden.

PLANK #3: ABOLITION OF ALL RIGHTS OF INHERITANCE
In a 2012 article for TheBlaze, Tiffany Gabbay wrote:

> What was most ironic about Marx's desire to abolish inheritance was that, if he had his way, citizens would not own anything of value to bequeath upon death in the first place. Nonetheless, his odd and arguably redundant tenet has worked its way into the American landscape via the estate tax.[2]

Think about it: the government taxes the items we accumulate and then taxes them *again* when we bequeath them to our loved ones when we die. The higher the death tax, the less motivated we are to accumulate savings and pass them on to our heirs.

PLANK #4: CONFISCATION OF THE PROPERTY OF ALL EMIGRANTS AND REBELS
The Second Amendment reads, "A well regulated Militia, being necessary to the security of a free State, the right of the people to keep and bear Arms, shall not be infringed." The Communist Manifesto advocates the opposite. According to this plank, anyone the government determines is an emigrant (foreigner) or rebel is fair game for arbitrary property confiscation by the government.

Before the Soviet government confiscated the property of their people, they first confiscated their guns. We cannot allow the US government to violate our Second Amendment rights, which could easily lead to the forfeiture of the rest of what lawfully belongs to us.

PLANK #5: CENTRALIZATION OF CREDIT

In 1913, the Federal Reserve Act of Congress created a national bank, which we call the Federal Reserve. The "Fed" sets our monetary policy and is supposed to combat inflation by raising or lowering interest rates.

Probably the greatest danger of the Fed's powers is their ability to print money at their discretion. The *Wall Street Journal's* Stephen Moore recently commented:

> One of the fundamental problems with the U.S. economy right now is the Federal Reserve thinks the answer to all our economic problems is printing money. We haven't created new jobs from all of this printing of money, but what we have produced is inflation in prices.[3]

PLANK #6: CENTRALIZATION OF THE MEANS OF COMMUNICATION AND TRANSPORTATION

On February 26, 2015, the Federal Communications Commission promulgated its new net neutrality regulations, under the heavy hand of the Obama administration. Acting directly contrary to federal law, the FCC has decreed that Internet service providers (ISPs) will be treated like public utilities. Previously, the Internet had grown up free of the heavy hand of regulators; now, under the Obama FCC, Washington bureaucrats are declaring for themselves the power to impose billions in taxes, set prices, regulate terms of service, and stifle innovation.

Likewise, in transportation we have the heavily subsidized AMTRAK passenger train monopoly. Instead of allowing market forces to determine pricing and quality, the US government funds this money pit. The result? An inferior-quality, overpriced passenger train system with poor service that runs on time. Occasionally.

PLANK #7: GOVERNMENT OWNERSHIP OF FACTORIES

Market corrections and recessions tend to weed out bloated businesses, making room for newer and more dynamic companies to take root and grow. For years, the auto industry has stood out as the poster child of bloated, underperforming businesses that need a fundamental overhaul.

So, when the Great Recession tightened its grip on the economy in 2009, President Obama and the US government began bailing out the auto industry. General Motors, for example, received a total of $49.5 billion in bailout funds, giving the government a stake in its business. Five year later, who benefited most? General Motors, to the tune of $22 billion. The American taxpayers, however, lost $10.5 billion on the deal, according to CNN in a 2014 report. How did that happen? Uncle Sam decided to purchase GM stock instead of giving it a loan and weighing it down with additional debt. The CNN article explains: "Although GM has been very profitable since 2009, its stock price never rose to a level that let Treasury to recoup that investment."[4]

Just as troubling, Tiffany Gabbay asks, "How [can] government . . . fairly regulate its own business?"[5] Regulating businesses in which it has invested a generous sum cannot avoid accusations of favoritism and corruption.

PLANK #8: EQUAL OBLIGATION OF ALL TO WORK

Labor unions and the US government have long partnered together to control wages. Union bosses largely support Democratic candidates for election, who then support the union bosses. The result is unions that focus only on preserving the power of the bosses.

Affirmative Action laws mandate that employers maintain quotas comprising women, minorities, and people with disabilities. However, by establishing these mandates, business may be forced by law to discriminate. And hiring and firing become more and more burdensome.

PLANK #9: COMBINATION OF AGRICULTURE WITH MANUFACTURING INDUSTRIES

Billions in federal agricultural subsidies work against a market-driven economy and impose billions more on consumers and taxpayers.

We're also seeing the combination of agriculture with manufacturing industries taking place. Apparently the goal of this plank was to reduce the number of family farms so the government could more readily control the production of food. If that's true, then this plank is rapidly becoming reality.

PLANK #10: FREE EDUCATION FOR ALL CHILDREN IN GOVERNMENT SCHOOLS

The government's intrusion into our schools through Common Core is a dangerous precedent (see chapter 11). Furthermore, the Department of Education—which should be abolished and left to the states—usurps the states' and local school districts' authority to educate students consistent with the values and standards of each community.

THOMAS JEFFERSON'S LETTER TO THE DANBURY BAPTIST ASSOCIATION

The address of the Danbury Baptists Association in the state of Connecticut, assembled October 7, 1801.

To Thomas Jefferson, Esq., President of the United States of America

Sir,

Among the many million in America and Europe who rejoice in your election to office; we embrace the first opportunity which we have enjoyed in our collective capacity, since your inauguration, to express our great satisfaction, in your appointment to the chief magistracy in the United States: And though our mode of expression may be less courtly and pompous than what many others clothe their addresses with, we beg you, sir, to believe that none are more sincere.

Our sentiments are uniformly on the side of religious liberty—that religion is at all times and places a matter between God and individuals—that no man ought to suffer in name, person, or effects on account of his religious opinions—that the legitimate power of civil government extends no further than to punish the man who works ill to his neighbors; But, sir, our constitution of government is not specific. Our ancient charter together with the law made coincident therewith, were adopted as the basis of our government, at the time of our revolution; and such had been our laws and usages, and such still are; that religion is considered as the first object of legislation;

and therefore what religious privileges we enjoy (as a minor part of the state) we enjoy as favors granted, and not as inalienable rights; and these favors we receive at the expense of such degrading acknowledgements as are inconsistent with the rights of freemen. It is not to be wondered at therefore; if those who seek after power and gain under the pretense of government and religion should reproach their fellow men—should reproach their order magistrate, as a enemy of religion, law, and good order, because he will not, dare not, assume the prerogatives of Jehovah and make laws to govern the kingdom of Christ.

Sir, we are sensible that the president of the United States is not the national legislator, and also sensible that the national government cannot destroy the laws of each state; but our hopes are strong that the sentiments of our beloved president, which have had such genial effect already, like the radiant beams of the sun, will shine and prevail through all these states and all the world, till hierarchy and tyranny be destroyed from the earth. Sir, when we reflect on your past services, and see a glow of philanthropy and good will shining forth in a course of more than thirty years we have reason to believe that America's God has raised you up to fill the chair of state out of that goodwill which he bears to the millions which you preside over. May God strengthen you for your arduous task which providence and the voice of the people have called you to sustain and support you enjoy administration against all the predetermined opposition of those who wish to raise to wealth and importance on the poverty and subjection of the people.

And may the Lord preserve you safe from every evil and bring you at last to his heavenly kingdom through Jesus Christ our Glorious Mediator.

Signed in behalf of the association,
Neh'h Dodge
Eph'm Robbins
Stephen S. Nelson

PRESIDENT THOMAS JEFFERSON'S RESPONSE TO THE DANBURY BAPTISTS:

To messers. Nehemiah Dodge, Ephraim Robbins, & Stephen S. Nelson, a committee of the Danbury Baptist association in the state of Connecticut.

Gentlemen

The affectionate sentiments of esteem and approbation which you are so good as to express towards me, on behalf of the Danbury Baptist association, give me the highest satisfaction. My duties dictate a faithful and zealous pursuit of the interests of my constituents, & in proportion as they are persuaded of my fidelity to those duties, the discharge of them becomes more and more pleasing.

Believing with you that religion is a matter which lies solely between Man & his God, that he owes account to none other for his faith or his worship, that the legitimate powers of government reach actions only, & not opinions, I contemplate with sovereign reverence that act of the whole American people which declared that their legislature should "make no law respecting an establishment of religion, or prohibiting the free exercise thereof," thus building a wall of separation between Church & State. Adhering to this expression of the supreme will of the nation in behalf of the rights of conscience, I shall see with sincere satisfaction the progress of those sentiments which tend to restore to man all his natural rights, convinced he has no natural right in opposition to his social duties.

I reciprocate your kind prayers for the protection & blessing of the common father and creator of man, and tender you for yourselves & your religious association, assurances of my high respect & esteem.

Th Jefferson, Jan. 1. 1802

To read this letter online as well as David Barton's commentary on the separation of church and state, go to Wallbuilders.com.

JONAS CLARK SERMON PREACHED BEFORE THE BATTLE OF LEXINGTON

Following is an abridged transcript of the sermon Rev. Jonas Clark preached on the heels of the Battle of Lexington, which was then distributed throughout New England. Reverend Clark's personal account of the Battles of Lexington and Concord follow the sermon. The spellings and stylings from the original document have been unchanged. To read this sermon and battle account in their entirety, go to Wallbuilders.com.

The fate of Blood-thirsty Oppressors, and GOD'S

Tender Care of his distressed People.

A

S E R M O N,

PREACHED AT LEXINGTON,

April 19, 1776.

To commemorate the MURDER, BLOOD-SHED and *Commencement of Hostilities*, between *Great-Britain* and *America*, in that Town, by a Brigade of Troops of George III, under Command of *Lieutenant-Colonel* SMITH, on the Nineteenth of April, 1775.

A BRIEF NARRATIVE of the principal Transactions of that Day.

By JONAS CLARK, A.M.

PASTOR of the CHURCH IN LEXINGTON.

The fate of blood-thirsty oppressors, and GOD's care of his distressed people.
JOEL, III. 19, 20, and 21.

EGYPT shall be a desolation, and EDOM shall be a desolate wilderness, for the violence against the children of Judah, because they have shed INNOCENT BLOOD in their land. But JUDAH shall dwell for ever, and JERUSALEM from generation to generation. For I will cleanse their blood that I have not cleansed; for the LORD dwelleth in Zion.
Next to the acknowledgement of the existence of a Deity, there is no one principle of greater importance in religion, than a realizing belief of the divine government and providence, to realize that God is Governor among the nations, that his government is wise and just, and that all our times and changes are in his hands, and at his disposal, will have the happiest tendency to excite the most grateful acknowledgements of his goodness in prosperity, the most cordial resignation to his paternal discipline in adversity, and the most placid composure and equanimity of mind in all the changing scenes of life . . .

This principle and these sentiments therefore, being of so great use and importance in religion, under the various dispensations of providence, one great design of the present discourse, is to rouse and excite us to a religious acknowledgment of the hand of God, in those distressing scenes of MURDER, BLOOD-SHED and WAR, we are met to commemorate, upon this solemn occasion.

The passage before us, it is humbly conceived, is well suited to confirm our faith, to excite our trust, and encourage our hope, under such awful dispensations, as it points out the method of God's government and the course of his providence towards the enemies and oppressors of his people, and the fate of those that shed *innocent blood*; and at the same time, represents his peculiar care of his church and chosen, and the assurance they have, when under oppression, of restoration and establishment,—and that *God himself* will plead their cause and both *cleanse* and *avenge* their *innocent blood*. "*Egypt* shall be a desolation, and *Edom* shall be a desolate wilderness, for the *violence* against the *children of Judah*, because they have shed INNOCENT BLOOD *in their land*. But *Judah* shall dwell forever, and *Jerusalem* from generation to generation. For *I will cleanse their blood*, that I have not cleansed; for the LORD dwelleth in Zion." . . .

In such public calamities, it is true, it often comes to pass, that as individuals, the innocent are involved and suffer with the guilty; and sometimes the innocent alone. But however unjust, or cruel the oppressor, and those that thirst for blood may be, in contriving and carrying into execution their wicked, oppressive, or *bloody* designs, they are no other than instruments in providence and the rod in the hand of the great Governor of the world, for the reproof and correction of his people. These things happen not by accident, or chance, but by the direction, or permission of that God, who is righteous in all his ways and holy in all his works. When Israel sinned and did evil in the sight of the LORD, it is said, "the anger of the LORD was hot against Israel, and he delivered them into the hands of spoilers that spoiled them, and he sold them into the hands of their enemies round about, and they were greatly distressed." Hence also the *Assyrian King* is expressly called "*the rod of God's anger*," for the correction of his people. And thus *Egypt* and *Edom*, in the prophecy before us, in committing violence upon the children of *Judah* and in shedding *innocent blood* in their land, are held up to view as the rod in God's hand, for the correction, reproof and instruction of his people. Agreeably, this is the language of a just and faithful God, in such dispensations, "*hear ye the rod, and who hath appointed it.*" . . .

Secondly, To observe the fate of oppressors, and the sentence of heaven against those that do violence to God's people and shed *innocent blood* in their land. *Egypt shall be a desolation, and Edom shall be a desolate wilderness, for the violence against the children of Judah, because they have shed innocent blood in their land.*

However just it may be in God to correct his people, and whatever right is ascribed to him of improving the wicked, as the rod in his hand to correct, or the sword to punish them; yet this alters not the nature of their oppressive designs, neither does it abate their guilt, or alleviate their crime, in these measures of injustice, violence or cruelty, by which the people of God are distressed . . .

The LORD is a God, that loveth righteousness and hateth iniquity, in whatever shape, or character it appears. Injustice, oppression and violence (much less the shedding of innocent blood) shall not pass unnoticed, by the just Governor of the world. Sooner, or later, a just recompence will be made upon such workers of iniquity. —Yea, though hand join in hand, in measures of oppression and violence, against God's people; and though their avarice, ambition, and lawless thirst for power and domination, may carry them on, 'till their steps shall be marked with *innocent blood*; yet certain it is, they shall not, finally, go unpunished . . .

Thirdly, To observe, in the prophecy before us, the peculiar care God takes of his church and people, and the assurance they have, even when actually suffering violence and under the cruel hand of oppression, of redemption, restoration and establishment; and that God himself will plead their cause, and both *cleanse* and *avenge* their innocent blood. Nothing can be more directly expressive of this sentiment, or a firmer ground of assurance, for the confirmation of the faith and hope of God's chosen people in the belief of it, than the promise and prophecy, concerning Judah and Jerusalem in the text . . .

Blood is said to be cleansed, or avenged, when justice hath taken place, and the murderer is punished. God may be said to cleanse the innocent blood, which may have been shed among his people, by the sword of oppressors, or enemies, when in providence he undertakes for them, avenges their blood upon them that slew them, and reduces them to reason or ruin.

The sword is an appeal to heaven, —when therefore, the arms of a people are eventually successful, or by the immediate interposition of providence, their enemies and oppressors are subdued or destroyed. — When a people are reinstated in peace, upon equitable terms, and established in the enjoyment of all their just rights and liberties, both civil and sacred: then may it be said, that the Lord hath cleansed their innocent blood, and then will it be manifestly evident, that their God is with them and dwelleth in the midst of them . . .

Nothing is more evident from history and experience, than God's care of his people, and the wisdom of his providence, in causing the violence and oppression of their enemies, to operate for their advantage, and promote their more speedy deliverance. This appears too plain, from various instances, to admit of dispute . . .

The *children of Israel* would not have been, so early, persuaded to have left the gardens of *Egypt* or the fertile fields of the land of Goshen, and in the face of every danger, attempted to free themselves from the *Egyptian yoke*, had not their burdens been increased to an unreasonable degree, by the violence and cruelty of those that oppressed them, in that house of *bondage*. And *Pharaoh and his armies* would never have met with that disgraceful defeat, and awful destruction, which overtook them in the *red sea*, had they not been infatuated to pursue their measures of oppression and violence, even after it was evident that their cause was desperate, and that God was against them . . .

Britons would never have resisted their kings, and flown to arms, in defence of their invaluable rights and liberties, had they not felt the weight of the iron rod of oppression and tyranny, and seen their danger and absolute necessity of such resistance to prevent the total deprivation, of all they held dear and sacred, as *Freemen, Christians* and a *free People* . . .

Our *fathers* would never have forsook their native land, delightsome habitations and fair possessions, and in the face of almost every danger and distress, sought a safe retreat, for the enjoyment of religious and civil liberty, among savage beasts and more savage men in the *inhospitable wilds of America*; had they not been drove from thence, by the violence and cruelty of persecutors and oppressors, in church and state . . .

But, alas! —Ill-judged counsels! —Ill-fated measures of *Britain*, and the *British administration*, with respect to *America*, have broken in upon the pleasing scene, and fatally destroyed the happy prospects of both *Britain* and *America*! . . .

Through the crafty insinuations, false representations and diabolical counsels, of the enemies of God's people and the common rights of mankind, in *America* and *Britain*, *acts of oppression* are made by the *Parliament of England*, in which we are not represented, which deeply affect our most valuable privileges. In open violation of our *chartered* rights, these acts of unrighteousness and oppression, are attempted to be carried into execution, in these *colonies* . . . And as one of the natural consequences of *standing armies* being stationed in populous cities, for such execrable purposes, many of the inhabitants of *Boston* are insulted. At length, under pretence of ill treatment, the streets of that once flourishing city, are stained with the *innocent blood* of a number of our brethren, wantonly or cruelly slain, by those sons of oppression and violence! . . .

New acts are passed to distress and enslave us. The lust of domination appears no longer in disguise, but with open face—The *starving Port-Bill* comes forth—[General Thomas] *Gage* arrives with his forces by sea and land, to carry it into execution, with vigour and severity. — And to complete the scene, and at once, to make thorough work of oppression and tyranny, immediately follow *the Bills*, that subvert the constitution, vacate our *charter*, abridge us of the right of trial by juries of the vicinity, in divers specified capital cases, and expose us to be seized, contrary to the laws of the land, and carried to *England* to be tried for our lives! . . .

At length, on the night of the eighteenth of April, 1775, the alarm is given of the hostile designs of the troops. The *militia of this town* are called together, to consult and prepare for whatever might be necessary, or in their power, for their own, and the common safety; though without the least design of commencing hostilities, upon these *avowed* enemies and oppressors of their country. In the mean time, under cover of the darkness, a brigade of these instruments of violence and tyranny, make their approach, and with a quick and silent march, on the morning of the nineteenth, they enter this town. And this is the place where the fatal scene begins! —They approach with the morning's light; and more like *murders* and *cut-throats*, than the troops of a *Christian king*, without provocation, without warning, when no war was proclaimed, they draw the *sword of violence*, upon the inhabitants of this town, and with a *cruelty* and *barbarity*, which would have made the most hardened savage blush, they *shed* INNOCENT BLOOD! — But, O *my GOD!* —How shall I speak! —or how describe the distress, the *horror* of that *awful morn*, that *gloomy day*! —*Yonder field* can witness the *innocent blood* of our *brethren slain*! —And from thence does *their blood* cry unto God for vengeance from the ground! —There the tender father bled, and there the beloved son! —There the hoary head, and there the blooming youth! —And there the man in his full strength, with the man of years! —*They bleed—they die*, not by the sword of an open enemy (with whom war is proclaimed) in the field of battle; but by the hand of those that delight in spoil, and *lurk privily that they may shed innocent blood*! —But they bleed, they die, not in their own cause only; but in the cause of this whole people—in the cause of God, their country and posterity. —And they have not bled, they shall not bleed in vain. —Surely there is one that avengeth, and that will plead the cause of the injured and oppressed; and in his own way and time, will both *cleanse and avenge their innocent blood*. —And the names of *Munroe, Parker*, and others, that fell victims to the rage of *blood-thirsty* oppressors, on that gloomy morning, shall be had in grateful remembrance, by the people of this land, and transmitted to posterity, with honour and respect, throughout all generations.

But who shall comfort the distressed relatives, —the mourning widows, the fatherless children, the weeping parents, or the afflicted friends? —May the consolations of that God, who hath hitherto supported them, be still their support! —Upon him may they still derive all needed supplies, in things spiritual and temporal; and yet more and more experience the faithfulness and truth, the mercy and goodness, of the God of all comfort.

May those that were wounded, and have since experienced the tender mercy of that God, "who woundeth, and healeth, and bindeth up." Be deeply impressed with a sense of his distinguishing goodness, that their lives were spared, while others were taken; and be persuaded, more entirely than ever, to devote them to God, his service and glory . . .

But this is not by us alone, that this day is to be noticed. —This *ever memorable day* is full of importance to all around—to this whole land and nation; and big with the fate of *Great Britain* and *America*. —From this *remarkable day* will an important *era* begin for both *America* and *Britain*. And from the *nineteenth of April*, 1775, we may venture to predict, will be dated, in future history, THE LIBERTY or SLAVERY of the AMERICAN WORLD, according as a sovereign God shall see fit to smile, or frown upon the interesting cause, in which we are engaged.

May that God, who is a God of righteousness and salvation, still appear for us, go forth with our armies, tread down our enemies, and *cleanse* and avenge our *innocent blood*. And may we be prepared, by a general repentance and thorough reformation, for his gracious and powerful interposition in our behalf; and then may we see the displays of his power and glory for our salvation. Which God of his infinite mercy grant, for his mercy's sake in Christ Jesus.

AMEN.

JONAS CLARKE'S ABRIDGED ACCOUNT OF THE BATTLES OF LEXINGTON AND CONCORD:

A NARRATIVE

As it was not confident with the limits of a single discourse, to give a full account of the particulars of this most savage *and murderous affair; the following* plain *and* faithful narrative of facts, *as they appeared to us in this place, may be matter of satisfaction.*

On the evening of the eighteenth of April, 1775, we received two messages; the first verbal, the other *by express, in writing,* from the *committee of safety,* who were then sitting in the westerly part of *Cambridge,* directed to the Honorable JOHN HANCOCK, Esq; (who, with the Honorable SAMUEL ADAMS, Esq; was then providentially with us) informing, "that *eight* or *nine officers* of the *king's troops* were seen, just before night, passing the road towards *Lexington,* in a *musing, contemplative* posture; and it was suspected they were out upon some evil design."

As both these gentlemen had been frequently and even *publicly,* threatened, by the enemies of *this people,* both in England and America, with the *vengeance* of the *British administration:*—And as Mr. *Hancock* in particular had been, more than once, *personally insulted,* by some officers of the troops, in Boston; it was not without some just grounds supposed, that under cover of the darkness, *sudden arrest,* if not *assassination* might be attempted, by these *instruments of tyranny!*

To prevent any thing of this kind, *ten* or *twelve* men were immediately collected, in arms, to guard my house, through the night.

In the mean time, said *officers* passed through this town, on the road towards *Concord:* It was therefore thought expedient to watch their motions, and if possible make some discovery of their intentions. Accordingly, about 10 o'clock in the evening, three men, on horses, were dispatched for this purpose. As they were *peaceably* passing the road towards *Concord,* in the borders of *Lincoln,* they were suddenly stopped by *said officers*, who rode up to them, and putting pistols to their breasts and seizing their horses bridles, *swore, if they stirred another step, they should be all dead men!*—The officers detained them several hours, as prisoners, examined, searched, abused and insulted them; and in their hasty return (supposing themselves discovered) they left them in Lexington.—Said officers also took into custody, abused and *threatened with their lives* several other persons; some of whom they met peaceably passing on the road, others even at the doors of their dwellings, without the least provocation, on the part of the inhabitants, or so much as a question asked by them.

Between the hours of *twelve* and *one*, on the morning of the NINETEENTH OF APRIL, we received intelligence, by express, from the Honorable JOSEPH WARREN Esq; at *Boston*, "that a large body of the *king's troops* (supposed to be a brigade of about 12 or 1500) were embarked in boats from *Boston*, and gone over to land on *Lechmere's-Point* (so called) in *Cambridge*: And that it was shrewdly suspected, that they were ordered to seize and destroy the *stores, belonging to the colony, then deposited at Concord*," in consequence of *General Gage's unjustifiable seizure of the provincial magazine of powder at Medford*, and other *colony stores* in several other places.

Upon this intelligence, as also upon information of the conduct of the officers as above-mentioned, the *militia* of this town were alarmed, and ordered to meet on the usual place of parade; not with any design of *commencing hostilities* upon the *king's troops*, but to consult what might be done for our own and the people's safety: And also to be ready for whatever service providence might call us out to, upon this alarming occasion, in case *overt-acts* of *violence*, or *open hostilities* should be committed by this *mercenary band of armed and blood-thirsty oppressors*.

About the same time, two persons were sent express to *Cambridge*, if possible, to gain intelligence of the motions of the troops, and what rout they took.

The *militia* met according to order; and waited the return of the messengers, that they might order their measures as occasion should require. Between 3 and 4 o'clock, one of the expresses returned, informing, that there was no appearance of the troops, on the roads, either from *Cambridge* or *Charlestown*; and that it was supposed that the *movements in the army* the evening before, were only a feint to alarm the people. Upon this, therefore, the *militia company* were dismissed for the present, but with orders to be within call of the drum,—waiting the return of the other messenger, who was expected in about an hour, or sooner, if any discovery should be made of the motions of the troops.—But he was prevented by their silent and sudden arrival at the place where he was, waiting for intelligence. So that, after all this precaution, we had no notice of their approach, 'till the *brigade was actually in the town*, and upon a quick march within about a mile and a quarter of the *meeting house* and *place of parade.*

However, the commanding officer though best to call the company together,—not with any design of opposing so superior a force, *much less of commencing hostilities*; but only with a view to determine what to do, when and where to meet, and to dismiss and disperse.

Accordingly, about half an hour after four o'clock, *alarm guns were fired, and the drums beat to arms*; and the *militia* were collecting together.—Some, to the number of about 50, or 60, or possibly more, were on the parade, others were coming towards it.—In the mean time, the troops, having thus stolen a march upon us, and to prevent any intelligence of their approach, having seized and held prisoners several persons whom they met *unarmed* upon the road, seemed to come *determined for MURDER* and *BLOODSHED*; and that whether provoked to it, or not!—When within about half a quarter of a mile of the *meeting-house*, they halted, and the command was given to *prime* and *load*; which being done, they marched on 'till they came up to the east end of said meeting-house, in sight of our *militia* (collecting as aforesaid) who were about 12, or 13 rods distant.—Immediately upon their appearing *so suddenly*, and *so nigh*, Capt. *Parker*, who commanded the *militia company*, ordered the men to disperse, and take care of themselves; and *not to fire.*—Upon this, our men dispersed;—but, many of them, not so speedily as they might have done, not having the most distant idea of such *brutal barbarity* and more than *savage CRUELTY*, from the troops of a *British KING*, as they immediately experienced!—For, no sooner did they come in sight of our company, but one of them, supposed to be an officer of rank, was heard to say to the troops, *"Damn them; we will have them!"*—Upon which the troops shouted aloud, huzza'd, and rushed furiously towards our men.—About the same time, three officers (supposed to be Col. Smith, Major Pitcairn and another officer) advanced, on horse back, to the front of the body, and coming within 5 or 6 rods of the *militia*, one of them cried out, *"ye villains, ye Rebels, disperse; Damn you, disperse!"*—or words to this effect. One of them (whether the same, or not, is not easily determined) said, *"Lay down your arms; Damn you, why don't you lay down your arms!"*—The second of these officers, about this time, fired a pistol towards the *militia*, as they were dispersing.—The foremost, who was within a few yards of our men, brandishing his sword, and then pointing towards them, with a loud voice said, to the troops, "Fire!—By God, fire!"—which was instantly followed by a discharge of arms from the said troops, succeeded by a very heavy and close fire upon our party, dispersing, so long as any of them were within reach.— *Eight were left dead upon the ground! Ten were wounded.*—The rest of the company, through divine goodness, were (to a miracle) preserved unhurt in this *murderous* action!—

As to the question, 'Who fired first?'—if it can be a question with any; we may observe, that though General Gage hath been pleased to tell the world, in his account of this *savage transaction*, "that the troops were fired upon by *the rebels* out of the *meeting-house*, and the *neighbouring houses*, as well as by those that were in the field; and that the troops *only returned the fire, and passed on their way to Concord*;"— yet nothing can be more certain than the contrary, and nothing more *false, weak,* or *wicked,* than such a representation.

To say nothing of the absurdity of the supposition, 'that 50, 60, or even 70 men, should, in the *open field, commence hostilities* with 12, or 1500, of the best troops of *Britain*, nor of the *known* determination of this small party of Americans, upon no consideration whatever, to begin the scene of blood —*A cloud of witnesses*, whose veracity cannot be justly disputed, *upon oath* have declared, in the most express and positive terms, '*that the British troops fired first*: —And I think, we may safely add, without the least reason or provocation.—Nor was there opportunity given, for our men to have saved themselves, either by laying down their arms, or dispersing, as directed, had they been disposed to; as the command to fire upon them was given almost at the same instant, that they were ordered, by the *British officers*, to disperse, to *lay down their arms*, &c.

In short, so far from *firing first* upon the king's troops; upon the most careful enquiry, it appears, that but very few of our people fired at all; and even *they* did not fire till after being fired upon by the troops, they were wounded themselves, or saw others killed, or wounded by them, and looked upon it next to impossible for them to escape.

As to any firing from the *meeting-house*, as *Gage* represents; it is certain, that there were but *four men* in the meeting-house when the troops came up: and they were then getting some ammunition, from the town stock, and had not so much as loaded their guns (except one, who never discharged it) when the troops fired upon the *militia*. And as to the *neighbouring houses*, it is equally certain, that there was no firing from them, unless, after the dispersion of our men, some, who had fled to them for shelter, might fire from them upon the troops . . .

Having thus *vanquished the party* in *Lexington*, the troops marched on for *Concord*, to execute their orders, in destroying the stores belonging to the colony, deposited there—They met with no interruption in their march to *Concord*.—But by some means or other, the people of *Concord* had notice of their approach and designs, and were alarmed about break of day; and collecting as soon, and as many as possible, improved the time they had before the troops came upon them, to the best advantage, both for concealing and securing as many of the public stores as they could, and in preparing for defence.—By the stop of the troops at Lexington, many thousands were saved to the colony, and they were, in a great measure, frustrated in their design.

When the troops made their approach to the easterly part of the town, the provincials of *Concord* and some neighbouring towns, were collected and collecting in an advantageous post, on a hill, a little distance from the *meeting-house*, north of the road, to the number of about 150, or 200: but finding the troops to be more than three times as many, they wisely retreated, first to a hill about 80 rods further north, and then over the *north-bridge* (so called) about a mile from the town: and there they waited the coming of the *militia* of the towns adjacent, to their assistance.

In the mean time, the British detachment marched into the center of the town. A party of about 200, was ordered to take possession of said bridge, other parties were dispatched to various parts of the town, in search of public stores, while the remainder were employed in seizing and destroying, whatever they could find in the *town-house*, and other places, where stores had been lodged.—But before they had accomplished their design, they were interrupted by a discharge of arms, at *said bridge*.

It seems, that of the party above-mentioned, as ordered to take possession of the bridge, one half were marched on about two miles, in search of stores, at Col. *Barret's* and that part of the town: while the other half, consisting of towards 100 men, under Capt. *Lawrie*, were left to guard the bridge. The provincials, who were in sight of the bridge, observing the troops attempting to take up the planks of said bridge, thought it necessary to dislodge them, and gain possession of the bridge.—They accordingly marched, but with express orders not to fire, unless first fired upon by the king's troops. Upon their approach towards the bridge, Capt. *Lawrie's* party fired upon them, killed Capt. *Davis* and another man dead upon the spot, and wounded several others. Upon this our *militia* rushed on, with a spirit becoming *free-born Americans*, returned fire upon the enemy, killed 2, wounded several and drove them from the bridge, and pursued them towards the town, 'till they were covered by a reinforcement from the main body. The provincials then took post on a hill, at some distance, north of the town: and as their numbers were continually increasing, they were preparing to give the troops a *proper discharge*, on their departure from the town.

In the mean time, the king's troops collected; and having dressed their wounded, destroyed what stores they could find, and insulted and plundered a number of the inhabitants, prepared for a retreat.

"While at *Concord*, the troops disabled two 24 pounders; destroyed their 2 carriages, and seven wheels for the same, with their limbers. Sixteen wheels for brass 3 pounders, and 2 carriages with limber and wheels for two 4 pounders. They threw into the river, wells, &c. about 500 weight of ball: and stove about 60 barrels of flour; but not having time to perfect their work, one half of the flour was afterwards saved."

The troops began a hasty retreat about the middle of the day: and were no sooner out of the town, but they began to meet the effects of the just resentments of this injured people. The provincials fired upon them from various quarters, and pursued them (though without any military order) with a firmness and intrepidity, beyond what could have been expected, on the first onset, and in such a day of confusion and distress!—The fire was returned, for a time, with great fury, by the troops as they retreated, though (through divine goodness) with but little execution.—This scene continued, with but little intermission, till they returned to Lexington; when it was evident, that, having lost numbers in killed, wounded, and prisoners that fell into our hands, they began to be, not only fatigued, but greatly disheartened. And it is supposed they must have soon surrendered at discretion, had they not been reinforced.—But *Lord Percy's* arrival with another brigade, of about 1000 men, and 2 field pieces, about half a mile from Lexington *meeting-house*, towards *Cambridge*, gave them a seasonable respite.

The coming of the reinforcement, with *the canon*, (which our people were not so well acquainted with then, as they have been since) put the provincials also to a pause, for a time.—But no sooner were the *king's troops* in motion, but our men renewed the pursuit with equal, and even greater ardor and intrepidity than before, and the firing on both sides continued, with but little intermission, to the close of the day, when the troops entered *Charlestown*, where the *provincials* could not follow them, without exposing the worthy inhabitants of that *truly patriotic town*, to their rage and revenge.— That night and the next day, they were conveyed in boats, over *Charles-River* to *Boston*, glad to secure themselves, under the cover of the shipping, and by strengthening and perfecting the fortifications, at every part, against the further attacks of a justly incensed people, who, upon intelligence of the *murderous transactions* of this fatal day, were collecting in arms, round the town, in great numbers, and from every quarter.

In the retreat of the king's troops from *Concord* to *Lexington*, they ravaged and plundered, as they had opportunity, more or less, in most of the houses that were upon the road.—But after they were joined by *Piercy's brigade*, in Lexington, it seemed as if *all the little remains* of humanity had left them; and rage and revenge had taken the reins, and knew no bounds!— *Clothing, furniture, provisions, goods, plundered, broken, carried off, or destroyed!—Buildings (especially dwelling houses) abused, defaced, battered, shattered and almost ruined!—And as if this had not been enough, numbers of them doomed to the flames!—Three dwelling houses, two shops and a barn, were laid in ashes in Lexington! —Many others were set on fire, in this town, in Cambridge, &c. and must have shared the same fate, had not the close pursuit of the provincials prevented, and the flames been seasonably quenched!—Add to all this; the unarmed, the aged and infirm, who were unable to flee are inhumanly stabbed and murdered in their habitations!—Yea, even women in child-bed, with their helpless babes in their arms, do not escape the horrid alternative, of being either cruelly murdered in their beds, burnt in their habitations, or turned into the streets to perish with cold, nakedness and distress! —But I forbear—words are too insignificant to express, the horrid barbarities of that distressing day!*

Our loss, in the several actions of that day, was 49 killed, 34 wounded and 5 missing, who were taken prisoners, and have since been exchanged. The enemy's loss, according to the best accounts, in killed, wounded and missing, about 300.

As the war was thus began with *savage cruelty*, in the aggressors; so it has been carried on with the same temper and spirit, by the enemy in but too many instances. Witness the *wanton cruelty*, discovered in *burning Charlestown, Norfolk, Falmouth*, &c. But as events which have taken place since the *ever memorable nineteenth of April*, 1775, do not properly come within the compass of this narrative, they must be left for some abler pen to relate.

FINIS.

RECOMMENDED RESOURCES

BOOKS, PAMPHLETS, AND PAPERS

Baldwin, Alice. *The New England Clergy and the American Revolution* (Kindle Edition). Amazon Digital Services, Inc., 2015.

Bastiat, Frédéric. *The Classic Works of Frédéric Bastiat* (Kindle Edition). Amazon Digital Services, Inc., 2013.

Bright, Bill. *The Four Spiritual Laws.* New Life Publications, 1993. http://crustore. org/four-laws-english/.

Cato, Brutus, Centinel (pseudonyms). *The Anti-Federalist Papers* (1790).

Cruz, Ted. *A Time for Truth: Reigniting the Promise of America.* New York: Broadside Books, 2015.

Díaz-Versón, Salvador. "Communist Threat to the United States Through the Caribbean." Testimony of Salvador Díaz-Versón, May 6, 1960, http://www. latinamericanstudies.org/us-cuba/diaz-verson.htm.

Díaz-Versón, Salvador. "When Castro Became A Communist: The Impact on U.S.-Cuba Policy," http://www.latinamericanstudies.org/diaz-verson.htm.

Friedman, Milton. *Capitalism and Freedom: Fortieth Anniversary Edition.* Chicago: University of Chicago Press, 2002.

Hamilton Alexander, James Madison and John Jay. *The Federalist Papers* (1788).

Hayek, F. A. *The Road to Serfdom.* Chicago: University of Chicago Press, 1944.

Headley, Joel Tyler. *The Chaplains and Clergy of the Revolution.* New York: Charles Scribner, 1864. (Classic Reprint, Forgotten Books, 2012).

Hudson, Charles. History of the town of Lexington, Middlesex County, Massachusetts, from its first settlement to 1868, with a genealogical register of Lexington families (Kindle Edition). Ulan Press, 2012.

Jefferson, Thomas et al, *The Declaration of Independence* (1776).

Madison, James et al, *The U.S. Constitution* (1788).

Metaxas, Eric. *Bonhoeffer: Pastor, Martyr, Prophet, Spy.* Nashville: Thomas Nelson, 2011.

Smith, Adam. *The Wealth of Nations* (1776).

von Mises, Ludwig. *Socialism: An Economic and Sociological Analysis.* Ludwig von Mises Institute, 2011.

ORGANIZATIONS

Alliance Defending Freedom (http://www.adflegal.org).

The American Renewal Project (http://theamericanrenewalproject.org).

The Jefferson Gathering (http://jeffersongathering.com).

National Black Robed Regiment (http://nationalblackrobedregiment.com).

Wallbuilders (http://Wallbuilders.com).

Washington A Man Of Prayer (http://washingtonamanofprayer.com).

WND (http://wnd.com)

ACKNOWLEDGMENTS

I want to express my appreciation to Keith Urban and his team for their advice and interaction throughout the writing of this book; to our publishers, WND Books; to Geoffrey Stone, editorial director; and Thomas Freiling, vice president, for their continuous editorial support; and to Michael J. Klassen for his invaluable research assistance.

The constant encouragement that I have received from my son, Ted; my daughter, Roxana; and my niece Bibi have been a tremendous source of strength that has helped to keep me on course and focused as I tried to navigate through my extremely busy schedule and find the time to work on this manuscript. Similarly, I have been inspired by the many, many people who have encouraged me to write this book.

Finally I offer praise and thanksgiving to my Lord and Savior, Jesus Christ, and to the divine inspiration of the Holy Spirit, not only in the writing of this book, but also in guiding my daily walk. To Him be all honor, glory, and praise!

NOTES

INTRODUCTION

1. John Adams, Letter to the Officers of the First Brigade of the Third Division of the Militia of Massachusetts, October 11, 1798, in *Revolutionary Services and Civil Life of General William Hull*, ed. Maria Campbell (New York: D. Appleton, 1848), 266.

2. Sylvia Rusin, Jie Zong, and Jeanne Batalova, "Cuban Immigrants in the United States," Migration Policy Institute, April 7, 2015, http://www.migrationpolicy.org/article/cuban-immigrants-united-states.

3. Ronald Reagan, Farewell Address, January 11, 1989. Transcript available online at the website of the Miller Center, at http://millercenter.org/president/speeches/speech-3418.

4. Ronald Reagan, address to the annual meeting of the Phoenix Chamber of Commerce, March 30, 1961.

5. The Declaration of Independence, signed July 4, 1776, emphasis added. Transcript available at http://www.archives.gov/exhibits/charters/declaration_transcript.html.

CHAPTER 2: BATISTA, CASTRO, AND MY FIGHT FOR FREEDOM

1. *I Love Lucy*, episode 148 ("Lucy in the Swiss Alps"), 1951, http://www.imdb.com/title/tt0043208/quotes.

2. "Cuba Facts," Institute for Cuban and Cuban-American Studies, University of Miami, December, 2008, http://ctp.iccas.miami.edu/FACTS_Web/Cuba%20Facts%20Issue%2043%20December.htm.

3. Ibid.

4. Vahakn N. Dadrian, *The History of the Armenian Genocide: Ethnic Conflict from the Balkans to Anatolia to the Caucasus* (Providence: Berghahn Books, 1995), 372 (n5).

5. Palash, Ghosh, "How Many People Did Joseph Stalin Kill?" *International Business Times*, March 5, 2013, http://www.ibtimes.com/how-many-people-did-joseph-stalin-kill-1111789.

6. Adolf Hitler, *Hitler's Table Talk, 1941–1944: His Private Conversations*, new ed., ed. Hugh Redwald Trevor-Roper, Gerhard L. Weinberg (n.p.: Enigma, 2008), 321.

7. "Strict Gun Control To Stay," The China Post, October 23, 2009, http://www.chinapost.com.tw/taiwan/national/national-news/2009/10/23/229755/Strict-gun.htm.

8. Jung Chang and Jon Halliday, *Mao: The Unknown Story* (London: Jonathan Cape, 2005), 569.

9. Dave Hodges, "Back to the Future: What History Teaches about Gun Confiscations," *The Common Sense Show*, December 29, 2012, http://www.thecommonsenseshow.com/2012/12/29/back-to-the-future-what-history-teaches-about-gun-confiscations/.

10. Robert K. Home. *Of Planting and Planning: The Making of British Colonial Cities*. (London: Chapman and Hall, 1997), 195.

11. "(1959) The American Comandante in the Cuban Revolutionary Forces: William Morgan * (1959) EL COMANDANTE AMERICANO en las Fuerzas Armadas Revolucionarias de Cuba," May 16, 2012, TheCubanHistory.com, http://www.thecubanhistory.com/2012/05/william-morgan-a-rebel-americano-in-cuba/.

12. "Fulgencio Batista," United States History, accessed September 19, 2014, http://www.u-s-history.com/pages/h1768.html.

13. Timothy P. Wickham-Crowley, *Exploring Revolution: Essays on Latin American Insurgency and Revolutionary Theory* (London: M. E. Sharpe, 1991), 63.

CHAPTER 3: MY ESCAPE TO THE LAND OF THE FREE

1. Herbert Matthews, *New York Times*, July 1959, in Humberto Fontova, "Fidel Castro Apologizes to Gays, MSM Accepts," *Townhall.com*, September 12, 2010, http://townhall.com/columnists/humbertofontova/2010/09/12/fidel_castro_apologizes_to_gays,_msm_accepts/page/full.

2. Walter Lippmann, *Washington Post*, July 1959, at ibid.

3. *Newsweek*, April 1959, at ibid.

4. *Look* magazine, March 1959, at ibid.

5. As quoted in Eliott C. McLaughlin, "Raul Castro may join Catholic Church, he says after Pope Francis meeting," CNN, May 14, 2015, http://www.cnn.com/2015/05/10/europe/italy-raul-castro-pope-francis-meeting/index.html.

6. Speech of Senator John F. Kennedy, Cincinnati, Ohio, Democratic Dinner, on the website of the American Presidency Project, http://www.presidency.ucsb.edu/ws/index.php?pid=25660.

7. Ibid.

8. Salvador Diaz-Verson, "When Castro Became a Communist: The Impact on U.S.–Cuba Policy," Institute for U.S.–Cuba Relations Occasional Paper Series, vol. 1, no. 1, November 3, 1997, at http://www.freerepublic.com/focus/f-news/952836/posts.

9. To view some film footage of the riots, see "Rioters Sack Bogota (1948)," YouTube video, 1:16, posted by "British Pathé," April 13, 2014, https://www.youtube.com/watch?v=FFIre7C9ONo.

10. See "School Children Taught to Praise Obama," YouTube video, 2:26, from a class at the B. Bernice Young Elementary School in Burlington, NJ, filmed around June 19, 2009, posted by "Educational Revolution," September 24, 2009, https://www.youtube.com/watch?v=FO3NBqT3LBc; and FoxNews.com, "Review Ordered of Video Showing Students Singing Praises of President Obama," Fox News Politics, September 24, 2009, http://www.foxnews.com/politics/2009/09/24/review-ordered-video-showing-students-singing-praises-president-obama/.

11. Diaz-Verson, "When Castro Became a Communist."

12. See the article "The U.S. Election of 2008: Year in Review 2008," on the website of *Encyclopedia Britannica*, accessed August 19, 2015, http://www.britannica.com/topic/US-Election-of-2008-The-1501373.

CHAPTER 4: DOES COMMUNISM WORK?

1. The following story and its quotations were taken from Patricia Cohen, "A Company Copes with Backlash against the Raise That Roared," *New York Times*, July 31, 2015, http://www.nytimes.com/2015/08/02/business/a-company-copes-with-backlash-against-the-raise-that-roared.html?_r=0.

2. Lennon–McCartney, "All You Need Is Love," performed by the Beatles (London: Olympic and EMI, 1967), vinyl.

3. "The Revolution Begins Now" (transcript of a speech by Fidel Castro on January 3, 1959 at the Cospedes Park in Santiago de Cuba), at Marxists.org, https://www.marxists.org/history/cuba/archive/castro/1959/01/03.htm.

4. Taylor Tyler, "Corruption Report 2014: Somalia & North Korea Among Most Corrupt Countries in the World," HNGN (Headline & Global News), December 3, 2014, http://www.hngn.com/articles/51617/20141203/corruption-report-2014-somalia-north-korea-among-most-corrupt-countries-in-the-world.htm.

5. Oliver Arlow, "Kim Jong-il keeps $4bn 'emergency fund' in European banks," *Telegraph* (UK), March 14, 2010, http://www.telegraph.co.uk/news/worldnews/asia/northkorea/7442188/Kim-Jong-il-keeps-4bn-emergency-fund-in-European-banks.html.

6. "Kim Jong-Un Net Worth: The Luxurious Lifestyle of the Most Notorious Dictator on Earth," My First Class Life, accessed September 19, 2015, http://myfirstclasslife.com/kim-jong-un-net-worth-luxurious-lifestyle-notorious-dictator-earth/.

7. "North Korea," The World Factbook, accessed September 19, 2015, https://www.cia.gov/library/publications/the-world-factbook/geos/kn.html.

8. "Kim Jong-Un Net Worth: The Luxurious Lifestyle of the Most Notorious Dictator on Earth," My First Class Life, accessed September 19, 2015, http://myfirstclasslife.com/kim-jong-un-net-worth-luxurious-lifestyle-notorious-dictator-earth/.

9. Transparency International, Corruption Perceptions Index 2014: Results: Rankings, accessed August 19, 2015, https://www.transparency.org/cpi2014/results.

10. Dexter Roberts, "China's Communist Party Admits It Has a Big Corruption Problem," *Bloomberg*, July 10, 2014, http://www.bloomberg.com/bw/articles/2014-07-10/nepotism-corruption-rampant-in-selecting-cadres-says-chinas-communist-party.

11. Jean-Louis Panné, Andrzej Paczkowski, Karel Bartosek, Jean-Louis Margolin, et al. *The Black Book of Communism: Crimes, Terror, Repression.* (Cambridge: Harvard University Press, 1999).

12. Alison Vicrobeck, "A Brief Overview of the Cuban Sugar Industry from 1590 to Today," accessed September 19, 2015, http://www.academia.edu/6820674/A_brief_overview_of_the_Cuban_sugar_industry_from_1590_to_today.

13. "Heroic Myth and Historic Failure," The Economist, December 30, 2008, http://www.economist.com/node/12851254.

14. "The Cuban Ration System: A Look Inside The Libretta," *Ruby's Cuba*, March 27, 2009, http://rubyweldon.blogspot.com/2009/03/cuban-ration-system-look-inside-libreta.html.

15. "The Cuban Money Crisis: The Biggest Change to The Island's Economy Isn't the Thaw In US-Cuba Relations," *Bloomberg*, April 1, 2015, http://www.bloomberg.com/news/features/2015-04-01/cubas-new-money.

16. Associated Press, "Cuba's Black Market Thrives Despite Raul Castro's New Market Reforms," *Huff Post Business*, July 5, 2011, http://www.huffingtonpost.com/2011/07/05/cubas-black-market-thrives_n_890307.html.

17. Yoani Sanchez, "Cuban Communist Regime Replaces Parents and Then Complains Its Children Are Badly Brought Up," *World Post*, March 7, 2014, http://www.huffingtonpost.com/yoani-sanchez/cuban-communist-regime-re_b_4922338.html.

18. Yoani Sanchez, "I Don't Want to be Like Che, Because Che Is Dead and I Don't Want to be Dead," *World Post*, March 18, 2010, http://www.huffingtonpost.com/yoani-sanchez/i-dont-want-to-be-like-ch_b_314190.html.

19. Oren Dorell, "North Korea ship held in Panama has a colorful past," *USA Today*, July 18, 2013, http://www.usatoday.com/story/news/world/2013/07/17/n-korea-ship-checkered-history/2524479/.

20. "Castro to Pocket 92% Of Worker Salaries From Foreign Companies," *Breitbart*, December 19, 2014, http://www.breitbart.com/national-security/2014/12/19/castro-to-pocket-92-of-worker-salaries-from-foreign-companies/.

21. Jeffrey Goldberg, "Fidel: 'Cuban Model Doesn't Even Work for Us Anymore,'" *Atlantic*, September 8, 2010, http://www.theatlantic.com/international/archive/2010/09/fidel-cuban-model-doesnt-even-work-for-us-anymore/62602/.

CHAPTER 6: HOW TO FIND TRUE FREEDOM

1. Laurie Goodstein, "Campus Crusade for Christ Is Renamed," *New York Times*, July 20, 2011, http://www.nytimes.com/2011/07/21/us/21brfs-CAMPUSCRUSAD_BRF.html?_r=0.

2. "#19 Campus Crusade for Christ," on the Ten Largest Charities page (as of 2014), *Forbes*, accessed August 20, 2015, http://www.forbes.com/companies/campus-crusade-for-christ-international/.

3. Press Kit: Campus Crusade for Christ Overview, on the Bill Bright page at CCCI.org, accessed August 20, 2015.

4. Rick Warren, "Bill Bright: A quiet giant," Crosswalk.com, July 31, 2003, http://www.crosswalk.com/faith/spiritual-life/bill-bright-a-quiet-giant-1212626.html.

5. "William R. 'Bill' Bright, Founder of World's Largest Christian Ministry Dies," CCCI.org, July 19, 2003, http://billbright.ccci.org/public/.

6. The four laws that follow are taken from Bill Bright, *Have You Heard of the Four Spiritual Laws?* ©1965–2009 Bright Media Foundation® (BMF) and Campus Crusade for Christ International® (CCCI®), as seen at http://www.4laws.com/laws/english/pda/the-files/4laws-foldout.pdf.

7. Ibid.

CHAPTER 7: BUILDING UPON THE SOLID FOUNDATION

1. The Africa Report, "The 50 most influential Africans: T. B. Joshua," *Africa Report*, September 20, 2012, http://www.theafricareport.com/west-africa/the-50-most-influential-africans-t-b-joshua.html.

2. "Celebrity Priests," *The Economist*, July 7, 2012, http://www.economist.com/node/21558298.

3. Abdulwahab Abdulah, Bartholomew Madukwe, and Victor Ogunsola, "'Synagogue building collapsed due to foundation overload,'" *Vanguard* (NG), March 5, 2015, http://www.vanguardngr.com/2015/03/synagogue-building-collapsed-due-to-foundation-overload/.

4. The Ten Commandments: Transcript, Prager University website, accessed August 20, 2015, http://prageruniversity.com/Ten-Commandments/#.VdXvKrJVhBc.

5. Stéphane Courtois, ed., *The Black Book of Communism: Crimes, Terror, Repression*, trans. Jonathan Murphy and Mark Kramer (Harvard University Press, 1999), x, 4.

6. John Adams, "A Defence of the Constitutions of Government of the United States," in *The Founders' Constitution*, ed. Philip B. Kurland and Ralph Lerner, vol. 1, chap. 16, doc. 15 (Chicago: University of Chicago Press, 1987), http://press-pubs.uchicago.edu/founders/documents/v1ch16s15.html.

7. Henry David Thoreau, "Walden," 1854.

8. Martin Bashir and Deborah Apton, "Rick Warren and Purpose-Driven Strife," ABC News, June 22, 2007, http://abcnews.go.com/print?id=2914953.

9. Charities Aid Foundation, *World Giving Index 2014* (November 2014), 3, 5, 10, https://www.cafonline.org/docs/default-source/about-us-publications/caf_wgi2014_report_1555awebfinal.pdf.

10. "Giving USA: Americans Donated an Estimated $358.38 Billion to Charity in 2014; Highest Total in Report's 60-year History," June 29, 2015, http://givingusa.org/giving-usa-2015-press-release-giving-usa-americans-donated-an-estimated-358-38-billion-to-charity-in-2014-highest-total-in-reports-60-year-history/.

11. "American Donor Trends," *Barna Group*, April 12, 2013, https://www.barna.org/barna-update/culture/606-american-donor-trends#.VgA6ZbQZh8j.

12. Ibid.

13. "How States Compare and How They Voted in the 2012 Election," *Chronicle of Philanthropy*, October 5, 2014, upd. January 13, 2015, https://philanthropy.com/article/How-States-CompareHow/152501.

CHAPTER 8: AMERICA'S SHAKY FOUNDATION

1. Humanist Manifesto II (1973), from the website of the American Humanist Association, accessed August 25, 2015, http://americanhumanist.org/Humanism/Humanist_Manifesto_II.

2. Michael Lipka, "Five Facts about Atheists," *Fact Tank* (blog), October 23, 2013, http://www.pewresearch.org/fact-tank/2013/10/23/5-facts-about-atheists/.

3. The official website of the American Humanist Association, accessed August 25, 2015, http://americanhumanist.org/.

4. J. A. Dunphy, "A Religion for a New Age," *Humanist* (January–February 1983).

5. D. Bostock, *Plato's Theaetetus* (Oxford, 1988).

6. John Calvin, *Institutes of the Christian Religion*, 2 vols., repr. ed. (Louisville: Westminster John Knox Press, 2006), 1:108.

7. "The New School Wars: How Outcome-Based Education Blew Up," *The American Prospect*, November 19, 2001, http://prospect.org/article/new-school-wars-how-outcome-based-education-blew.

8. U.S. Code § 7 - Definition of "marriage" and "spouse" from Pub. L. 104–99, § 3(a), Sept. 21, 1996, 110 Stat. 2419, as listed on the website of the Legal Information Institute, https://www.law.cornell.edu/uscode/text/1/7.

9. Mark Hodges, "Christian couple loses business for refusing to participate in gay 'wedding,'" LifeSiteNews, June 25, 2015, https://www.lifesitenews.com/news/christian-couple-loses-business-for-refusing-to-participate-in-gay-wedding.

10. Brandon Rittiman, "Court: Cake shop discriminates against gays," 9News, August 13, 2015, http://www.9news.com/story/news/2015/08/13/appeals-court-ruling-lakewood-baker/31608003/.

11. Rick Scarborough, "Anti-Same-Sex Marriage Pastor Rick Scarborough: 'We Do Not Hate Homosexuals,'" *Variety*, June 30, 2015, http://variety.com/2015/biz/news/rick-scarborough-marriage-equality-pastor-1201530925/.

12. David Jackson, "Obama signs hate-crimes law rooted in crimes of 1998," *The Oval* (blog), October 28, 2009, http://content.usatoday.com/communities/theoval/post/2009/10/620000629/1#.VdxwxfZVhBd.

13. Chelsea Schilling, "Obama Signs 'Hate-Crimes' Bill into Law," WND, October 28, 2009, http://www.wnd.com/2009/10/114305/.

14. Tom Strode, "UPDATED: Obama signs hate crimes act," Baptist Press, October 29, 2009, http://www.bpnews.net/31577.

15. Bob Unruh, "For Now, Pastors Can Still Oppose Sin," WND, October 20, 2012, http://www.wnd.com/2012/10/for-now-pastors-still-can-oppose-sin/.

16. United States Commission On Civil Rights letter dated April 29, 2009, http://www.marylandthursdaymeeting.com/Archives/SpecialWebDocuments2009/Civil_Rights_Comm._Ltr-1.pdf

17. F. A. Hayek, *Law, Legislation and Liberty*, rev. ed. (Abingdon (UK): Routledge, 2012), 258.

18. "Remarks by the President at a Campaign Event in Roanoke, Virginia" (press release), from the website of the White House Office of the Press Secretary, July 13, 2012, https://www.whitehouse.gov/the-press-office/2012/07/13/remarks-president-campaign-event-roanoke-virginia, emphasis added.

19. Friedrich Hayek, *Economic Freedom and Representative Government* (Chicago: University of Chicago Press, 1976).

20. Friedrich A. Hayek, *Law, Legislation and Liberty: The Mirage of Social Justice*, vol. 2, rev. ed. (Chicago: University of Chicago Press, 1978), 83.

CHAPTER 9: IT'S TIME TO AWAKEN THE SLEEPING GIANT

1. Eric Metaxas, Bonhoeffer: Pastor, Martyr, Prophet, Spy: a Righteous Gentile vs. the Third Reich (Nashville: Thomas Nelson, 2010), 141, 139.

2. Ibid., 321.

3. Letters Between Thomas Jefferson and the Danbury Baptists (1802): Thomas Jefferson's Letter to the Danbury Baptist Association, January 1, 1802, on the website of the Bill of Rights Institute, http://billofrightsinstitute.org/founding-documents/primary-source-documents/danburybaptists/. You can read the exchange of letters between the Danbury Baptist Association and President Jefferson in their entirety in appendix 2.

4. As quoted in David Barton, "Church in the U.S. Capitol," WallBuilders, November 10, 2005, http://www.wallbuilders.com/libissuesarticles.asp?id=90. To learn more about the Founding Fathers' recognition of the Christian church's role in the government and society, go to WallBuilders.com. WallBuilders, "an organization dedicated to presenting America's forgotten history and heroes," disproves the myth that the United States Constitution insists on the separation of church and state. See http://wallbuilders.com/ABTOverview.asp.

5. Ibid.

6. The weekly "Jefferson Gatherings" and the annual "Washington—a Man of Prayer" services can now be seen globally on the Daystar Television Network and at WND.com.

7. See "The Restriction of Political Campaign Intervention by Section 501(c)(3) Tax-Exempt Organizations," IRS.gov, upd. January 6, 2015, http://www.irs.gov/Charities-&-Non-Profits/Charitable-Organizations/The-Restriction-of-Political-Campaign-Intervention-by-Section-501(c)(3)-Tax-Exempt-Organizations.

8. Alliance Defense Fund, "The History of the Johnson Amendment," October 29, 2012, https://www.youtube.com/watch?t=18&v=3sWK1z6mXcQ. See also "Editorial: Repeal the Johnson Amendment," The Washington Times, May 20, 2013, http://www.washingtontimes.com/news/2013/may/20/repeal-the-johnson-amendment/.

9. Ibid.

10. Alliance Defense Fund, "The Pulpit Initiative: Executive Summary," December 23, 2009, http://adfwebadmin.com/userfiles/file/Pulpit_Initiative_executive_summary_candidates%203_11_10.pdf, 1–2.

11. "Houston Mayor Withdraws Subpoenas, but Political Intimidation Continues" (news release), Family Research Council, October 28, 2014, http://www.frc.org/newsroom/houston-mayor-withdraws-subpoenas-but-political-intimidation-continues.

12. Phone interview, August 21, 2015.

13. John Quincy Adams, The Bible Lessons of John Quincy Adams for His Son, ed. Doug Phillips (San Antonio: Vision Forum, 2000), 14.

14. Abraham Lincoln, "Reply to Loyal Colored People of Baltimore upon Presentation of a Bible," from Collected Works of Abraham Lincoln, vol. 7, at http://quod.lib.umich.edu/l/lincoln/lincoln7/1:1184?rgn=div1;view=fulltext.

15. Harvard Graduate School of Arts and Sciences Christian Community, "Shield and 'Veritas' History," Harvard GAS Christian Community website, accessed August 31, 2015, http://www.hcs.harvard.edu/~gsascf/shield-and-veritas-history/.

16. "History of Yale," All About…, http://www.allabouthistory.org/history-of-yale.htm.

17. "Religion and the Founding of Princeton," Princeton University website, accessed September 22, 2015, http://etcweb.princeton.edu/campus/Campus/text_founding.html.

18. "Jonathan Edwards," Encyclopaedia Britannica, http://www.britannica.com/biography/Jonathan-Edwards.

19. "Standing Columbia: the Founding of King's College," Columbia University website, accessed September 22, 2015, http://www.college.columbia.edu/cct_archive/sep03/cover.php.

20. "College of William and Mary," Encyclopaedia Britannica, http://www.britannica.com/topic/College-of-William-and-Mary.

21. "Brown University," Encyclopaedia Britannica, http://www.britannica.com/topic/Brown-University.

22. "Rutgers, The State University of New Jersey," Encyclopaedia Britannica, http://www.britannica.com/topic/Rutgers-The-State-University-of-New-Jersey.

23. "Eleazar Wheelock," Encyclopaedia Britannica, http://www.britannica.com/biography/Eleazar-Wheelock.

24. David Barton, "The Effects Of The 1962 Court Decision," America's Godly Heritage, http://www.skatewhat.com/russhowell/10-EffectsOfThe1962CourtDecision.html.

25. Tom Meagher, "The Cost of Crime Fighting: Reading Between the Line Items of Department Budgets, Past and Present," The Marshall Project, https://www.themarshallproject.org/2015/02/12/the-cost-of-crime-fighting.

26. Patricia McDonough, "TV Viewing Among Kids at an Eight-Year High," Nielson, http://www.nielsen.com/us/en/insights/news/2009/tv-viewing-among-kids-at-an-eight-year-high.html.

27. "Media Literacy: Fast Facts," Teen Health and the Media, http://depts.washington.edu/thmedia/view.cgi?section=medialiteracy&page=fastfacts.

28. "Martin Niemöller: 'First they came for the Socialists . . .'" Holocaust Encyclopedia, upd. August 18, 2015, http://www.ushmm.org/wlc/en/article.php?ModuleId=10007392.

29. Chris Woodward, "Barna: Many pastors wary of raising 'controversy,'" OneNewsNow, August 1, 2014, http://www.onenewsnow.com/church/2014/08/01/barna-many-pastors-wary-of-raising-controversy.

30. Larry Eskridge, "How Many Evangelicals Are There?" Institute for the Study of Evangelicals, accessed September 22, 2015, http://www.wheaton.edu/ISAE/Defining-Evangelicalism/How-Many-Are-There.

31. George Washington, farewell address, September 19, 1796, posted at csnnews.com, http://www.cnsnews.com/news/article/president-george-washington/george-washingtons-farewell-address.

CHAPTER 10: THE ROLE OF PASTORS IN THE AMERICAN REVOLUTION

1. "In the Wake of the Great Awakening," *Christian History Magazine-Issue 23: Spiritual Awakenings in North America* (Worcester, PA: Christian History Institute, 1989).
2. Benjamin Franklin, "Benjamin Franklin on George Whitefield 1739," National Humanities Center Resource Toolbox, http://nationalhumanitiescenter.org/pds/becomingamer/ideas/text2/franklinwhitefield.pdf.
3. Harry Stout, "Preaching the Insurrection," *Christian History*, no. 50 (1996), http://www.christianitytoday.com/ch/1996/issue50/5011.html, 1.
4. Ibid., 2.
5. James L. Adams, *Yankee Doodle Went to Church: The Righteous Revolution of 1776* (Old Tappan, NJ: Fleming H. Revell, 1989), 22.
6. J. T. Headley, *The Chaplains and Clergy of the Revolution* (New York: Scribner, 1864), 82.
7. Maurice W. Armstrong *et al*, eds., *The Presbyterian Enterprise: Sources of American Presbyterian History* (Philadelphia: The Westminster Press, 1956), 85.
8. This Day in Presbyterian History, April 20: Rev. John Craighead, http://www.thisday.pcahistory.org/2013/04/april-20/, accessed September 14, 2015.
9. The following quotes, among others, are listed on the website of the National Black Robe Regiment. See "History of the Black Robe Regiment," http://nationalblackroberegiment.com/history-of-the-black-robe-regiment/, accessed September 14, 2015.
10. "Episode 5, Muhlenberg Robe, Philadelphia and Colonial Williamsburg, VA," *History Detectives*, Oregon Public Broadcasting, http://www-tc.pbs.org/opb/historydetectives/static/media/transcripts/2011-05-13/505_muhlenbergrobe.pdf.
11. Alice M. Baldwin, *The New England Clergy and the American Revolution* (New York: Frederick Ungar, 1958), 170, 134.
12. Cassandra Niemczyk, "Christianity and the American Revolution: Did You Know?," *Christian History*, no. 50 (1996), http://www.christianitytoday.com/ch/1996/issue50/5002.html.
13. "Religious Affiliation of the Founding Fathers," Adherents.com: National & World Religion Statistics - Church Statistics - World Religions, http://www.adherents.com/gov/Founding_Fathers_Religion.html.
14. Although only fifty-six men signed the Declaration of Independence, you may have noticed that the sum of these numbers is sixty-two. Some of the signers shared multiple religious affiliations, so they are counted twice.
15. David Barton, "How many signers of the Declaration were ministers?" Frequently Asked Questions, "America's Founding Fathers," May 2015, the WallBuilders website, http://www.wallbuilders.com/libissuesarticles.asp?id=100766#Top.
16. Benjamin Franklin, Constitutional Convention Address on Prayer, Philadelphia, June 28, 1787 (public domain), quoted on the American Rhetoric Online Speech Bank, http://www.americanrhetoric.com/speeches/benfranklin.htm.

CHAPTER 11: FIVE DANGERS IF AMERICA DOESN'T CHANGE COURSE

1. See Randy Sly, "Obama Moves away from 'Freedom of Religion' toward 'Freedom of Worship'?".

2. Russ Hepler, "New U.S. Citizenship Exam Shreds 1st Amendment," *The Federalist Papers Project*, http://www.thefederalistpapers.org/us/new-u-s-citizenship-exam-shreds-1st-amendment.

3. Ashley E. Samelson, "Why 'Freedom of Worship' Is Not Enough," *First Things*, February 22, 2010, accessed September 12, 2015, http://www.firstthings.com/web-exclusives/2010/02/why-ldquofreedom-of-worshiprdquo-is-not-enough.

4. Chai R. Feldblum, "Moral Conflict and Liberty: Gay Rights and Religion," *Brooklyn Law Review* 72, no. 1 (2006): 120, 123, http://scholarship.law.georgetown.edu/cgi/viewcontent.cgi?article=10 80&context=facpub.

5. Tribune Media Wire, "University Encouraging Students to Use Gender-Neutral Pronouns Like 'Ze' and 'Zirs,'" WNEP 16, August 28, 2015, http://wnep.com/2015/08/28/university-encouraging-students-to-use-gender-neutral-pronouns-like-ze-and-zirs/.

6. "About the Standards," *Common Core State Standards Initiative*, http://www.corestandards.org/about-the-standards/.

7. "Race to the Top Executive Summary," U.S. Department of Education, November 2009, http://www2.ed.gov/programs/racetothetop/executive-summary.pdf

8. "Standards in your State," *Common Core State Standards Initiative*, accessed September 22, 2015, http://www.corestandards.org/standards-in-your-state/.

9. Lindsey Layton, "How Bill Gates Pulled Off the Swift Common Core Revolution," *The Washington Post*, June 7, 2014, http://www.washingtonpost.com/politics/how-bill-gates-pulled-off-the-swift-common-core-revolution/2014/06/07/a830e32e-ec34-11e3-9f5c-9075d5508f0a_story.html.

10. Lauren Camera, "PDK/Gallup Poll Finds Rising Awareness, Majority Opposition to Common Core," *Politics K–12* (*Education Week* blog), August 20, 2014, http://blogs.edweek.org/edweek/campaign-k-12/2014/08/pdkgallup_poll_finds_oppositio.html.

11. "Joint Statement of Early Childhood Health and Education Professionals on the Common Core Standards Initiative,"*Alliance For Childhood*, March 2, 2010, http://www.edweek.org/media/joint_statement_on_core_standards.pdf.

12. Carol Burris, in Valerie Strauss, "Four Common Core 'flimflams,'" *Answer Sheet* (blog), September 17, 2014, https://www.washingtonpost.com/blogs/answer-sheet/wp/2014/09/17/four-common-core-flimflams/.

13. Diane Ravitch, "The Biggest Fallacy of the Common Core Standards," *The Blog*, August 24, 2013, http://www.huffingtonpost.com/diane-ravitch/common-core-fallacy_b_3809159.html.

14. "English Language Arts Standards » Introduction » Students Who are College and Career Ready in Reading, Writing, Speaking, Listening, & Language," *Common Core State Standards Initiative*, accessed September 22, 2015, http://www.corestandards.org/ELA-Literacy/introduction/students-who-are-college-and-career-ready-in-reading-writing-speaking-listening-language/.

15. Allie Bidwell, "Behind the SAT: The Good and Bad of the 2016 Redesign," *U.S. News & World Report*, March 10, 2014, http://www.usnews.com/news/articles/2014/03/10/behind-the-sat-the-good-and-bad-of-the-2016-redesign.

16. Ibid.

17. Patrick Shannon, "An Evidence Base for the Common Core," accessed September 22, 2015, http://www.personal.psu.edu/pxs15/PShannon/PShannon/Thirty_Years_of_Resistance_files/An%20Evidence%20Base%20for%20the%20Common%20Core.pdf.

18. See the website of FoSE (Future of Sex Education) at futureofsexed.org.

19. David Barton, "Revisionism: How to Identify It In Your Children's Textbooks," *Wallbuilders*, http://www.wallbuilders.com/libissuesarticles.asp?id=112.

CHAPTER 12: RESCUING AMERICA FROM AN AGE OF LAWLESSNESS

1. Maolis Castro and Keial Vyas, "Venezuela's Food Shortages Trigger Long Lines, Hunger and Looting," *Wall Street Journal*, August 28, 2015, http://www.wsj.com/articles/venezuelas-food-shortages-trigger-long-lines-hunger-and-looting-1440581400.

2. Sandy Fitzgerald, "Obama Admits: You May 'End Up Having to Switch Doctors," Newsmax, March 14, 2014, http://www.newsmax.com/Newsfront/keep-doctor-obamacare-promise/2014/03/14/id/559637/.

3. Louis Jacobson, "Barack Obama says that what he'd said was you could keep your plan 'if it hasn't changed since the law passed,'" PolitiFact.com, November 6, 2013, http://www.politifact.com/truth-o-meter/statements/2013/nov/06/barack-obama/barack-obama-says-what-hed-said-was-you-could-keep/, emphasis added.

4. Grace-Marie Turner, "51 Changes to ObamaCare . . . So Far," Galen Institute, June 9, 2015, http://www.galen.org/newsletters/changes-to-obamacare-so-far/.

5. M. Northrop Buechner, "Obama's Disdain for the Constitution Means We Risk Losing Our Republic," *Forbes*, November 19, 2013, http://www.forbes.com/sites/realspin/2013/11/19/obamas-disdain-for-the-constitution-means-we-risk-losing-our-republic/.

6. Ibid.

7. The full report can be found at: www.cruz.senate.gov/ObamaLawlessnessReport.

8. See http://www.usgovernmentdebt.us.

9. Monthly Statement of the Public Debt of the United States, The Bureau of the Public Debt, https://www.treasurydirect.gov/govt/reports/pd/mspd/2008/opds122008.pdf.

10. Sheldon Filger, "The U.S. National Debt: Can the Federal Reserve Perform Fiscal Alchemy Forever?" *The Blog*, May 28, 2014, http://www.huffingtonpost.com/sheldon-filger/the-us-national-debt-can-_b_5375040.html.

11. Kevin Liptak, "How could Obama have 'underestimated' ISIS?," CNN, September 30, 2014, http://www.cnn.com/2014/09/29/politics/obama-underestimates-isis/.

12. See Julie Hirschfeld Davis, "It's Either Iran Nuclear Deal or 'Some Form of War,' Obama Warns," *New York Times*, August 5, 2015, http://www.nytimes.com/2015/08/06/us/politics/obama-urges-critics-of-iran-deal-to-ignore-drumbeat-of-war.html?_r=0.

13. See Paul Kengor, *God and Ronald Reagan: A Spiritual Life*, repr. ed. (New York: Harper Perennial, 2004), 153–54.

14. Ronald Reagan in a speech given to the Phoenix Chamber of Commerce March 30, 1961, https://archive.org/details/RonaldReagan-EncroachingControl.

15. Jeffrey Scott Shapiro, "Broken promise? Obama's America better for Wall Street than Main Street, stats show," *Washington Times*, January 4, 2015, http://www.washingtontimes.com/news/2015/jan/4/obama-economy-welfare-dependency-peaks-as-rich-get/?page=all.

16. Ibid.

CHAPTER 13: A CALL TO ACTION

1. John McManus, ""A Republic, if You Can Keep It,'" *New American*, November 6, 2000, http://www.thenewamerican.com/usnews/constitution/item/7631-a-republic-if-you-can-keep-it.2.

2. Seth McLaughlin, "David Lane's American Renewal Project mobilizing pastors to run for office," *Washington Times*, June 15, 2014, http://www.washingtontimes.com/news/2015/jun/15/david-lanes-american-renewal-project-mobilizing-pa/?page=all.

3.   Rick Scarborough, *Enough Is Enough* (Lake Mary, FL: FrontLine, 2008) 186–87.

4.   Vision America, "About Us," accessed September 15, 2015, http://visionamerica.us/?page_id=1483.

EPILOGUE

1.   Nate Cohn, "Why Ted Cruz Is Such a Long Shot," *TheUpshot* (blog), March 23, 2015, http://www.nytimes.com/2015/03/24/upshot/why-ted-cruz-is-such-a-long-shot.html.

APPENDIX 1: TEN PLANKS OF THE COMMUNIST MANIFESTO

1.   Ross W. Gorte et al., *Federal Land Ownership: Overview and Data* (Congressional Research Service, February 8, 2012), summary, https://fas.org/sgp/crs/misc/R42346.pdf.

2.   Tiffany Gabbay, "Are We Headed Toward the Constitution or the Communist Manifesto? This Breakdown Tells You," TheBlaze, April 22, 2012, http://www.theblaze.com/stories/2012/04/22/are-we-headed-toward-the-constitution-or-the-communist-manifesto-this-breakdown-tells-you/.

3.   Doug McKelway, "Critics Say Fed Policies Devalue the U.S. Dollar," Fox News, April 26, 2011, http://www.foxnews.com/politics/2011/04/26/critics-say-fed-policies-devalue-dollar/.

4.   CNNMoney, "GM made $22.6 billion. We lost $10.6 billion," CNN Money, May 29, 2014, http://money.cnn.com/2014/05/29/news/companies/gm-profit-bailout/index.html.

5.   Gabbay, "Are We Headed Toward the Constitution or the Communist Manifesto?".

INDEX